Revealing and Healing

3 Women's Stories of Survival

Rhasha Hoosier • Angenita Childs • Delina Hill-Brooker

Lioness
Vizions

First published in 2009 by Lioness Vizions, Columbus, Ohio

ISBN-13: 978-0-615-33089-1
ISBN-10: 0-615-33089-4

Library of Congress Cataloging-in-Publication Data
Data applied for

10 9 8 7 6 5 4 3 2 1

Printed in the United States of America

Contents

Foreword

Revealing and Healing: 3 Women's Stories of Survival is a compelling mix of the lives of three women. Their life struggles and disappointments make this book a must read for men and woman alike who have been abused, yet suffer in silence. This book shows the awesome power of God that brings healing, deliverance, and reconciliation to a person who has been deeply broken and wounded.

Minister Paul Bateman

Acknowledgments

First and foremost, we have to thank God, because without Him, none of this would have been possible. We would like to thank our husbands, James, Mikel, and Shawn, for their undying love and support through all the late nights, phone calls, and long days. Where would we be without you? We would also love to thank all of our children, all fourteen of you.

To Jason Pearce and the team at Newgen, words cannot express the gratitude we have for you. Thank you so much for supporting our dream, and for all your hard work.

To Paul Bateman and Rev. Elaine Walters, we thank you for your spiritual and business expertise, and most of all your guidance.

Reign

I FELT HOPELESS, worthless, on the verge of death. I told myself I didn't deserve to live. Everyone around me was trying to hurt and use me. Even my friends and family couldn't help me with the pain and the deep depression that constantly haunted me. I turned to alcohol, sex, and suicide attempts to ease the pain. I felt like the world had turned its back on me and there was nothing left for me. I was on the edge of destruction.

I am coming at you raw and transparent; straight, no chaser. I want you to feel every inch of my life, the struggles, and the triumphs. There will be some roller coasters where I scream through the loops. There will be victories and obstacles overcome.

In the face of adversity, do I sit back and allow my life to be taken? Do I give my power to another? Do I fight like hell, or do I just stand? These are questions I asked myself and I am sure many of you have also asked.

Well, I have done it all. Anything you are going through most likely is nothing new for me. My story is for anyone who has felt like they have hit rock bottom and wants to rise again like the phoenix.

Don't just read my story; learn from it. After you have digested it, pass it on to someone else who needs their life transformed. My goal is to help someone who doesn't have a mother to talk to or whose daddy is not around much. My story is for those of you who want someone to finally do what she says and keep it real.

I am not perfect, but I am still here and still strong. The odds were stacked against me, but I beat the hell out of the odds and came out golden. This is *my* story. No one can tell it like I can. I am Miss Victim, Mrs. Depressed, and Ms. Perfectionist.

Miss Victim

JUST LIKE EVERY FRIDAY for the past month, it was raining again, and just like every Friday, I was dancing and singing after leaving the babysitter's house. Mom paid as she did every Friday. *I wonder if I am going to Dad's this weekend?* As I walked out to the car, I wondered if my mom noticed I had a boyfriend. Although I was only nine years old, I was in love. He didn't tell anyone I was his girlfriend. He didn't hold hands with me or even take me places, but he kissed me deeply. He put his fingers inside me and he let me hide his penis.

These are the first memories of my childhood that I can recall. Me and D—that was what I called him. D was a little overweight, but I think I liked that. He was handsome, always had a nice haircut, and smelled nice all the time. He bounced me on his knee and made me laugh. He was my babysitter's son, and he had been molesting me for a year.

Each time he had sex with me, I focused on Victor Newman's face. I listened to *The Young and the Restless* theme music, and I waited. At twelve-thirty p.m. every day my babysitter and all of the young ones napped. As soon as Victor Newman went off, it would all be over. The first time, there was blood, but after a while, it didn't hurt at all. Like he said, "This is what boyfriends and girlfriends do." I just wondered why he wouldn't tell everyone, so they would know that we 'went together.' He paid me no attention unless we were alone. It hurt me, because I was proud of our soap opera love affair. I couldn't for the life of me figure out why he wouldn't tell anyone we were boyfriend and girlfriend.

I was used to our physical relationship. We usually did it in the first room on the left. I think that was D's sister, Natalie's, room. He laid down a blanket. It was the same blanket I was supposed to use for my nap. It would double as a catch for all of the juices from our bodies.

We were both silent during each episode. He never made a sound, and I didn't either. I mostly watched. It felt like I was outside of my own body, watching myself. I could see my face, my eyes, and my hands. The first time, I was scared, but after a while, I just waited. D seemed to like it, and that made me happy. *I guess I am here to make him happy.* In the back of my mind, I still wondered why we always met in secret at the same time every day.

After he finished and "peed" inside of me, he would sneak into the bathroom then rush back every time to carefully wipe me off with a blue washcloth. He never said "Sorry" or "Don't tell anyone." We never spoke of it—ever. I didn't think about it until the next time. I figured it was our thing, and I kept it to myself. I am not sure why I never told anyone about it.

Throughout my childhood, I kept the secret of the violations that were happening at the hands of D. For a while, I thought it was normal and that everyone was doing what I was doing at age nine. I was just like the ladies from the movies. I had a boyfriend. The only difference was D was ten years older than I was.

My next vivid memory is of my dad. Every other weekend, I visited with him and my stepmother, Momma Lisa; my brothers, Al, Freddy, and Dave; and my sister, Nala. My dad was a great cook. He and Momma Lisa taught me how to make a lot of great foods. I especially loved making breakfast. We prepared eggs, smoked sausage, pancakes, and freshly squeezed orange juice.

I loved being around my dad and brothers. Dad picked me up on Friday evenings and brought me home on Sundays. I took on the sister role and gave my little brothers hell. I tormented my brother Al. I bullied him and made him call me "Queen," but when someone messed with him, it was on. Once a boy called him "fat" and tried to punk him. I went down to the boy's apartment and beat him up.

While over Dad's house, I enjoyed taking care of my baby brother, Freddy. Dad trusted me to keep an eye on him while he went on short trips to pick up Momma Lisa from work or make runs to the store.

During the summers, I stayed with my dad, and I was able to care for my brothers for the whole day. One of the scariest moments of watching Freddy occurred one winter evening, while Dad was gone to pick up Momma Lisa. Al and I were chasing three-year-old Freddy around the couch. He was laughing and we tickled him when he came around the corner.

"Come on, Freddy, get me, man."

I ran to the end of the hallway with Al behind me. The next thing I heard was a bloodcurdling cry from Freddy. I turned to see blood running down his head. He had hit his head on the side of the couch. There was a sharp end that had pierced his temple. I ran and grabbed a towel. I pressed down hard to apply pressure, but the thick blood oozed around the towel. No sooner had I applied one towel than I needed another, as each quickly became drenched with blood.

Freddy screamed out in pain and kicked his legs. I tried to keep him calm, but Al and I were in tears. Those were the days before cell phones; only doctors had cell phones, so I waited for Dad and Momma Lisa to get there. They arrived about ten minutes later. I met them at the door and tried to explain. When Momma Lisa saw her baby, she was livid. I felt so bad for letting them down. They rushed Freddy to the hospital, while Al and I stayed home worrying.

Later that night, they came back from the hospital with Freddy wrapped up in a blanket, with a white dressing above his eye. He looked to be unconscious. I thought he was dead. I was frantic and began to cry. I lost my mind.

"Reign, he is fine, baby. It was an accident. He had to get stitches, but he will be fine."

Dad didn't seem angry at all. He held my brother down close to me. I gave him a kiss and they put him to bed.

My oldest brother, Dave, always took good care of me. Once, we went on a long bus trip from Indiana to Memphis. I talked the whole way and got on his last nerve. We made many stops during the trip, and Dave made sure I was safe when going into the restrooms and eateries. He protected me. I felt secure around him. In Memphis, we stayed with my nanny, granddaddy, and my Aunt Ruth. I loved our trips to Memphis. At night, when I would get scared, Dave would tell me stories and make me laugh. He was eight years older than I was, so when I went for my weekend visits with Dad as I got older, Dave was busy driving and dating. I didn't see him regularly, but whenever I did, it was a real treat.

My younger and only sister, Nala, was a joy to be around. We played school and choir. She had a nice voice and sang in the Indianapolis Children's Choir. I bossed her around and told her to start over when she messed up the words to a song. She was very pretty, and the time we spent was precious.

I missed my siblings when I was not with them. I wished they could come home with me. I hated living with no siblings, no kids my age. I didn't want just the weekends with my dad, brothers, and sister. I wanted my parents to live together and for all of us to be a family. *I hate my life; it's horrible. When I am older, I am going to stay with my husband and have kids and never get a divorce no matter what happens. I want all of my children with me and their dad. I guess my parents didn't love me enough to stay together.*

Despite the sexual abuse by D and my parents being split up, in my mind my life was much like everyone else's. I did okay in school and enjoyed it. I made friends easily in elementary and middle school. On Sundays, we went to church and I sang in the choir. I enjoyed the Baptist church. Our small congregation was like a family. Most Sundays, we would get to clapping and stomping our feet. The drums would get to going and folks would sing and shout well into the afternoon.

When I was at my dad's, we went to his Catholic church. It was a lot different. The service was serene. There were spoken rituals and songs sung. I liked being a part of both worlds. Where the Baptist church was charismatic and lively, the Catholic church was peaceful and calming.

Mom and I had lots of fun. On weekends, we would go to the movies. On the way, we would stop for snacks, drinks, and popcorn. Most times, we would see two movies and then afterwards have dinner at my favorite restaurants, Rally's or Rax.

Holidays were always cool. I can recall us watching all of the *Charlie Brown* holiday movies—whether it was Halloween, Thanksgiving, or Christmas. On Thanksgiving and Christmas, we would visit Mom's side of the family. We spent the holidays with my Aunt Betty, Uncle Cleo, and Nana.

Family was very important to me at this point in my life. Being an only child at home was boring. I often longed for my mom to have more children so I would have someone to play with. When I became restless, Mom let me visit Uncle Cleo and Aunt Betty. It was always a blast over there. I had twin cousins, Brianne and Brendan, who were a year younger than I was, and an older cousin, Kyle, whom we drove crazy.

My cousins and I were always getting into trouble. Aunt Betty pretty much let us get away with murder when I visited. She took us to the park and let us swing and slide for hours. Afterwards, she took us to Dairy Queen for blizzards. I always liked the Reese's Peanut Butter Cup blizzard. I would eat mine slowly and savor every bite.

Uncle Cleo and I got along well. He was so much fun and easy to talk to, and he gave great advice. He spoiled all of the girls. When Christmas came, Uncle Cleo would get us everything on our list. He loved seeing our faces when we opened our gifts.

We were mischievous children. One night, we were bored. We came up with a plan to knock on doors in the neighborhood and run when the door was answered. In the 'hood, we called this 'nigga knocking.' Aunt Betty and Uncle Cleo were at work, so we got dressed and got ready for trouble.

We ran two doors down and knocked. We waited and hit some houses across the street. Then we went to the home of a crazy man who lived four doors down. We knocked, ran, and were surprised when he opened the door and yelled at us. As we got back to the house, we realized someone had locked the door. We were locked out. No one would be home for hours. We had no clue what to do. We decided to go to a friend's house and ask for some tools. Brendan tried to get the door open with various tools. A neighbor kid tried to help. We couldn't get the door open.

Brianne was the first to speak.

"Now what are we gonna do, smart ones?" Brianne was upset, and she had to use the restroom. Brendan had an idea and we agreed. He would have to bust out the window and get into the house. Brendan climbed into the window and let us in through the front door. The three of us thought we could cover the broken window with cardboard and not get caught. My uncle and aunt were livid when they came home and saw cardboard covering the window. I got away unharmed, while Brendan and Brianne both got a whooping. It seemed that every time I should have gotten a whooping, I got out of it.

If I wasn't at Uncle Cleo and Aunt Betty's house, I was at Nana's. I loved to hang with her because we would talk for hours. Sometimes we agreed; sometimes we disagreed. She also taught me to speak up for myself. My cousins and I visited Nana's house often. We cut up over there. Nana didn't care if we blasted MTV on the television or if we ate all of her cake.

We drove our uncles crazy. Uncle Pete was always the quiet, reserved one. We bugged him as he got ready for dates. We checked out his clothes and cologne, cleaned out his car, and stole his change. He would yell at us, "Go on now, gals!"

Uncle Jim, the playful free spirit, would laugh as we terrorized him. Brendan would ask him all about music. Brianne and I tore up his drums and shredded on his guitar. He never really got mad at us. He just clowned around with us. He even let us go on some of his dates with him. Although my life was abnormal in some ways, my extended family life was pretty normal. I always felt loved and appreciated. I was loved at Dad's house, I was cherished at Uncle Cleo and Aunt Betty's, and I had a place in Nana's heart.

Once while I was at my dad's for a weekend visit, I asked Momma Lisa, "Can I go to the store?"

"Who are you going with?"

I lied and told her, "I'm going with my friend Tijuana."

"Okay, as long as you guys go together."

I went to the neighborhood store on 30th and Tacoma Street and got my candy. On the way back I crossed the street. The next thing I knew, I was flying through the air. I had been hit by an oncoming car. I got up, and when the driver got out of his car, I started hitting him and pulled his stocking cap off his head.

"Why did you hit me, muthafucka?" I got in his face.

He tried to talk to me, but I walked away.

"Hey, little girl, where are you going?"

I turned around and looked at him as if he were a fool.

"It looks like your arm is broken. I have called you an ambulance."

I just wanted to keep my candy. I started to open the wrapper on my Starburst when the man grabbed my hand to stop me.

"You can't eat anything. Just wait for the ambulance to get here."

It was my first time in an ambulance. I heard the sirens and the cars stop as we ran the intersection. We arrived at the hospital and the doctors performed surgery on my arm. I gave the nurse Mom's work number.

When Mom arrived, I had one question: "Am I gonna be on the six o'clock news?"

She laughed, and so did the doctor.

"I guess you are okay, huh, baby?"

She smiled and took my good arm in her hands.

I was fine until they started setting my arm. I had a few scratches on my face and a broken arm. They put a soft cast on my arm and sent me home.

Mom took me to Dad's, and when we pulled up, he came out with red eyes. Momma Lisa had been crying and Al was calling my name. At that time he called me Raya, because he couldn't pronounce Reign.

"Raya, what happened?" His eyes were sad as he pointed to my arm.

"I'm okay, Al. Don't be sad."

My eyes were glued to my dad. I could see the concern and the fear in his eyes. I always had the notion that since my mom and dad were not together, they didn't love me. I blamed both of them for how I felt. When I was with Mom, I missed Dad, Momma Lisa, and my siblings. When I was with Dad, I missed Mom. I think, deep inside, I thought my dad didn't love me as much as he loved my brothers.

That day was one of many when I realized Dad and Momma Lisa loved me very much. Momma Lisa kept saying she was sorry and hugging my mom. She looked upset and worried. It wasn't her fault. I had gone to the store alone, against her wishes. I had not been careful.

In the midst of all the craziness that was my childhood, I had a special friend to whom I could always turn. I was never hurt by this friend. It never turned its back on me. It would help me through Mom and Dad's divorce, the abuse, and the accident. It was my best friend … music.

I was introduced to music at a young age. I remember my mom had an old wooden box that contained records: Patrice Rushen and her long braids, Steveland Morris (better known as Stevie Wonder), Aretha Franklin, and a woman I adored, Chaka Khan. On Saturdays, we would clean up, and Mom would blast old music from the cassette deck. The local radio station, WTLC POWER 105 Indianapolis, would play all of the old jams. I listened to the sounds, and to me they were like colors. The soprano notes were bright reds, the full altos were oranges, and the husky tenor and bass notes, blue. I loved to hear the riffs and runs when the vocalist was really feeling things.

At my kindergarten graduation ceremony, I sang the final song. Me with my long braids, my glasses pushed up on my nose, wearing my cap and gown. I held the mic like a pro. To me, it was having fun pretending to be Aretha or Chaka. My feelings came out in song. I remember listening to the Isley Brothers and being able to connect with the heartbreak they sang about. I wanted to go to Atlantis with Ron, Ernie, and the guys. The guitar riffs danced along my spine many an evening.

I come from a long line of musicians. My grandfather played piano, taught music, and sang with a band that played at a small hole-in-the-wall called the Bluebird. My grandfather was known by the name Maestro. Aunt Betty sang in Tech High School's show choir and was in many theatre productions. She was very active in high school and sang in a band that toured the country.

Then there was Uncle Jim, who was a professional musician. He was a guitar and keyboard player. He wrote, produced, and arranged music. He saw something in me and my cousins at a young age. Brendan, Brianne, and I decided to start a group. Uncle Jim bought us shirts, and as Christmas presents he bought us keyboards. I often dreamed of being an entertainer, but where I am from, dreams don't come true. To me, I was just a little girl who came from a broken home, was sexing a grown man, and was hit by a car, all by the age of nine.

My close and extended family had always been important to me. At one point, family was the most important thing to me, but as I grew up, I grew out of family. I shut them out and ran away, never to look back. I guess you could call me the prodigal daughter. It was time for me to see what the world had to offer. What was the use of staying around people you loved? You only ended up being Miss Victim.

Reality

HAVE YOU EVER BEEN SO CONFUSED by life that you didn't know what to do? Have you seen things as a child that are etched in your memory forever? Is the one thing you've craved for the most in your life the only thing you didn't give yourself? I may not have all the answers, but I've been there.

Not ever belonging was an issue for me. I wanted love—and not just any love. Deep, passionate, lusty love that you see on *The Young and the Restless* or read in Danielle Steel books. That Cinderella love, equipped with Prince Charming. The kind of love that makes you wake up and sing, and say, "Hello Morning. How are you today?"

There was another love I was missing, though. Well, make that a few. I missed the love of my father. The first man available to me. The first man I saw with my own eyes. The first man I ever knew. The first man who was supposed to teach me how a man should treat a woman. And so I searched for it. I longed for it. And in doing so, I lost love for me.

I imagined a life for myself. I imagined that I would find a man to love me. I imagined that I would have the kids, the house, the fence, the dog, the career, and the husband who would provide nice things for me. I imagined my life as perfect. I would be all grown up and happy all the time. I wouldn't subject my kids to the things I saw. I would ban fighting. My man would never hurt me. I wouldn't walk around with fist prints on my eyes or wear funny-looking makeup. I would have four kids: boy, girl, boy, girl. My husband would love our daughters. Each girl would have a big brother to protect her. My girls would have long pretty hair. My boys would be handsome and strong. Life, in my head, would be all right.

I conjured these fantasies without knowing who I was, or how life could really be. Reality took those fantasies and made them true disappointments. They came so hard and so fast, and I wasn't prepared for the aftereffects. They led me down a path that was not meant for me—or was it?

Little Country Gal in a Big City

ONE TWENTY-FOUR SOUTH 16TH STREET, West Memphis, Arkansas. The first home that I ever knew was also the first home where I witnessed various kinds of abuses: physical, mental, and emotional.

I can also remember the days of happiness. The days when I helped my dad wash the car, and he sprayed me with the water hose. The days when I would go with my mother to the Laundromat and when I would help her pick greens. The mornings when my dad would come pick me up in the company truck to take me to school, or the walks my mom and I shared when she took me to school. I remember parties, and the playfulness of being a kid, but I also remember the dark times.

My first recollection of my mother's abuse was at the young age of seven. I awoke to her and my dad in the middle of a heated argument.

"You out all damn night!" my mother said.

"I'm the man, dammit. Hell, you giving your pussy away to another man!"

"Naw, that's you in somebody else's pussy. Not me."

I heard a loud smack.

I opened my bedroom door to see my dad standing over my mother, pounding her with his fists. He turned around and saw me. I will never forget the look in his eyes when he said to me, "Go back in your room."

The next morning, he came to my room and stated, very sternly, "Don't you tell nobody what you saw last night, hear me?" I nodded my head yes.

"'Cause if you do, you gonna make me hate you. You don't want me to hate you, do you?" I shook my head no as he walked out of the room.

After that, I tried my best to show my father that I loved him. All I wanted was for him to love me back, and he would, when he wasn't mad. When he was mad, it seemed like I was the reason he was in the situation he was in.

I was told that my mom got pregnant with me in or around July 1975. She and my dad married that October. I came along in March. Nicknamed "Angel" because my dad said I looked like a little angel. You would think that he would have treated me like one. Instead, he was an abusive man who just wanted to have absolute control to be able to do whatever he wanted with whomever he wanted to do it with.

One day, while my mother was in the house cooking dinner, I skipped around the house to the backyard. My dad was there, playing on the basketball court. I sat on the yellow swing set and watched him, like I'd always loved to do. Then, this strange woman appeared from nowhere. My dad stopped and smiled at her. He walked over to her and hugged her. I was thoroughly confused because I thought you should only do that to your wife. They leaned up against the house, between my brothers' bedroom window and my parent's window. He told me, "Go on around to the front, and don't tell ya momma. Remember what I told you?"

"Yeah," I said.

"Good. Now go on."

I ran around to the front of the house and stood on the porch, bewildered. I wanted to tell my mother, but I didn't want my dad to hate me. Talk about situations. I just saw my dad hug a woman like he hugged my mom, but I couldn't tell? If I did tell, he would hate me?

I learned that my dad had a plethora of women. They would call my home and harass my mother. A woman actually came to our front door to talk to my mother about my dad. Some women even had the nerve to call her at her job; one told her, "I could have blown your head off right then and there. You don't even know who I am." Another woman vandalized our car by pouring used motor oil in the backseat. Through all of the drama, my mother stayed with him.

While my mother worked, I stayed at home with my brothers. There were times when a strange man would call the house and say nasty things to me. He would always ask for my dad by name.

"He's not here."

"Oh, do you know what a pussy is?"

"No."

"You got one. It's between your legs."

"Who is this? I can give him a message."

"You are about eight or nine, right? I got a daughter your age. Does anybody touch you on your pussy?"

"Um, I gotta go."

"I touch my daughter's and I wanna touch yours."

The first time, I didn't say anything about it, but it continued for about three days. I finally told my mother, and we developed a system to answering the phone. She would call, let the phone ring once, then call right back. I'm not sure if my dad knew or not. I wondered if he cared anyway. The person knew him because they called him by name.

The phone calls made me curious. I wanted to know why someone would say things like that to me. It seemed like, after that, I started hearing more and more things of that nature. I remember one day I was playing house with my brother and one of the neighborhood boys, who was older. My brother was the baby, I was the momma, and the neighborhood boy was the daddy.

"Well, since I'm the daddy, you gotta give me something."

"What?"

He pointed to my private parts. I was confused.

"How can I give you that? That's a part of me."

"Like this."

He pulled my pants down and pulled his down. He lay on top of me and humped. This confused me even more. My mother was in the next room and didn't hear anything. I didn't feel anything. The whole ordeal felt weird. He got up, put his pants on, and left.

In the midst of all this, the abuse continued on a pretty regular basis. My dad would pick any reason to fight my mother. I remember one particular time when he chased her out of the house, but she was too quick for him. She laughed at him, and it was good that she got away, because he was piping mad.

Dad would have these spells when he would collapse in the bathroom. He would pass out and vomit everywhere. Mom would sit there and hold him through it. One time, he hit his head and had a gash above his eye that bled pretty badly. She took him to the hospital and stayed by his side through it all.

I wake up early in the morning, the sun shining through my window. I'm thirsty, so I go to the kitchen and get some water. Grandpa Robert is sitting on the couch. "Mornin'" he says. "Mornin' Grandpa." I say. I go back to my room and lie down. Momma comes out of her room, and I hug her tightly. She kisses my forehead and tells me, "Mornin' love. How is my sunshine?" "I'm fine." She walks into the kitchen. I see Dad's yellow and white robe moving, but Daddy isn't in it. I peer from my door and follow the robe. His hair is a funny shade of gray, and his ears look funny. Daddy sits on the couch, and Grandpa leaves. Momma is gone too. Daddy calls out, "Reality. Reality, come here." "Yes, Daddy?" He turns to me, and I see big ears, a long snout, and cat whiskers. His eyes are beady, and he has gross teeth. I realize what he looks like! He is a RAT!

I woke up, jumped out the bed, and ran to my parent's room. Dad and Mom were sleeping soundly. *My daddy is not a rat. That was a weird dream.* I closed their door, climbed back in my bed, and went back to sleep.

One day, my dad fell from a moving van and got hurt pretty badly. Mom rushed to the hospital to be with him. To me, she was the epitome of strength. He abused her, disrespected her, and ignored her, yet in his time of need, she was right there by his side.

My mother's thirty-third birthday was a sad occasion. Dad never came home to spend time with her; instead, he was spending his time with one of his other women. My mother wasn't a drinker at all, but she polished off two half pints of Bacardi rum. I was ten, and the next day I had to play a bigger and more mature role in the household. My mother was so sick from drinking that she couldn't cook dinner. She sent me to the store to buy some groceries. I also had to cook the meal. Dad wasn't paying any attention to her, and I remember thinking, *Daddy must not love Momma. He ain't taking care of her and he knows she's sick.*

There were times my dad would accuse my mom of poisoning him. He would go buy Church's Chicken, Captain D's, or Sonic and eat it in front of us. If she poisoned him, wouldn't she have poisoned us, too? We all ate from the same pot; all the food was cooked together. I looked at my own food more closely.

The last straw came in July 1987. My "uncle" was living with us. I quote "uncle" because he is my father's brother, but I do not claim him as a relative.

Mom's uncle, Uncle Charlie, came to our house and stayed a while. I had noticed a change in my mother. Her vibrant liveliness was gone. Uncle Charlie asked her to take him home. He lived in the rural part of Arkansas, as least thirty to forty-five minutes away. She piled me and my brothers into our '85 Thunderbird, and we drove off. I could overhear their conversation, although I wasn't supposed to be listening. I'd just turned eleven, and I was nosy as hell.

"You should leave him," Uncle Charlie said.

"I got these kids, Charlie. I can't just up and go."

"You can, Margie. Don't let that man kill you."

My mother had tears in her eyes. What I didn't know was that since my father's brother had come to stay with us, the beatings had become more frequent. When we pulled up into the driveway, I could sense something was wrong. We walked into the house and the argument started.

"Where the hell you been?"

"I took Charlie home."

"And it took you that long."

"Damn, you acting like he live around the corner or something."

He punched her hard in her face, right in front of us. He dragged my mother into their bedroom but didn't close the door. He beat her mercilessly, hitting her with all of his strength over and over as she cried and begged him to stop. I ushered my brothers into their room as I cried out for him to stop. The looks on my brothers' faces ate at me. I don't know which was worse, to witness the beating or the horrified look in their eyes. We all cried and continued to beg him to stop, but he wouldn't. He wanted to have the final word and the upper hand. She was now hanging off the edge of the bed, and he drilled her face over and over. I ran to get his brother to make him stop, but he just laughed and said, "That's what she get." If I had been a little bit taller, I would have kicked his ass.

My mother cried hysterically as she tried her best to fight him off, but it didn't help. I think it made him angrier, because the more she fought back, the worse he got, until he just stopped and stood up with a look of satisfaction on his face. He walked out of the room, and I ran in and hugged my mother. Her body shook because she sobbed so hard.

"I'm okay, baby. Go get me the alcohol."

I ran and got it from the bathroom, and my dad and his brother were laughing. My mother limped into the front room and sat down, still in tears, trying to soothe her pain with the alcohol.

"Go to bed," he said to me.

I couldn't understand why he talked to my mother like she was nothing. She bore him three children. He had a clean house, clean clothes, clean and healthy kids. She cooked for him and held him down when he got sick. He treated her like crap.

A few days later, Mom summoned me into her room. Dad was at work, and his brother was in the neighborhood somewhere.

"Baby, I need for you to do something. Take as many clothes as you can and put them in this trash bag," she said.

"Why?" I asked.

"We are leaving. Don't tell your dad. Don't tell your brothers because they would just tell him."

"Okay. Where we goin'?"

"Indianapolis. Put the trash bag in your closet and hide it there. Don't touch it or move it."

A day or two later, my dad took the car to his job. Mom walked to his job and used her set of keys to steal the car. When she got back home, we packed up the car, right under my "uncle's" nose. *Pretty clever*, I thought to myself.

We took food from the refrigerator and cabinets, pillows, covers, and the majority of our clothing. We went to her job and picked up her ninety-three-dollar check, then headed up the highway to Indianapolis. When Dad finally realized what had happened, we were tucked up safely 500-plus miles away.

When we made it to Indianapolis, I was elated. We didn't have to worry about Daddy anymore. I knew that she had planned on going back home after things cooled down, but he threatened to kill her if she came back, so we just stayed. It was just my mom, my brothers, and me.

I got the chance to really hang out with my "city" cousins, who often complained that I talked too loud and had no sense of style. In their eyes, I was country. I had just turned eleven that March. My older cousins, who were young teenagers, were already using foul language, and they pressured me to do so. I was floored, but I wanted to fit in, so I did it. Where I came from, if you said a cuss word, you got a beatdown. It was disrespectful. I just knew that I would get caught and get in trouble. I was scared to say "bitch."

Within the first month of living in Indianapolis, I said my first cuss word, had my first smoke, wore makeup in public, and had my first kiss from a boy who wasn't in my family. (It was a kiss on the cheek, but a kiss nonetheless.) Talk about fast—this was a whole lot faster than back home. The expectations were so high here. I had to be grown just to be able to hold my own.

We stayed with different family members for the first few months. Finally, we moved to Brightwood (a notorious drug haven) with my Aunt Suzie and my younger cousin, Teddy. It was there that I started middle school and had my first real crush. Even though I lived in the 'hood, I went to a middle school that was predominantly white. The majority of the black kids there were bused in. This atmosphere was different for me. I wasn't used to changing classes or being around so many white people. It was bad enough that I was poor, but being around white folks made my poverty stand out even more.

When school started, my mother bought all the necessary supplies she thought a sixth grader would need: crayons, markers, notebooks, and pencils. One day, my pencil box fell out of my hands, and all my crayons spilled. All of the kids in the hallway laughed at me. One person said, "What do you think this is? Elementary school?" There was another time this one white guy and I got into it because he thought he was better than I was and wanted everyone to feel the same. We were in class, and there was a mention of having a computer at home. When I told my teacher that I didn't have one, he yelled out, "Oh my goodness. You don't own a computer! You must be poor." I was stunned into silence.

A white girl named Kelly spoke up for me. "Just because someone doesn't own a computer doesn't mean they are poor. Have you ever thought that maybe she just doesn't want one?"

"May I go to the restroom, please ?" I asked the teacher. I slammed the stall door and cried my eyes out until the bell rang to go to the next class.

I vaguely remember a day in our science class when they split the boys and girls into two separate rooms and showed us this film about menstrual cycles. I remember not paying attention to it because I couldn't fathom ever bleeding from there. That was disgusting and I didn't like it at all. Besides, if that was going to happen to me, then why hadn't my mother ever told me about it? Instead, I opted to read a book.

I had my first major crush while still in the sixth grade. His name was Ben, and he was so cute. He looked like the singer Prince to me. I loved Prince, and I loved Ben too. Ben had a gorgeous smile and was in the eighth grade, but his parents were so strict that he could never come outside. My friend Brenda and I used to sit on her porch and watch his house to see if he would come out in the yard. At that time, I began really listening to music. I began to feel the power in the words of songs. Roger and Zapp's "I Wanna Be Your Man" stayed on my lips, only it was "I Wanna Be Ben's Girl." Keith Sweat's "I Want Her" became my "I Want Him." I didn't fully understand the meanings of the songs when I sang them. I just knew that Ben should be my boyfriend. It never happened, although I never quit wishing for it.

Ben walked me home one day and kissed me on the cheek, while stealing a peek into my newly formed bosom. I beamed like a lighthouse the rest of that day. Nothing could wipe the smile off my face. That was pretty much the gist of our 'relationship,' but I will always remember him, because there is nothing like your first crush.

We stayed in Brightwood about half the school year. My mother packed up my brothers and me, and we moved across town to Oak Tree Apartments on Post Road (another dangerous area). The four of us shared a tiny two-bedroom apartment. I started out sharing a room with my brothers, but I ended up in the room with my mother. It was not ideal, but it was comfortable. We had decent furniture, cable, and a thirteen-inch black-and-white TV. MTV and BET quickly became my addiction. I knew every song that came on, and my love for music grew. Hip-hop wasn't all that new to me, because rap was in the South when we left there. This was different because I had access to it. Back in Arkansas, I watched MTV, but the majority of the music shown was rock. BET was relatively new and played mostly R&B soul. The show *MTV Raps* gave a new face to hip-hop with the likes of Kwame, Doug E. Fresh, and of course, LL Cool J.

I made friends quickly, which shocked me because that had never happened to me before. My friends became my life, but the things they talked about I had never heard of. They asked me if I was a virgin. I stared at them blankly. I had no idea what a virgin was, and I was twelve years old by then. I asked them what that meant, and they laughed at the little country gal from Arkansas. I was thoroughly embarrassed, so I looked it up in the dictionary and got some random definition. I still didn't understand what a virgin was. When I got home, I asked my mother, "Mom, what does virgin mean?" I could tell that she really didn't want to touch that subject, and she replied, "It's not important, Reality. You don't need to know that right now."

I went to a predominantly black public school when we moved. This school was totally different from the middle school because sixth grade was considered to be elementary. I stayed in one room all day, with the same group of kids. There was one boy who always talked about how big my titties were, and I couldn't stand him. There was another boy, Sam, who was so dreamy-eyed and had the prettiest colored brown skin I had ever seen. I considered Sam my crush number two. I never told anyone about it, but I think he knew, even though he never said anything.

We went to camp in sixth grade with other schools in our district. The clique from my school got into it with a clique from another public school. One boy stood up with us against all these girls. I realized that he was the same annoying little twit who always talked about my titties. He became my best friend.

I graduated from elementary school and entered junior high, which was rough for me. The kids were more adult-looking and intimidating. I was tall and awkward. My clothing didn't match, and near the end of my seventh-grade year I had a short Jheri curl.

I wanted to be one of the popular kids, because they seemed to have it all. Everybody knew them, and each of them had a relationship. I wanted one, too. I wanted to have all that attention, and all that acceptance, they had. My friends were okay, and we had fun, but none of us was really popular, and none of us had a boyfriend. I felt like an outcast.

The boys in junior high were different, and I liked what I saw. Their roughness, in talk and otherwise, was what I was attracted to. The boys were so fine that I quit talking when they came around. I smelled cologne on them that knocked me off my feet. The only problem was that none of them saw me. I had several crushes, but I lacked style and finesse. Who would want to be with the tall, lanky, country gal with a Jheri curl?

My best friend was so short, and I used to call him Little Duckie because he looked like a duck to me. He always aggravated me, but I didn't mind. I would get him in trouble in all the classes we had together, which was close to all of them. If I hadn't been so green, I would have known that he had the hugest crush on me. I didn't pick up on certain clues: always messing with me, or me messing with him in class, eating lunch together, walking the halls together, clowning around all the time, really deep phone conversations, always visiting me, and always there when I needed a shoulder to cry on. My mother used to tease me all the time about him: "Ya'll gonna mess around and get married." I couldn't see that happening and would always say, "Yeah right! Me and Duckie? Never that, Mom! He is just a friend."

One day, in school, I found a letter dropped in my locker that was from someone named Mario. I was flattered by the thought that someone liked me, but he never would approach me in person. The letter said: "Hey Reality, I think you are pretty and I want to get to know you better. Write your number down and give it to my cousin Linda. We can keep in touch with letters for now."

My heart leaped. *Somebody noticed me?* I wrote him back, gave the note to Linda, and got another one the next day. The notes went back and forth for weeks. We even talked on the phone. His voice was really deep. He was much older than me: I was almost thirteen; he was sixteen. He seemed like a really nice guy, and we decided to meet up at Linda's house after school.

I was given a blindfold to put on before I could go into her apartment. I thought it was going to be a fun game. I was ushered in and taken back to a room. He just talked to me. When I asked about the blindfold, he said, "You'll see me soon enough." I thought it was fun. The routine with the blindfold added suspense and mystery to our new relationship. It would be one of the constants of our relationship as well. I would visit him at Linda's house at least once a week. He came into her house through the patio door because he didn't want anyone to see him. He might get in trouble if people knew about our age difference.

After Mario and I were an item, I told a few friends about our relationship. Torie and Ashley drilled me. "Do you wear a blindfold?"

"Yes."

"Have you really seen him?"

"No."

"That's not Mario; that's Linda."

"How can that be Linda? She's a girl, and she's our friend. Friends don't do that to each other. Ya'll just mad 'cause I got a boyfriend." I didn't believe them, because I figured that Linda was my friend. She wouldn't do that to me.

Things progressed steadily over the next month or so. Mario would kiss me and touch me, but we never went all the way. I was scared, but willing because he really liked me. He told me so all the time.

He kissed me and talked to me. I was still wearing the blindfold, and it added to the excitement of the act. He undressed me, kissed me, and caressed me. I got a feeling that I had never had before, and it scared me. I trembled, and he noticed. He held me close to him for a while—just long enough for me to stop shaking. He laid me on the bed and got on top. Then I felt it. He stroked about five times before I asked him to stop, which he did. It hurt. He got up and carried me to the bathroom and washed me up. I tried to sneak a peak, but he wouldn't let me. I went home; I was bleeding and scared. What if my mother found out?

A few weeks after losing my virginity, I remember my stomach hurting badly. I lay around that whole day and that evening. The next day it was still hurting, and I had to use the bathroom. When I went to the bathroom, I thought that I was bleeding to death.

"Momma! Look!"

She said, "You just got your period. You are going to be all right. Now you can get pregnant." She went to the closet and gave me a pad. I took a bath and put the pad in my underwear. She immediately got on the phone and called all the women in the family, like this was some big event or something. I was confused and angry at the fact that this was even happening to me. I had so many unanswered questions. *How much longer do I have to deal with this? How can I get pregnant?* I was clueless, and I wanted to know more, but I didn't want to ask my mother. I felt like she brushed too many things off. I asked the questions, but I didn't get the answers. None that I wanted to hear, anyway.

I started having suspicions about Mario. We had been together for at least two months and had already started having sex, but I was still always blindfolded every time I came over. I never saw what he looked like. I only had the pictures that Linda gave me. One evening when we were having sex, he flipped me on top and I sneaked a peek under the blindfold. I was bewildered to learn that he was a she, and that the she was actually my friend Linda. Instantly I stopped and jumped off. "I-I-I want to go home," I stuttered. She put my clothes back on and led me to the door, and I ran home.

I was freaking out. *How could I be so dumb? A girl? She even asked me if I was a virgin.* About an hour later, Linda walked across the way and knocked on my door, as if nothing had happened. I opened the door.

"I'm not coming out right now. I don't feel very good." She still didn't know that I knew.

A week later, "Mario" broke up with me. He called me early in the morning.

"I don't think I can do this Reality."

"What?"

"I can't be with you anymore," he said and hung up the phone.

I was distraught over the breakup, but I wasn't sure why. I called "Mario" back and asked if I could come over one last time. "Mario" agreed and I went to Linda's house. As usual, "Mario" blindfolded me. Once inside the apartment, I turned around and yanked off the blindfold. She stood there, dumbfounded.

"What is this, Linda?" I asked. "You've been doing this to me for months. Why did you betray me?"

Linda stood there, speechless. Her game had been found out.

"You are a girl pretending to be a dude!"

She stared at me and said, "I'm sorry."

Being gay was never something I thought I could be. I loved boys, not girls. But I didn't know what else to do when she kissed me. I was so confused, and I still wanted her to be my friend. *She had to like me a lot to go to this extreme.* I would still go to her house and hang out. We would kiss, and she would touch me sexually. I seriously thought I was gay, and I struggled with it. My cousins and friends all thought that I had lost my virginity to "Mario."

One day, I was sent home with a hickey on my neck. Momma saw it, and that's when she realized I wasn't a virgin. I got my ass beat. Technically, I was still a virgin; I just didn't know it. What I couldn't understand was the reason behind the ass whooping. I mean, exactly what kind of information had I been given, really? Could it be that I had been given the information and had chosen to ignore it? (That's what Mom says.) I know I should have obeyed her when she said don't do it. I was obviously curious about it, or I wouldn't have asked her about it. It was a topic my mother shied away from, even with my brothers.

Linda and her mother moved to a different apartment complex. We still kept in touch via the telephone. Sometimes, she would come to the 'hood, but she didn't really have a reason to, other than me. Most of our friends had already moved away.

In 1989, we moved from our tiny apartment to the projects; only my mother didn't realize it was the projects until it was too late. This was another new adventure for me. I had my own room, but we had roaches so bad that I was afraid to sleep half the time. The apartment was huge, and the people were a whole new breed. "Cut from a different fabric," Momma used to say. This was my first real taste of the 'hood, a lifestyle that I really didn't know about. I had always heard that the areas that I lived in were bad, but I never saw that side. The projects would definitely show you that side, and wouldn't care who was watching.

The first day of school was so weird. Everybody was trying to be friendly to me, passing me notes, smiling and waving and shit. I didn't know how to handle it, because it was so different from the last school. The teachers were impressed with me and felt the need to tell the students that I came from John Marshall Jr. High with straight A's. I really didn't bite, but I was curious to know why everyone was trying so hard to be my friend. I was apprehensive, as usual.

I befriended a set of twins who lived next door. I figured they could be cool to hang with. Unbeknown to me, there was animosity between the twins and Maya, a girl who lived in a house across the street. So when the older twin, Karen, and Maya jumped in each other's faces, I didn't know what was going on and I broke it up. I was standing in the middle trying to be the peacekeeper, but that made me public enemy number one. The twins turned on me. Their mother told the other kids to jump on me and leave her daughters alone.

One act of peacekeeping turned a mob of teens against me. I was followed home one day by the whole bus of kids, though they didn't do anything to me. I wasn't afraid; I walked home with them behind me, yelling and cursing me out. I stood in the doorway facing the mob, and Maya drew her hand back to hit me, but she didn't. I slammed the door in her face.

I was jumped by two girls, one of whom was on the basketball team with me. I didn't know why. I had to fight a girl over a boy that

I didn't like, though he obviously liked me. I couldn't have cared less about him. I had doors slammed on me, my books knocked out of my hand, and my locker slammed shut while standing at it. I tried to keep my cool. I got threats that if I didn't quit the basketball team someone would beat me up. (I didn't quit, and I dared them to step up.) I was isolated. Honestly, I had no clue as to why they wanted to fight me so bad. In my opinion, it had something to do with the fact that I was a new face and the dudes paid attention to me. There was one dude who was in high school and had a girl pregnant. Now this pregnant chick wanted to fight me so bad because her 'baby daddy' was checking for me. However, I didn't even *like* him, let alone give him the time of day. This new world was crazy to me, and I didn't understand how or why people were like that.

I still talked to Linda. We wrote letters back and forth and talked on the phone. One day, I caught the bus to her house. I had my shirt off, but she was fully dressed. Her mother came home and caught us in Linda's room. Her mother put me out and went off on Linda. I was stuck in the cold because the bus didn't run on a regular schedule. The bus took me downtown. I had to call Mom to come get me. I stood outside for hours in the freezing cold. By the time I made it home, I was a popsicle. Linda's mother called my mother and told her what happened. My mother, in a state of shock, asked me, "What's wrong with you?"

"Nothing."

"Nothing? What the hell were you doing?"

"Nothing."

"Reality, if you need some help, I will find you some."

"Help? For what?"

She would never come out and ask me if I was gay. She danced around the whole thing. I was so tired that I just gave one-word answers or just repeated everything she said to me. Mom sent me to my room. I didn't talk to Linda for a while.

About two months later, out of the blue, Linda called me. She had moved in with her dad, and he had put her out. She asked me if she could stay at my house. I knew my mother wouldn't have it, but I told her to come anyway. She caught the bus to my house, and she was there for a week before she was discovered. We covered our tracks very well. She left right after my mother, so as not to be discovered by my brothers, and she came back when everybody was asleep. I had no idea that she had run away and that her father had filed a missing person's report on her. I felt betrayed.

I never got over that, though, and it plagued me for a long time. I questioned my sexuality. I never went down on her. I never fondled her. I never did anything of a sexual nature to her but kiss. She did them all to me. I still, to this day, have no idea what she screwed me with; all I know is that it was big. Deep down, I knew that I liked boys. I loved me some male species. I loved their voices and how they looked in their clothes. I liked their swag, and I knew that something was missing from my sexual encounters. I knew that Linda could not be with me; I knew I needed a he, but I just couldn't stop things with her. I secretly wished she could be a guy. I mean, we knew each other very well, always had good conversations. We were tight. She loved me. I loved her, but I couldn't love her like that. That's when I knew that I wasn't a lesbian. I couldn't fall in love with her. When boys hugged me, it felt so different; it just felt right. I knew where it was I was supposed to be … with a man … a dude … a ding-a-ling.

After the Linda ordeal, I started hanging with my older cousins a lot more. When they drank, I drank. It was fun to feel funny like that. I started with wine coolers and worked my way up to hard stuff. One night, while riding around town, I met this guy named Darrell. He was really dark with big eyes and big lips, but I didn't realize it at the time because I had been drinking. We exchanged numbers and started talking. He had a really deep, sexy voice and a sexy laugh. Soon after, he became my first real boyfriend.

Darrell was sweet. He went to the high school that I would go to after junior high. He loved Babyface's "Whip Appeal," and he always sang it to me, albeit always off-key, and I thought it was cute. He talked about his dreams and what he wanted to be. He liked the fact that I was smart and funny. He would visit me while my mom was there. Mom didn't like him, but that made me like him even more.

The summer of 1990, I got a summer job at a local hospital. I would catch the bus to work, and sometimes Darrell would meet me downtown. We'd walk in Union Station, a popular teenage hangout, and around downtown, laughing and talking for hours. My first real French kiss (from a guy) came from him. His lips were so soft, and he held me so tight. He gave me a ring, black with gold accents and trim. With this gesture, I thought I was in love, but I wasn't so sure. The next time he came over, Mom wasn't home. He stayed over almost the whole day. We made love twice, and I was smitten. He told me that he really liked me. As the bus was taking off with Darrell on it, my mother was rounding the corner coming home.

A few weeks later Darrell and I started having problems. His attitude changed.

"I didn't start talking to you because you were cute, because you aren't. You are sweet and that's what I like about you. You really ain't all that," he said.

"Go to hell!" I told him. *How dare he! I'm not cute? Yeah right. He even gave me a ring!* I thought to myself.

A few weeks later, I spent the night at my Aunt Clara's house, and my cousin's friend, Todd, came over. He was looking for my cousin, Jake, and I was the only one up. He seemed really interested in me for some reason.

"Are you hungry?" he asked.

"Yeah, a little." He left and returned with a burger combo meal.

We talked for a while about general things, like age. He was seventeen; I was fourteen. The subject changed, and he put the pressure on to sleep with him. He told me that he liked me. He even gave me his phone number, and told me that he would like me even more if I slept with him. Todd kissed me on my cheek then kissed me again on the lips. He started rubbing my neck and whispering in my ear. I loved what I was hearing and feeling. We had sex on the floor.

I would visit Aunt Clara's house all of the time just to see him. When he knew I was visiting, we'd have sex. He wasn't my boyfriend, but he really liked me. I could tell because he kept coming back.

During all this, Mom and I were not getting along. I felt that since I was doing such a good job in school, I should have some type of freedom, like spending the night over friends' houses or going to the mall. She relented on the mall, but sometimes I felt like I was being wronged. Now that I look back, I should have been able to do a little more, but not much. The community center in the apartments where we lived gave parties for the teens. I couldn't participate, and the center was about a hundred feet away from our front door. I couldn't understand her reasoning. I wasn't particularly bad; I made good grades all the time, and I figured that's all she really wanted from me. I started rebelling.

One particular time, I wanted to stay at Aunt Clara's house, secretly hoping I would run into Todd. I wasn't ready to go home, but my mother made me.

"If you don't get your ass in this car, Reality!" she yelled.

"I'm not ready to go! Why do I have to?"

"Because I said so!"

I surrendered and got into the car. My mom drove toward the interstate. We argued until we got close to the interstate.

"I wanna go live with my daddy. I know he won't treat me like this," I smirked.

"I'm sick of you acting like that. Shut up or I'ma put you out this car."

"I'll get out," I retorted, and jumped out the car right before we exited on the highway.

My mom turned the car around to come and get me.

"I'm sending your ass to your daddy," she sighed.

I smiled, like, "Cool, Daddy's gonna take care of me, and I won't have to worry about a thing."

Grandpa, my mother's father, picked me up at the bus station in Memphis, Tennessee. He didn't recognize me at first. It had been about four years since he last saw me. We got in the car and headed to rural Arkansas. A usual thirty-minute ride took about two hours, as his eyesight and health were failing him. When we arrived at the house, Grandma was there, greeting me with open arms and a home-cooked dinner. I felt so at home, but at the same time there was no action there, no one who could really relate to me. My first night back in Arkansas I spent at my grandparents' house. When I awoke the next morning, I called my father and told him to come and get me.

Later that day, Dad picked me up and took me to my Aunt Lisa's house, where all my cousins lived. I missed them so much! We caught up on what was going on with everyone, and we did some heart-to-heart talking. I was surprised to learn that things were not good in their world either.

"What's for dinner?" I asked, and was greeted with funny looks.

"Dinner? You know yo' Auntie ain't gon' cook!"

Apparently, Aunt Lisa hadn't cooked dinner in a few months. She simply refused to cook. Instead, she sent us to the store. We bought granola bars and went to Dairy Queen for her so that she could get a hamburger. There was no soap at the house, so I used the little money that I had to buy soap and a few meals from Dairy Queen. I had a Jheri curl, so I also had to buy my hair juice.

My father left me at my Aunt Lisa's house for two months and went to stay with his girlfriend in another town. I was out of my own personal money and I literally starved for the whole time.

Dad would visit every once in a while. When he did, I would ask him for money.

"Daddy, I'm hungry. All I ate was a granola bar," I whined.

He told me, "You're aight. You need to lose some weight anyway."

"Well, I wanna go with you."

"Naw now," he replied.

"Daddy, take me, Tina, and Nala with you."

"Aight, I'll take you this time. Go get your stuff."

That was the first and last weekend I spent with him the whole time I was there. I was confused. *I am his little girl, right? Why does he treat me like this?* I truly felt as if I were more of a burden than his daughter. That Sunday he took me back to Aunt Lisa's house.

I loved hanging out with my cousins. We stayed outside, playing with the neighbors, and would go for walks in the Arkansas heat. I was rough and a true tomboy at heart. I would jump on people's backs, play-fight, and climb trees. I got cussed out when they called some boys over and snuck them in the house, because I wouldn't have sex with one of them. I just said, "So, I don't know you, I don't know anything about you, and I definitely don't like you." I had a crush on Cameron, their very chocolate next-door neighbor. He was so cute, and we almost had sex, but he came in his pants before we could do anything. I guess that was a good thing, though.

I quickly grew tired of being hungry and playing all the time. I longed for home, a home-cooked meal, a good book, and I missed my brothers. I called my mother and told her I was ready to come home. She wired the money for my ticket. Dad took me to the bus station, we said our goodbyes, and I was headed back to Indianapolis.

Three years after we left Arkansas, and a few months after my trip there, the divorce was final. It really hurt me; even though I knew my parents wouldn't get back together, I still held on to the hope that maybe one day, they would get it right. The finalization of the divorce killed my whole spirit. To this day, my dad doesn't realize the pain he caused me. My mom doesn't realize the pain she's caused me. I know she left for her life, and I understood that, but my understanding of the situation didn't ease the pain of it.

IF YOU WERE TO MEET ME TODAY and knew nothing of my past, you would probably say, "Wow, she's got her life together; she probably only has 'normal' problems in her life, if any." It seems that way now, but that's not the way it always was.

I started life with the 'picture perfect' family. A man and woman who each had a child from a previous marriage, joined together, living in the middle-class suburbs of Indianapolis. A total of five kids, a German Shepherd, a fenced-in backyard with a swing set. Our neighbors were nice and helpful. We were living in a real-life Pleasantville, or so it seemed. My mother was a housewife, and my father worked out of town on the railroad. In reality we were a dysfunctional family with a plethora of secrets. All of the signs were there, if you really looked.

A chosen victim, I was subjected to sexual abuse from the time I was four until I was eight and in the third grade. The two who started my cycle of abuse were the two closest males in my life, my father and my oldest brother. They were the first out of seven men who would attempt or 'succeed' in 'messing' with me. The two people in the whole world you would think were there to protect me from things of this nature were the ones doing these horrible things to me and encouraging each other to spread this demonic spirit throughout my family. This was the stem of a tree that would grow in my life. In my adult years, I vowed to cut it down.

Because of the abuse, my mother was a single mom through the duration of my childhood. I had a misconstrued sense of relationships and men. I thought that all men abused their children, girls and boys alike.

I watched as my mother, once a stay-at-home mother, struggled to keep a roof over our heads, food on the table, clothes on our backs, and presents under the tree. I remember being in the programs where the local fire department would adopt our family for Christmas so that we could have new things and even got to make a Christmas list. Not all of our requests were granted, but most of them were.

When my dad was around, I never knew of any money problems. Not to say we didn't have them, but I never saw it. We still went on vacations, had fun, went to the movies, and were able to buy snacks. When it was just Mom, it was obvious that we didn't have much. We would sneak popcorn, snacks, and drinks into the theatre or watch free movies at the library.

We were near poverty, even though I didn't realize it at the time.

Poor Little Rich Girl

MY EARLIEST CHILDHOOD MEMORIES are good for the most part. I was daddy's little girl. Wherever he went, I went. We would ride his motorcycle around town. My best friend and I would ride in the back of his gray pickup truck on hot summer days. He taught me how to read at the age of two, along with simple addition and subtraction. I was way ahead of my kindergarten class. I would play with my brothers and sisters: the two oldest, Derrick and Tisha, myself, then Keenan, and the youngest, Kevia. We would run outside and be carefree, play tricks on each other, and occasionally have sibling rivalry. Every holiday the whole family would go to Grandmere's house for a BBQ or a nice formal dinner for Thanksgiving. Almost every Sunday after church, we went out to eat. Our favorite restaurant was PoFolks. I loved it because they used Mason jars instead of drinking glasses. Other Sundays we would visit my father's family for dinner.

We had a very open home—opened to friends, family, and visitors. Aunt Mary spent the night when Mom went to the hospital to have Keenan. Aunt Mary wasn't our blood aunt; she was a friend of the family we called Aunt. Grand Pap stayed with us before he moved back to Ohio with Dad's family. I remember one time Dad and I drove all the way to Beaver Falls, Pennsylvania, to pick up Cousin Tammy. I did not remember having met her before, but I was in awe of the mountain scenery. The day we headed back home, the whole family stood outside, waving and saying their goodbyes. There were so many people, too many to count. "Wow, Dad, we have a big family."

"Yes, there were eighteen of us growing up, including four sets of twins."

"Wow! How did Grand Pap feed all of ya'll?"

"We lived off the land."

I knew his mother had passed away long before he and Mom were married. I also knew he was a twin, because every time we would come to Beaver Falls, we would visit Dad's twin, Uncle Steve. I would tease them, "You guys aren't twins. You don't look alike." They would just laugh. Uncle Steve would say, "You're right, Dream, I'm bigger than he is, so maybe I should beat him up."

Even though Uncle Steve was bigger than Daddy was, I did not think he could beat him up.

"My dad is Superman! No one can beat him up."

When we got back to Indianapolis, Tammy settled right in. She and I shared a room, and she got a job working at the McDonald's a mile away. Each week she would bring me the latest Happy Meal toy. She would play with my hair and braid it into two French braids with ribbons in them. I felt beautiful. I liked it so much better than the 'boof balls' Mom put in my hair. When I went to school, everyone would ask how I got the colors in my hair, and I would happily say, "My cousin Tammy."

One day, when I came home from school, Tammy was not there, and all of her stuff was gone. "Where's Tammy?" I inquired.

"She went back home."

She didn't say goodbye. She just up and left. Something's not right. I knew by the tone in my father's voice that I should not pry for more answers and left it at that.

For my fifth birthday, Mom and Dad threw me a big party. All of my friends and family were there, including Aunt Mary, her daughter Nyla and my best friend, Michelle. We had a blast. We played, laughed, joked, and ran around.

The next morning I was awakened by Dad picking me up and carrying me to the car. He laid me down in the back seat. He got in the car and started the ignition. I peered through my sleepy eyes and saw Mom in the passenger seat. They started praying for God to watch over us while we were away from home. "Where are we going so early?" I asked.

"It's a surprise, Dream. Go back to sleep, okay."

I woke up again after we got to the Tennessee state line.

"Look, Dream, it's Tennessee."

"We're going to Tennessee?"

"No, we are going to Disney World."

"Disney World!"

I could not contain myself. "Are we there yet? Are we there yet? How much longer?"

We arrived at Disney World. I rode all of the kid rides, petted a boa constrictor, and rode an elephant. "Can I pet the goats, Dad?"

"Sure, go ahead." My parents watched outside the gate as I went to make friends with the goats. I could overhear them talking: "Goats eat any and everything." Their voices faded as I went further into the pen. I was rubbing one of the goats' heads when I felt a harsh tug behind me. I turned around and screamed, "Ahhhhh! Help! Help!"

There was a goat behind me who had eaten off the back of my dress, exposing my panties for all of Disney World to see. My heart was crushed as I watched the blue polka dot fabric disappear into his mouth. I watched as Dad jumped over the wooden fence to rescue me. I was too stunned to run, but I let out another blood-wrenching cry. Dad seemed so far away, and the goats just looked at me like I was crazy. Dad chuckled to himself. As he reached down to pick me up, the goat took a bite out of his pants. "Get! Get! Get out of here, ya dumb goats!" I giggled and said, "Dad, I don't like the goats. I don't want to be at Disney World. I wanna go home."

I used to wake up before the crack of dawn every morning. I would play in my room until someone else woke up to keep me company, but this morning was different. Just thinking about it, I get a lump in the back of my throat just like I did that day. Although I was very young, no matter how hard I've tried to forget, I will always remember. My father walked into my room, kneeled down, and kissed me, but it wasn't a normal kind of kiss. It was on the lips, no tongue, but just different from a kiss from a father to his daughter. Now that I am older I'd say it was a more passionate kiss. I was confused because it just didn't feel right; I got that 'uh-oh' feeling in my stomach. *That's my dad, and he would never do anything to hurt me, right?* He wore a burgundy crushed velvet–type robe that was halfway tied around his waist. As he kissed me, he opened his robe and exposed himself. He was naked underneath. I thought nothing of it, really. I had seen him naked on a few occasions, but more by accident … or not. I remember I used to peek through the crack in the door sometimes when he would pee, but I was curious as to why he could stand up and pee and I couldn't. I don't think he ever saw me. Or did he? *Was it my fault because he saw me looking at him?* He laid me down on the floor; he was shaking. I was nervous. *Why is he shaking?* He fondled me with his fingers, made me give him oral sex, and did the same to me; he masturbated until he came. He put it in his hand and said, "Dream, this is our secret, okay; you can't tell anyone."

Okay, I thought to myself, fighting back the tears, and I didn't even know why I wanted to cry. *Why is it so hard to swallow this big lump in my throat?* Even though I didn't know what we did, I would keep his secret. Why wouldn't I? He was my father, and I loved him.

A lot of times Dad and I would go outside on mile-long walks and he would molest me in the woods. One time, he and I went on a trip to Pennsylvania and it was night. We parked on the side of the highway. He molested me there. Then we went to sleep. A policeman knocked on the window and woke us up. He asked why we were sleeping there; my father's reply was that he didn't want to pay for a hotel, and the policeman left. I wished silently to myself that the policeman could just know about my 'uh-oh' feelings, but he didn't. I still hadn't figured out why I felt so scared and weird every time we did 'our little secret.'

The incident between my father and me that sticks in my mind the most was one day we were home alone. He told me to tell him when I had to pee because he wanted to see how I peed. Being the young child that I was, I forgot to tell him, partially because I waited until the last minute to go. I went running down the hall to the bathroom, and when he found out what I was doing, he came charging down the hall and threw open the door. He yanked my legs apart and grabbed my vagina, squeezing it, trying to twist and turn it so he could get a better view. He stuck his fingers in my virgin parts. It felt like my insides were bleeding and were going to fall out of my newly discovered holes. That was the roughest he had ever been. He wasn't even that rough when he was spanking me. The majority of the time he would lay me on the floor and rub up against me, moving his hand back and forth on his privates until he came on my stomach. We would stay butt naked on the floor until he saw my mother backing into the driveway in our blue LTD Crown Victoria. He would wipe me off quickly before my mom came in, but I would still be sticky and uncomfortable until my bath.

I can also remember my older brother, Derrick, molesting me on several occasions. I'm not exactly sure when it happened, or when the first time actually was. Maybe it had always been; I don't really know. He mostly would make me give him oral sex. It was nasty. He tasted dirty. I didn't like it, nor did I understand why I had to keep doing these things that had to be kept a secret.

One night, as my older sister, Tisha, and I were falling asleep in our bed, we had a heart-to-heart talk. I told her what had been going on with Daddy and Derrick. From that moment we had a silent bond that no one could get through. It was the kind of bond that didn't need words; we would just look into each other's eyes and that would say all we needed to say.

Some time shortly after that, I told my mother what had been happening. I really don't know what motivated me to, but I did. Mom was cooking pancakes for breakfast. Somehow we ended up in her room and it all came out. I don't remember her response in words or if she had any at all. I do remember her walking back into the kitchen, finishing breakfast over tears. My dad's eyes met mine, and somehow I think he knew that I had told. After that it was like my life was another person's life. I felt like I was walking in a strange girl's body and her name just happened to be Dream too.

Just as I remember the day the abuse from my father started, I also remember the day that it stopped. I was in the third grade and in the gifted and talented program. During class one day the principal came in my class and got me. My teacher, Mr. Green, told me, "You have to go so that we can keep you safe." I didn't understand. *Safe from what?* A social worker came to pick me up from school. Her name was Kate. She was a white lady with blonde curly hair. We left school and she took me to McDonald's. "You can order whatever you want." As I ordered a cheeseburger kids meal she continued to talk. "My job is to keep children like you safe ..." My mind started to wander.

Why is everyone trying to keep me safe when I'm not in any danger? She told me some of what would happen next for me.

After we left McDonald's, Kate took me to the Guardian Home. It was a place where abused kids and runaways lived. When I first got there, it was big and scary. Kate walked me down a long and empty hallway with couches and chairs against the walls like they have in hospitals and doctors' offices. There were no children or grown-ups around. The echo of Kate's heels clicking against the floor was excruciatingly loud. She led me to a room with about eight beds. The bed that designated for me was to the left of the emergency door. The room monitor told one of the girls that had already been there a while not to try to run away again. I was so scared. *What kind of place is this where kids want to run away?* I just wanted to go back home. I still didn't understand how or why I was in any danger. I figured that if I was, I could handle it.

The next morning, the sound of giggling girls awakened me. A black lady named Miss Ann was watching us then. Apparently they had different shifts to watch us. There were only a few black girls there. Miss Ann would grease our hair and scalp with a lot of grease. She would give me a lot of ponytails all over my head with rubber bands. I was mad because my mother never put rubber bands in my hair because it would break it off. We had to wear the Guardian Home's clothes and even their underwear. Our clothes were put into a big trash bag with our name written on masking tape until we went home. I was okay with wearing their clothes, but I never got used to wearing their underwear. I longed to go home so I could be with my own family and wear my own underwear. I didn't trust that just because they washed them, they were clean. *I bet everyone in my room has worn the underwear I have on.* All of the clothes had this weird smell to them. I never got used to the Guardian Home lifestyle, and I refused to be 'institutionalized.'

The bathroom in our dorm had a lot of tubs and one shower in it. There was a line of toilets on one wall, and the bathtubs were in the middle of the floor, with the shower in the corner. I hated bath time because everyone was in the bathroom at the same time, taking a bath, using the bathroom. I was so insecure and didn't understand why. My body had gotten me into this place. I was embarrassed and ashamed and didn't want anyone to look at me. There was absolutely no privacy. I would wash, but I still felt dirty all the time.

Each dorm was grouped by age. We would have to line up for breakfast, lunch, and dinner. We would go into the cafeteria to eat. I always ate in silence. I didn't know why, but I didn't plan on being there much longer. I think secretly I was trying to figure out how I was going to run away without getting caught like that other girl did.

One morning, we were lined up on our way to the cafeteria and I saw my older sister, Tisha, in line too. That really brightened my day. She smiled at me, but it was like our special bond. She was worried about something, but she pretended for my sake not to be. One day, one of our caregivers came over to me and said, "Congratulations, your sister had her baby!" I just smiled.

"Thanks," I said. *A baby?* I asked myself. *I didn't even know that she was pregnant.* I was speechless, but Tisha had left the Guardian Home and was living with Aunt Yvonne. I later overheard that she had given the baby up for adoption. I also soon discovered that my mother, Keenan, and Kevia were living in a shelter until my father moved out. I also learned that my father had molested Derrick and Tisha as well.

My social worker, Kate, took me to the doctor to prove evidence of molestation in court. I was not told exactly what they would do until the doctor was performing the procedure. I had my first Pap smear at the age of eight. It was horrible. I had a male doctor who wasn't gentle at all. He was frustrated with me because I wouldn't be still. I couldn't keep still because the lamp he had between my legs was burning me. He told me it was 'our friend' and gave it some cheesy name that didn't help me relax; if anything, it made me tense up even more. After all of the stretching and poking of the Pap smear, they drew blood for more tests. I remember another black girl—I believe her name was Megan—had been molested too. She cried when she had her blood drawn, but I didn't; but then again, I wasn't me.

Kate picked me up for my court dates. We would go to McDonald's, bond, and talk. One day, we went to court and my Aunt Yvonne was there. Just like Aunt Mary, Yvonne wasn't our blood relative, but she and Mom grew up together, so we called her Aunt. She had already come and picked up Tisha from the Guardian Home. Aunt Yvonne brought me my favorite stuffed bear, named Snuggles. He helped me through lonely nights at the Guardian Home.

One evening, I remember all of us children sitting on the steps lining the hallways in a devotional session. We were taking random turns at picking songs that we wanted to sing. My song was "Kum Ba Yah." I started the group off by singing, "Kum ba yah, my Lord, kum ba yah. Kum ba yah, my Lord, kum ba yah. Kum ba yah, my Lord, kum ba yah. O Lord, kum ba yah." The older kids that were sitting around looked at me in amazement and told me that I had a really good voice. I always knew that I could sing, but I guess that's when I first wanted to be a singer.

One day Kate came to check on me. We found a quiet spot where we could talk. She was just about the only one that I trusted, so I asked, "Kate, when can I go home?"

"Well, sweetie," she answered, "it's not that easy. Your mother is not quite ready to take care of all of you guys yet. As soon as she is ready,

I will come and take you home." There was a glimmer of light when she told me, "What we can do is, you can stay with your Grandmere until your mother is in a better position for you to come back home."

It wasn't the news that I wanted to hear, but it was a lot better than my current situation. Grandmere was my mother's mom, and I loved her dearly, but I wanted to go home. But I didn't hesitate. Any place was better than the Guardian Home. I got my garbage bag of clothes with my name on it and put my underwear and coat back on. My clothes smelled funny, but I knew my Grandmere would be able to get them to smell fresh again.

Grandmere enrolled me in the third grade, and I started school again. This school was different from the school I was used to. I finished my third grade year at school #55. The public schools were so different from the township schools that I was used to. I wondered why the public schools were numbers but the township schools had actual names. I never asked anyone, because I didn't want them to think that I was dumb. In the township schools it was a cafeteria-style lunch. You got to choose what you wanted to eat. In the inner-city public school we had metal trays with one cold plate and one hot plate. The food tasted gross. Everyone else seemed not to mind, but I did. Maybe it was just that I wasn't at my school, the school I was used to, because no cafeteria food is good really. I didn't like doing the work, because the things they were doing I had already done in my gifted and talented program. The majority of the time I didn't even pay attention in class. Even though I loved being around other kids at school, just to have people around me that were my age, I kept my distance. I already felt like an outcast. I felt ugly and awkward. I felt like everyone knew what had happened to me, even though I was still unsure of what had happened.

Life was very different over Grandmere's. I couldn't go outside and play with the other kids, and I could play in the fenced-in backyard only if Grandmere was out there too. I was bored unless I was at school, because all Grandmere would do was watch soap operas and play solitaire. She taught me how to play and gave me my own deck of cards. We would play a million games of solitaire. I would get frustrated when I kept losing; it was something about losing to yourself that I just couldn't adjust to. She did teach me how to shuffle cards. It always amazed me because she would do it so fast, she never dropped one, and all of the cards always seemed to fall right into place. I would see Mom, Keenan, and Kevia on occasional weekends. If they weren't visiting, Aunt Yvonne would let me stay the weekend at her house with her family, where I would get to see Tisha.

Mom set it up for the whole family to get counseling to cope with everything. We would all go together, but I would have one-on-one counseling or counseling with my peers and family counseling. During my first session, the counselor pulled out some ugly dolls that had private parts. She told me, "Make the dolls do exactly what your father did to you." I went through the motions of the man doll's privates on the girl doll's face and made them rub on each other. I still didn't see what the big deal was. *He only hurt me that one time in the bathroom, but I deserved it because I didn't do what he told me.*

When I went to fourth grade, I got to move back in with my family, which now consisted of my mother, Keenan, and Kevia. Tisha was still with Aunt Yvonne, and I'm not sure where Derrick was. When I went back to my old school, I felt so stupid. I was taken out of the gifted and talented classes and was back in regular classes. I was so far behind from going to the public schools and not doing any work. I wasn't used to studying extra hard; every subject had used to come to me so easily, and I could retain the information. I lost my desire and love for learning. I would do enough just to pass and make it to the next grade. If I did well, that was great, but a C was quite alright with me, too.

My father went to jail for what he did. When I went to counseling, all of us girls had to write letters with questions and feelings to our offenders. Most of them were our fathers; some were uncles and grandfathers.

In his response to me, he said that he thought he was holding the family together. I didn't understand. *How did he think that he was keeping the family together, and how did he feel in his heart that no one would get hurt?* Even still I loved my father. I still thought of myself as lucky. All of the other girls who were in therapy with me had it worse than I did, so it seemed. Their offenders were rough and actually had sex with them. I hadn't experienced that. They also told us that since we had been molested and raped, there was a greater chance that we would do the same thing. I thought to myself, *That's the craziest thing that I ever heard. Why would I do that to someone when I hate it?*

Now that I was back at home with my family, things were different, very different. My mother seemed happy at times, but it didn't take much to make her upset. She wasn't working at the time, money was tight, and my father was in jail. She never said not to tell anyone, but we knew not to let the cat out of the bag. No one really talked about it. I had already had my birds and bees talk in group therapy. I got the talk again in school, and the teacher told us that if someone gives you a 'bad touch' you need to tell someone. I told a friend that I sat next to, "I already told, and it messed up my family and my life." *I'm the reason that Mom and Dad broke up. I'm the reason we are poor now and Mom is on welfare. It's my fault there's no dad in the house. If I had never said anything, we could've kept living our perfect suburban life. Why didn't I keep my secret?* I was so mad at myself. I rationalized the possible scenarios. *Derrick and Tisha are already out of the house. I could've withstood the abuse he gave me, just to keep everything else going smoothly.* Even though the counselors and therapists told us it wasn't our fault, I still felt like it was my fault, and it was too late to turn back the hands of time.

One day, Mom and I were at the mall shopping. I peaked over the comforters that were for sale and saw my cousin Tammy. I was excited; I hadn't seen her or heard from her since she had left so suddenly. "Hi, Tammy! Where have you been?"

"Oh hey, Dream." She didn't seem too excited to see me or Mom.

I wonder why she's actin' like she's not excited to see me. We were so cool when she lived with us.

"Do you want to come over for dinner tonight?"

"I don't know; I have to ask my husband."

Why she gotta ask her husband? If he says no, does that mean she won't come over? That's crazy! Just 'cause that's her husband doesn't mean he can tell her what to do.

"You're married! Where is he?"

"Over there."

She seemed so distant, as if there was something she was hiding, but her eyes told it all. Tammy and her husband never came over that day. It always stayed in my mind how she reacted to seeing us. *I wonder if dad messed with her too. That's messed up, because she's not even his child.*

The summer before I was to start the sixth grade, Mom enrolled me in a program called Young Scholars at IUPUI. We would go to the college campus and pick two programs of study. The coordinator urged us to pick something we wanted to be when we grew up. There was dentistry, art, architecture, etc. I chose song writing and dance. In the writing class we learned how important and fun writing could be. We made up silly songs and poems and expressed our innermost feelings. The last week of the program, we sang and recorded each other's songs. When it was time to do my song, I wanted the class to sing it, but not me. "But you have a beautiful voice, Dream. I think you should sing it with us."

"No, I'm okay." I wasn't sure why I didn't want to sing along with the class. I didn't feel nervous; I just didn't want to do it. I sang the song to them to give them the melody, and they started to sing into the microphone. The instructor sang and played along on the guitar. The guitar was hooked up to a printer that printed out the sheet music for the music being played. I watched as my original thoughts printed out on paper. I was amazed and thought, *That's the coolest thing I've ever seen.* When they were done recording, the instructor popped out the cassette tape and handed it to me. "This is for you. Keep it and you'll always have a record of your very first song." I held the tape in my hand.

Wow, this is my song, on tape, just like the songs on the radio. This is my song.

When I got home, I went in my room and listened to the recording. *This is* not *how this song was supposed to go. The melody is all wrong, and they can't sing! Ugh! I should've sung it by myself; at least that way it would sound good and the melody would be right.*

I always had musical talent; it came naturally. Everyone on my mother's side of the family was musically inclined in one way or another, but the older kids at the Guardian Home told me I was great. I would record songs off of the radio because we didn't have the money to buy tapes. I would write down the lyrics of all of the songs I liked, and I would dissect them. Mariah Carey's "Vision of Love," Whitney Houston's "Greatest Love of All," "I Believe (When I Fall in Love)" by Stevie Wonder, to name just a few. I would study the words, how they were put together, and how they flowed. I'd write them down, paid attention to the rhythm, and studied what made that song great. I would count the bars to see how everything fell into sequence. I was a sponge, and I soaked it all in. Music was my drug of choice. I've never felt the need to try cigarettes, drugs, or alcohol; give me some nice ear candy and I'm good. I could drown myself in my problems by listening to something sad or close to what I was going through, or pick myself up with a happier song. At first I would listen only to R&B and rap that was on the radio. I started broadening my horizons. I listened to pop, jazz, gospel, rock and roll, classical music, and even opera. I fell in love with the sounds of Ella Fitzgerald, Billie Holiday, U2, Aerosmith, Collective Soul, and old-school Aretha Franklin. I would put on my headphones, close my eyes, and paint a picture in my mind. I didn't know what the opera singers were saying, but I could feel the emotions of the song and loved the piercing high notes. I wanted to hit that high note too, so I'd scream and strain, trying especially with the Mariah Carey songs, until I eventually hit the note effortlessly. With the classical music I could see myself on stage dancing to the music in front of an audience in awe of my talent. In my music I was in my own perfect and happy world. I also studied the one-hit wonders and tried to figure out why one song did well but the album didn't. Most of all I studied the harmonies of En Vogue, Boyz II Men, Adoration-N-Prayze, and Take 6. I'd learn every part and could sing all of the notes. I loved to watch musicals and could see myself on a Broadway stage as Little Orphan Annie. I even auditioned for the play. I was the only black girl and was mad when not only did I not get the role of Annie, but I didn't even get cast as an orphan! I was crushed, but I kept my spirits up. I said to myself, *That's okay; when I get grown I'll play Miss Hannigan!* I loved Carol Burnett in that movie, and to me it was the next best role to Annie. I loved music because I could impress people with my singing without really trying, and if I put my heart and soul into it, Oh Lord, hold on! Everyone would ask, "How does that big ole voice come out of that little bitty body?" I was only about eighty-five pounds soaking wet. I would write down the words to the number one hit songs in my notebook alongside my poems and original songs to have the success rub off on my work.

Diary Entry, *July 10, 1991*

On the 4th of July I found out that Tisha was pregnant, she's due in September. Anyway, Aunt Mary and her kids want me to spend a week at their house, but Mom said I probably won't be able to go. I think it's because Dad would have to take me and you know what he did. But with his back and all he can barely do anything he has to go to the doctor every other day 'cuz he was in a car wreck and his back went out and he couldn't move. Plus I'm strong and he wouldn't do nothin' to me, but I wouldn't tell on him if he did 'cuz that's my dad and I don't want to go through all that stuff again, not living with my mom, living in the Guardian Home, then living with Grandmere, going to camp, not seeing my dad for a year or two because he went to jail …

I completed my middle school years as normally as possible, focusing mostly on music, choir, and the performing arts. It was so much fun to become someone else instead of my not-so-normal self. It was the same for high school. I was a great student when I wanted to be and made honor roll a few times; other times I just didn't care and only did enough to be able to go to the next grade.

Throughout my school years I had several interactions with my father, but they were never really consistent. I would stay after school when I was a freshman for various programs and ride the late bus home. One fall evening, while in the sixth grade, I got off the late bus and headed home. The late bus would drop us off at the end of the street and not closer to your house, so I had to walk a bit. It was dark outside, but the street lights were on. There was a man walking down the street, and although my past was always in the back of my mind, I didn't really think anything of it until he walked up on me and stopped me from walking down the street. Once again, I had that lump in my throat, like the one I'd get when my father would mess with me. He introduced himself and said his name was Daniel. He told me I was cute and tried to sweet talk me into coming to his house. He kissed me on my neck. He told me that he lived down the street in the house with all of the cars in the driveway. He told me he had money and lots of cars and I could have one or anything I wanted if I would come by and visit him from time to time. I held my ground as best I could and told him, "No thank you." I knew the game he was playing, but I wasn't having it. I didn't even know this man, and he was old and ugly too. Once he saw that I was not going to bite his bait, he grabbed my arm and tried to pull me close to him, telling me, "Just touch it. It's okay, just touch it."

Damn! Why did my daddy mark me like this? He started getting aggressive, and I started to assess my situation. My house was only two doors down. If I couldn't do anything else, I could run. If something happened and I fell or he got me, I'd scream. All my neighbors knew me; I'd be okay. As he kept trying to reel me in, I waited for the exact moment for my escape. I couldn't be too close because he'd get me, but he was moving in closer, so I had to do something fast. I stepped back and, like a football player, faked left and dashed right. He didn't chase me; I'm not really sure where he went, because I didn't look back to see. But I was nervous; this man lived on my street and he'd just seen where I lived. *What if he comes back to get me?* I ran in through our side door. Mom and Tisha were in the kitchen at the table with my niece. As soon as I walked in the door I slammed it behind me. Trying to catch my breath, I knew I had 'the look' on my face, the look that every child has when they have been abused. Tisha looked up at me, and her facial expression changed. Mom looked at me and said, "What's wrong baby?" I burst into tears.

Here we go again. "There was a man outside who tried to mess with me!" Mom ran outside to see if he was still there; Tisha jumped up and put her arms around me, holding me tight, and she cried with me. She said, "I don't know why this keeps happening to you."

Yes you do: Daddy marked me, and you too! My mother sat me down and told me, "Dream, no matter what or how many times this happens, I will always believe you. Don't ever think that I won't believe you."

We called the police, and the detective came over to get my report. The detective sat on our brown striped couch. "Okay, sweetie, tell me what happened."

I cried as I went through the story again. Although nothing sexual had happened, it very easily could've. The detective gave me his card. "Call me anytime if you think of anything else. We will have to take Daniel to court and press charges. I'll call you and let you know when they schedule the court date."

"Can you not have it during my Christmas break?"

"Unfortunately our judicial system doesn't work quite that fast, so you should be okay." He chuckled to himself.

During lunch the next day, I fainted. I was stressed and nervous that Daniel hadn't been caught yet and that it would be just a matter of time before he came and got me. I was carried into the nurse's office, and they called my mother. She came and picked me up from school. Not only had I passed out; my hands were peeling, and I just didn't feel good. I went to the doctor, who told me it was stress.

Mom told the pastor of the church what had happened, and he prayed for us. He also assigned his assistant pastor to be with us during all of the meetings with the prosecutor and at the trial. We sat down to devise a plan so that I could keep my extracurricular afterschool schedule without fear of walking home by myself in the dark. The plan was I could stay after school still and ride the late bus home. My dad would be there when I got off at the bus stop, pick me up, and drive me home. My mother was in college at the time taking night classes. My father mumbled to himself, "I don't play that, ain't nobody goin' to be messing with my daughter!"

So, it's okay for you to mess with me, but no one else can? Our pastor had no idea about my father's past. To him, he was an outstanding member who was very active in the church and always volunteered on committees, so it seemed like a great plan. Yes, after my father got out of jail, he came back to our church. We had changed pastors, so the new pastor had no idea. When we went to trial, Daniel's family would try to stare me down and look at me like I did something wrong. My mother rolled her eyes at them and said, "I can't believe this mess!"

I agreed to let Daniel plead guilty to a lesser charge so that I wouldn't have to testify. He pled guilty to attempted battery and served a light sentence. The trial was over, but it was just another notch in my belt, so to speak. My mark hadn't been erased, and now it was shining bright again.

Reign

Mrs. Depressed

AS I WENT THROUGH MIDDLE SCHOOL, there were many changes and transitions. We moved from the far eastside projects to the township district. I hated moving away from all of my friends. I didn't like being the new girl. After school, I'd finish my homework, turn on my keyboard, and write. Most of the songs I wrote back then were sad. I wrote about my new apartment, about missing my old friends, about the changes I was going through.

Brianne and I started our group and named it the Party Patrol. You couldn't tell us nothin'. We walked through the mall with those shirts on.

We stayed at Nana's the entire Christmas break. During winter break, we wore our Party Patrol shirts from December until January. If you think Nana washed them every day, you better think again. Her large wooden table was our stage. We took Uncle Jim's huge boom box and brought it in the front room. There was a drum set, microphones, and guitars in Nana's basement.

Brianne and I rehearsed in the basement and then did shows for the family upstairs. I remember us practicing to BeBe and CeCe Winans. Our love of music was something we shared as a family. I thought of it as our legacy. Singing for me had always been like breathing. To sing a note was like taking a big breath. It had always been that easy and cleansing. Many times I would be stressed about things, and I would hum a little bit and feel better.

In middle school, I was in my first talent show. I sang my favorite song, "Let's Chill," by the group Guy. My best friend, Erica, and I sat in the bathroom. You could hear the harmonies down the hallway. When we came out of the bathroom there was a small crowd gathered outside.

"Dang, ya'll can sang. I ain't never seen skinny chicks who could blow. That's a trip." A girl named Tiffany, who was in a dance group, looked us up and down.

"You Reign, right? You don't ever talk on the bus or nothing."

"Yeah, I'm Reign. You Tiffany right? I've seen you 'round the corner."

"Yeah, I'm T and chile you can sang."

I was proud that folks liked my voice, but I couldn't stand when they called me skinny. I knew I was thin. *Do I have to always be reminded?* I admired the bodies of the other girls in my school. They were curvy and had hips and booty for days. I stared down at my flat chest. *Hmm that's cool. I'm skinny huh? I betcha I will get some attention for something more than my body. I am gonna sing, and people are gonna come to my shows. I am gonna sign autographs and act. I will be the next Whitney.*

"Reign, come in here and get dressed. The show starts in one hour."

Mom ironed my clothes. I was fierce. Erica and I would be dressed in black. We had on our black MC Hammer pants, patent leather shoes, and shiny black-and-silver blouses.

The gym was full of students. It looked like all of Belzer Middle School was in attendance. The crowd became quiet, and we took the stage. I began a riff that brought applause from the start.

"Ooohhhhhhhhh owwwww leeeeeetttttt's chilllll baaaaayyyy-bayyyyyyyyy."

The music dropped in, and we began our steps. I felt so free while on stage. I was in a beautiful, unstoppable trance. We bowed and sat on the bleachers.

Throughout middle school, music played a major part in my life. I always sang in the church choir. Mom had me in Youth in Arts at the Madame CJ Walker Building, in the historic Indiana Avenue area. It was a program that provided voice lessons and theatre classes. I was singing at the Parks Department talent shows and festivals around the city. I also took dance classes to perfect my overall performance. I competed in solo and ensemble competitions and always received high scores.

One event my friend Lashanda and I signed up for sticks out in my mind. Mom took us to a local festival. We were set to sing at eleven o'clock. We chickened out a little after ten. Our plan was that when the lady called our names, we would just ignore her and act like we had left. We let my mom in on the plan and got ready to watch the show.

"Reign and Lashanda are up next. Ladies, are you here?"

The announcer waited, and everyone looked around. Somewhere in the back of the park the elderly woman who signed us up to sing called out.

"There they are; there are my girls, over there." She pointed directly at us. Mom almost died laughing.

We hung our heads and laughed. Then reluctantly we hit the stage. The After 7 track played. My rich alto tone flowed.

"Last night I made love for the very first time, it's true and for the last time."

My mom cranked her neck back

"Last night what happened?"

The elderly woman patted her hand. "Sweetie, it's just a song they singing. They ain't made no love."

"Where am I?" I looked around the room. Everything was unfamiliar. I could hear machines beeping, and I saw a blurry face.

"Momma, what's going on?"

She told me I was in the hospital and I had attempted suicide. "Reign, why would you drink fingernail polish and take a whole bottle of aspirin? Why would you want to take your life? God wants you to live."

I had no answers. During my stay at the hospital, I was asked many questions about why I had attempted suicide. I told the therapist I was sad and angry most of the time. There was a team of doctors, and I was assigned to two of them. One was a woman, Dr. Stevens, and the other a man, Dr. Sven. Dr. Stevens was the 'medicine woman.'

Her job was to figure out what was wrong with you, prescribe the medicine, and make you take it. Other than that, she didn't seem concerned with me at all. As long as I took the medicine, she was fine.

Dr. Sven questioned me for hours about my life, beginning with my childhood. Soon he knew it was sexual abuse; his next question was, Who? First, he made up his own scenario.

"Is it your dad who is molesting you? Is that who it is?"

What is he talking about? I have no clue what molesting is; I'm lost.

After an hour of questions and answers, I told him about D. I didn't tell him his name, but I told him what had happened.

"You will need to write a letter to your mom unless you want to stay at the hospital another seven days."

"Okay, I will. I don't want to, but I will."

I wrote the letter and was released. I gave the letter to my mom when we got home.

Mom, I hope this letter doesn't upset you. I have been keeping this secret for so long. Sometimes I think I should just keep it forever. First, I want to say that I love you very much. You have always taken good care of me. I have always respected the fact that you work hard to make a life for us. Back when I was going over Aunt Peaches's house during the week D molested me. Momma he took my virginity and for two years, he had sex with me on a regular basis.

My mother dropped the letter and began to weep. I could hear her in the other room. Maybe it was a bad idea to tell her. I never wanted to hurt her, but it was time for me to let her know why I had so many issues and why I didn't trust anyone, even God. *What has He done for me? Why would God allow such things to happen to a child?*

I heard Mom talk about how some of the children she worked with were abused sexually and physically. She'd tell me why they had problems with boundaries, stealing, and relationships. I had those same problems. I stole from my mom, even if I didn't need the money. I'd do and say anything around anyone. *Maybe if I told it would get better.*

Someone said that, didn't they? I had kept the secret for years; why did it matter now?

Mom asked me exactly what happened. I told her about the blood and the washcloth, *The Young and the Restless*, and Victor Newman. I told her everything that happened.

I had kept this secret for so long; it was my freshman year, and I couldn't take it anymore. She told me about the laws and asked me what I wanted to do. I didn't know at the time. I actually still liked D. The thought of him going to jail and me being on the witness stand scared me. I had seen those shows where the victim is blamed for everything. I also wanted to make sure Aunt Peaches never knew what her son had done to me. She was a foster and adoptive parent. I knew that revealing a secret publicly could put those kids in harm's way.

For years, there was a picture that I had. It was me and D, and I was looking up at him lovingly. The sky was up above and looked so heavenly. I used to look at the picture often and say to myself, *Look at me and my boyfriend.* I looked at that picture for hours, and then I made a decision. I could not ruin the lives of my family, D, and his family. *My life is already ruined. Why make things worse?*

I decided to do nothing. I would not go to counseling. I would just get over it. During my hospital stay, they told me I was a manic depressive. I was placed on Haldol, an antipsychotic used to treat schizophrenia. I just accepted what they told me and took the medicine. I didn't have any feelings about the diagnosis. I did have a feeling about the Haldol: I hated it. It made me feel out of it and tired all day. I felt like a zombie, and unlike myself.

I spent a lot of time with Aunt Betty and Nana around this time. I loved being around them. They made me feel comfortable and listened to me. I also hung out with my dad and brothers on days I was too sick to go to school. After a while, I stopped taking the medicine and started feeling physically and mentally better. Telling Mom about the abuse made me feel free and brought us closer together.

She was happy to take me off the medicine since it made me feel awful. Things seemed back to normal, until I began having sex.

I met a young man named Junior, whom I thought I fell in love with. We were both sophomores and went to the same school. We were inseparable; I felt like he loved me. He held my hand when we walked. He always worried about my safety and gave me his jacket when he thought I was cold. He took me out every weekend and didn't look at other girls when we were together.

He told me I took all of his energy and he loved that. He was my first true lover, but he never believed me, because I didn't bleed when we had sex. There had been rumors that I had been with many guys at the high school. They were not true; however, I never denied them. The most I had done was let a few guys suck on my breasts and get on top of me, but only D and Junior had ever been inside of me.

Junior and I were going strong. We were popular at school and always together. We were having sex on a regular basis and doing exciting things. The more sex we had, the more I felt he loved me. We were always careful and used condoms. One day he called me from his job at a portrait studio in Glendale Mall and asked me to come have sex with him. We had sex where the babies posed for pictures. Every week we met there and had sex. We had sex in cars, outside, and in the apartment's clubhouse. I loved all of the excitement. There were times we had sex and our parents came home five minutes later, or they were in the next room. One day, after the state fair, we had sex outside by the picnic table. This time neither of us had a condom. I got on top, and it was the most powerful feeling I had ever felt. He came inside of me.

"We are gonna do it like this from now on okay," I whispered in his ear. His mom picked us up three minutes later. I still had his sticky cum in my panties as I climbed in the backseat of her beat-up Charger.

I was lounging in my loft, blasting my radio, when Mom's voice startled me.

"Reign, your Uncle Jim is on the phone."

I plopped down on my bed.

"What up man?"

Uncle Jim had moved to Atlanta, Georgia. He had been there for ten years when he called with an idea. He was putting a group together and wanted me to be in it. I was so excited.

"Heck yeah, I am down. Junior will be so happy. It's about time I live my dreams and make it big."

I hung up and began to daydream. I could see myself on stage as a lead singer. I had the mic in my hand, threw my head back, and wailed. *I love to be on stage.* I felt the music in my chest. The crowd swayed back and forth. My voice captivated them. It was my time, and I was ready. A few weeks later, a woman named June called me.

"Hello, Reign, I am putting the group together. Take down this number. There's a girl named Tomika I want you to connect with."

As soon as I hung up, I quickly dialed her number.

"May I speak to Tomika? Hey, this is Reign, the girl starting the group. How old are you?"

"This is Tomika. I am eighteen, and I live on my own."

"Oh, cool, so when can we meet up?"

"Well, I have a one-year-old son, so I will need to find a sitter. We can probably hook up on Friday."

I was excited to meet her. From what I heard, she could blow.

Tomika and I got along well. She was silly, and I fell in love with her son, Damieon. We met June face to face. She would manage and write songs for us. We immediately began recording in the studio, and things moved fast. June had two other girls she knew who could sing. We met them and we became the group Baby Girl. The group consisted of Tomika, Melissa, Amber, and me. Melissa had a smooth voice like Aaliyah and was beautiful. Amber was not as good a singer, but she had other strengths. She was a cheerleader and a good writer.

We began to practice songs our manager, June, wrote. We were in the studio at her home once a week. We sounded good together, had a nice blend, and got along well. I enjoyed being around the girls and considered them friends. We talked on the phone even when we were not singing. Being an only child at home, I loved to interact with them.

That spring Uncle Jim came from Atlanta with some tracks for us. He stayed in Indianapolis for a week, and we were in the studio nonstop. I loved being in the studio. If we were not singing, we were clowning, eating, and dancing. I liked the long studio sessions; sometimes we were there for ten hours. It worked perfectly because Junior helped me a lot. He would take me to practice and pick me up at night. He always supported me in my dreams.

We were becoming less like a group and more like a family. Tomika would bring her son sometimes, and he became like my nephew. One of the girls in the group found a singer name Elisha. We set up a meeting at TRC studios to meet with her. I remember this small, cute girl walking in. She had a squeaky voice,

"I am gonna sing a gospel song okay?"

When she opened her mouth, she had a surprisingly strong voice. *That girl can sang.* We recorded a song that night. It was official: Elisha was in the group.

After Elisha joined the group, things moved even faster. We learned three songs and recorded them in three weeks. Uncle Jim was coming home on a regular basis. The great thing about us was the five of us could hold our own, and our weakest singer could write. We would all have a part on each song. Elisha and Tomika blended well on the hook and shared the bridge. Most times, I started the song. I enjoyed being the first voice you heard. I would let you know to listen up. Melissa's voice was smooth and sweet. You always felt like she was singing right to you. Melissa had curves too, and she could dance her butt off. Tomika, Amber, and I had a more difficult time learning the dance steps. Once I was taught, I was okay. Elisha and Melissa were made to dance and picked up our choreography quickly.

I was still attending high school and becoming more popular. I felt like a star at school. I would dress in Baby Girl gear, and my hair was always fly. People would ask me when our album was coming out, and I would always say "soon." One weekend we had a group photo shoot. We went to a nice hair salon and got the latest styles. I had a similar style to Coko from SWV, with a full eyebrow arch and full makeup. My hair was bone straight with a middle part. We had on all black for the pictures and silver shoes.

I went to school that Monday feeling like a million bucks. Junior was bragging to all of his friends.

"My baby is 'bout to be a star. She is 'bout to blow up. She is 'bout to be wifey and superstar."

I wore shirts showing my six-pack abs and low-cut tops to show my cleavage. I gained a lot of attention from the whole school. I thought I was the shit.

It was October, and the annual Circle City Classic was in town. Most people in the city were going to the game, including my mom. Junior and I had a plan. When Mom left for the parade, we made love on the steps of my apartment building. The next morning I threw up. My stomach hurt and I felt queasy. I thought back to the fair and the absence of the condom. I knew it: I was pregnant. A month later, a test confirmed what I already knew.

After I found out I was pregnant, my life seemed to be looking up. Junior got a job, and we were still doing well in school. Although we were living a grownup life, I still wanted to hang out with friends. After a while, Junior began to hassle me. We began to argue about my hanging out while he was working. One afternoon, I was with my friend Brian. As I walked back to my apartment, Junior confronted me.

"Where are you going, and where have you been?"

I was startled when I heard his voice. "Um, I was with my friend Brian."

Why does he care? I thought to myself. *He is always at work, and all we do is argue.*

"Brian came to see me, and we walked over to the clubhouse."

As I walked up the steps, Junior was behind me. I felt my body falling down and realized Junior had pulled me. I was six months pregnant, and it was the first time I had ever been hit. He told me that I better stay away from Brian and any other boy who tried to talk to me. I tried to explain, but he walked down the stairs and got into his car.

"Please don't be mad at me. Don't leave me."

He yelled out of the window: "The only way you are leaving me is in a body bag."

Things were off and on between us. One thing we had in common was that we wanted to make things work for our unborn baby. We argued and fought, and the next day we were best friends. Junior went to most of my doctor's appointments with Mom and me. My pregnancy was going pretty good, even with all of the stress I was under.

Since I was a soon to be mother, Uncle Cleo thought I should learn how to drive. He took me to an empty parking lot and started teaching me the basics. It was rough riding.

"What do you do when you get into the car?"

"Put my seatbelt on." I did so.

"Okay, what next?"

The car was in park. I put my foot on the gas and punched it. The car didn't move. I was confused.

"Oh, Reign, this is gonna be hard, sweetie. You need to learn how to drive, but you know nothing."

"Well, Junior said he can take me everywhere I want to go. So far, that's what he does. We are gonna be together, so getting around won't be a problem."

"Sweetheart, you have to be independent. You can't always rely on Junior or your mom."

That word independent scared me. I needed Junior, and I liked being able to count on him. We drove around the parking lot for a while. I was comfortable and felt safe in there. When Uncle Cleo asked me to go onto the main road, I panicked. My hands started sweating, and I could hardly breathe.

"We will stop for now, but we have to come back to this. We have to get you mobile."

On the night of May 4, 1994, I was at home with Mom. We were watching a little TV when I felt a sharp pain in my stomach.

"Ma, my stomach is hurting. I think I need to take a bath."

This happened a few times during my pregnancy. Once I had to be rushed to the ER, but it was a false alarm. The other time I ate a bad orange that messed up my stomach. I usually took a warm bath. So that's what I did.

"It's still hurting, and so is my back. Oh, it feels like I am about to pee on myself."

My mom started getting dressed. Alex Trebek announced the daily double. I watched the rest of *Jeopardy*, and we left for the hospital. We both thought we would be back, so we didn't pack. I was only seven months pregnant. Actually, I wasn't sure how many months I was. Junior and I had sex all of the time, so I could have gotten pregnant at any time. When we got to the hospital, they examined me. Someone called the doctor, and he said, "We have to stop the baby."

They were about to give me the medicine to stop the contractions when my mucus plug came out, and seconds later my water broke. They checked me again, and I was dilated to ten centimeters; the baby was coming and quick. They asked, "Do you want any medicine for pain?"

"No, I am fine. I'm not in too much pain. It just feels like I have to make a number two."

Junior was kept out of the room until the very last minute. The doctor never seemed to like Junior. Maybe it was the fact that he was a boy who had knocked up a girl. Maybe he knew what I kept hidden, that Junior and I were physically fighting.

They gave me a local anesthetic, and my baby girl was born minutes later. I pushed three times and there she was. I thought she looked funny. They showed her to me and then rushed her away. They said they would have to hook her up to machines because she was premature at four pounds nine ounces. I was fine and just wanted to take her home and begin to bond. I named her Princess Denice.

They took her to the NICU right away. She was jaundiced, so she had to stay under a heat lamp for weeks. The doctor told me jaundice was a condition that makes the skin appear yellow. Princess was in the hospital for a month. I would sit near her for hours, singing and reading to her. She was funny even at that young age. She would pull the bandages from her eyes. Just imagine a tiny baby with little arms pulling at her eyes. They had to tape them to her little forehead. She had a full head of hair. It was jet black and looked like it was finger-waved. Her eyes were slanted, and she appeared to be of Hispanic descent. She had an extra finger on her hand that the doctor had to tie off. It looked like a little pimple, but to me she was absolutely perfect. She was the most beautiful thing I had ever seen, and she belonged to me.

For the next month, I learned how to hold and feed her. I went to school every day, and then in the afternoon Junior and I came and sat with Princess. At night, Mom and I sang to her and prayed. She always looked at us and darted her eyes at night. Mom and I always joked that she was looking at the clock, like, *What is wrong with you guys? It's ten o'clock at night.* With the help of my family, I managed to go to school, keep my grades up, and see my daughter two times a day. Before, I hadn't cared about school, but after having Princess, I knew I had to do my best. I had something to live for.

After four weeks, Princess came home. She was eating well and had gone from four pounds nine ounces to six pounds. Her skin was an olive color instead of the sickly yellow caused by the jaundice.

When I finally got Princess home, I tried to get accustomed to the new baby routine. One night I was sleeping soundly when I heard a noise and wondered how a cat had gotten into my small loft. It kept purring, and I was annoyed. I woke up and remembered it was my daughter. She was no longer in the hospital but under my care. I went into 'mommy mode.' I enjoyed feeding her and kissing her. I would sit up for hours, smell her, and touch her hands.

Junior spent the night during the week and helped with Princess. Many nights, Junior stayed up with her. He seemed to be taken by her. He had helped raise his siblings, so caring for her was nothing for him. We sat and held her and talked baby talk. We laughed at her funny faces, and everything she did seemed so cute. She was so goofy and would make monkey sounds and copy what we did.

Parenting wasn't always a joy for me. At the beginning, Princess was sick and had colic. She would cry and scream for no reason. When she yelled and shook, I would cry with her and try to think of things to soothe her. Many times, Mom and Junior's mom, Sophia, would come and help. After I learned how to do things to make Princess comfortable, she would fall asleep in my bed.

She was the most beautiful part of both of us. We vowed to make sure she had the best in life, starting with a mom and dad who were together. We promised never to be the hated baby mommas and daddies we saw on Maury and Ricki Lake. *Naw, we are better than that.*

That spring, we went to the prom, took the SAT, and graduated together, with our daughter looking on in the crowd. Little did our family and friends know baby number two was in my belly as I walked across the stage and received my high school diploma.

Mom knocked on my door and said she wanted to talk with me. I sat down and lay in her lap.

"What up Mom Dukes?"

"Reign, we have got to get you driving. You have a new baby, and you need to be able to take her to daycare or the hospital if something happens to her."

"Nope, I'm straight. Junior got me if I need to take Princess anywhere. I hate driving and have no desire to learn. It scares me. I don't like having that much control."

"Come on, baby, give it a try. Uncle Cleo has been telling you for years, if you learn he will get you a car."

"Aight, but when I wreck your new car, then what?"

Mom took me to a local Village Pantry and got out. We traded seats, and I took the wheel. I thought back to the accident when I was nine. *I don't want to hit anyone, and I don't want to get hit. Here goes nothing.* I put my foot on the brake and put the car in drive. I had seen Mom, Dad, Junior, and Uncle Cleo drive enough times to know how to do it. The car began to coast. I put my foot on the gas and floored it.

"Slow down, Reign, just tap the gas. You are doing well."

I got in the lane and got ready to turn onto Emerson Avenue. I panicked. My hands started shaking and became sweaty. It was hard to breathe, and I screamed. I let go of the wheel, and the car careened to the left side.

"Get out of my car, Reign. You can't lose control. You can't scream and let go of the wheel. Then what? What happens if you let go of the wheel in the middle of the street?"

"I will kill someone, or they will kill me. I told you this was a bad idea."

Driving lesson over.

On Aunt Peaches's birthday, she invited everyone from the old days to come over. It was nice to see all of the others who called her Auntie. She had adopted a set of beautiful girls. My mind began to race. *Her daughters seem fine, but so did I. They're around the age I was when the abuse began. I can't allow myself to think about the possibility.*

Everyone cooed at how beautiful Princess was. Junior came along, and I introduced him to the family. D kept eyeing Junior, but he didn't say a word. D shook his hand like he was a nice guy, but I knew different.

I went to a back room to change Princess's diaper and felt eyes on me. D put his hand on my shoulder. The coldest chill went down my spine and then all over my body. I looked back, and he said, very dry, "Don't worry, Reign, I won't hurt you. Don't be scared anymore."

I nodded my head and went into the living room like nothing happened. Junior knew all about the abuse, but he sat there and talked with D. *How can I blame him? I am acting like nothing is wrong.*

That night Junior and I argued. He said I was lying about the abuse, and I thought he should have done something. I wanted to hurt D, but I was afraid. I felt like someone should fight for me, but as usual, no one did. I had been a victim so long I didn't know any other way to live.

The summer of my graduation, Uncle Jim suggested we go to a showcase in Atlanta. We packed a truck and all of our stuff and set off for the A. It was to be an all girl-trip: the girls and our manager, June. Junior surprised me by telling me he was coming too. We dropped Princess off at Sophia's house and got ready to leave. After packing up the car with clothes, shoes, food, and everything else we could think of, we realized Junior couldn't fit. There wasn't even room to move. Junior would have to rent a car and come later.

Ten hours later, we arrived in Atlanta. Uncle Jim had a nice crib. He took us on a tour and told us to make ourselves at home. He has always been the cool, fun uncle, and the girls didn't waste time taking advantage of that. We were not there three days before we started tearing his house up. Amber called her boyfriend long distance like she was at home. I let her have it, as did the other girls. Someone was on their period and dripped blood on the carpet. It couldn't have been me, since I was quietly four months pregnant. We decided to clean up the blood with some cleaner. No one read the label, and minutes later the light beige carpet was bleached white. We hid the spot with a rug.

I was frustrated, so I called Junior. He and his cousin Malik arrived in Atlanta and stayed at his Aunt Sadie's house. I asked them to pick me up, and we cruised around the city. The girls seemed jealous, but I didn't care. *I need a break from these hens.* We rehearsed for hours each day, with a vocal coach and choreographer, leading up to the showcase. We went over the show so many times that I was sick of all of the songs. Elisha helped write one of our songs. She added "Baby girl yeah we be rollin'" in the hook. It became the Baby Girl anthem. It was fun and full of energy. We must have sung that song a hundred times.

Finally, the night before the showcase arrived. All of the girl groups and female soloists went to the hair salon. We grabbed some food and piled on the floor of the shop. We were there for eight hours. It was worth it, though, because when we came out, we looked good. We left and went to bed. I was antsy and couldn't sleep; plus the baby inside me was restless and wouldn't be still. For the most part, I did a good job hiding my pregnancy. Even in Atlanta, where it was eighty degrees most days, I had on a heavy hoodie. Uncle Jim asked, "Why are you so overdressed?"

I told him, "The air in your house gives me the chills."

I went to the bathroom constantly and told the crew it was the sweet tea I loved so much. They were so naive. At four months pregnant, I was definitely showing. I guess sometimes you see what you want to see.

In the middle of the night, I called Junior.

"There is nothing in the house to eat, and this baby is starving. I don't feel good either, and all of this dancing is wearing me out."

"I will be there soon," Junior replied.

When he got there, he had no food. I was upset but didn't want to wake anyone in the house. I drifted off to sleep with an empty stomach.

The next morning Elisha woke up first.

"It's show time, ladies, wake up. I am starving I'm gonna make some Ramen noodles."

I had never heard of these noodles, but I was starving. Elisha boiled some water and got in the shower. I added the noodles and got ready to drain them when they were done.

"Reign, what are you doing? You don't drain Ramen girl. Look at this girl, ya'll." They all started laughing.

"I thought it was like spaghetti." I was ashamed that they were laughing at me. The girls explained the concept to me and cracked up.

"Well, if it's cheap, how do you know about it, Elisha? You too, Melissa?"

Both of them are uppity. They both lived in very nice homes and had both parents. Tomika, Amber, and I were from poor backgrounds and seemed to be more urban.

"Girl, this is Ramen. Everybody knows about this." Elisha shook her head and walked away.

Melissa grabbed the bowls and scooped hearty amounts in them. That was breakfast.

We got ready to leave and headed to the spot. We sang a little bit of each song, making sure to preserve our voices for the big show. I was nervous; our outfits were cut off and tied at the stomach. The pants were very fitting. I wondered if I could zip and button them over my stomach. The hardest part would be sucking my stomach in for the fifteen-minute performance. We pulled up to the hall. *No time to be scared. It's performance time.*

There were groups, celebrities, and record label executives at the showcase. Among them was young singing sensation Monica, whom I adored. I loved her song "Don't Take It Personal." Keith Sweat was sitting in the front row, along with other musicians I didn't know. We went into a dressing room on the side and got prepared. *Today is the first day of the rest of our lives.* We had confidence that we would be signed to a major label soon.

The entire crew from the showcase was hype. We held hands and prayed. I went into a private bathroom while the other girls got dressed in the common area. I couldn't risk them finding out; I had come so far in hiding the secret. We watched the other artists perform and stayed backstage. We were fourth, so we had a little time to chill.

"Okay, girls, it's about that time."

June stuck her head in the back. We held hands and prayed again. *This is it, Reign.*

The announcer introduced us, and I heard the music drop.

"Hello, Atlanta, we are Baby Girl. Watch us work."

We finished the first song. I thought it went well. The ballad was next, and we always impressed everyone with that one. Elisha shined on that, and we backed her up with spot-on harmonies. The fast cut was next, and we hyped up the crowd.

"Thank you, Atlanta," Elisha and I said in unison, as planned.

What a rush, I thought.

"Great job, girls." Uncle Jim hugged us all.

Now all we had to do was wait for the phone calls. The next day we headed back to Indianapolis.

Before we hit home, Uncle Jim called June.

"Reign is pregnant, and the entire showcase knew it."

She talked to me in private, and I confirmed it. She said she would keep my secret and not let the girls know. They wouldn't find out until after my second child was born.

A few weeks later, we reviewed the tape of the show. What we thought and how we did in the show were two different things. As we watched the tape, we realized someone was sharp on the entire first hook, but we corrected it on the second hook. The ballad went well as always; however, the last song was just okay. Between that and my pregnancy, no label wanted us. *It's my fault that we didn't get a deal. If I hadn't gotten pregnant, things would have been fine.*

There were many events going on in our family. The pressure of being adults began to take its toll on us. Junior and I had a one-year-old daughter and a baby on the way, and now my singing dream was crushed. The physical abuse escalated on both sides. Every day we were fighting, but neither of us was strong enough to leave the other. We hated each other and what we had become together. As children of divorced parents, we forced it to work. No matter what happened, we didn't want to let go.

There I was again in the bathtub, stomach hurting. Junior was at work, and Princess was at Sophia's. I called Junior's job and talked with his boss. The man couldn't believe it; he thought I was some chick calling.

"Who is this? Junior is with Reign, and she is not pregnant. Who are you, trick?"

I can't believe this.

"Damon, this is Reign, and I am having a baby." I was forgetting no one knew I was pregnant.

"Junior, I think I am having this baby now!"

"Reign, why are you calling me at work? You know it's not time to have that baby yet. Finish your bath and quit bothering me, damn." Junior hung up the phone. I was in so much pain, but not enough to cry. I knew the baby was coming. I had to do what I hated to do. I had to call my mom and tell her I was pregnant and needed her help.

"Ma, please come. I am having a baby. Junior will not come home and get me. He says he's working and ..." She hung up the phone and was there in minutes.

"Reign, I knew you were pregnant. Why didn't you just tell me? Why didn't you trust me?"

I couldn't answer her; I was rolling around on the floor holding my stomach.

"I'm calling an ambulance." She picked up the phone and dialed.

"Please don't, Momma. I don't want people on this street looking and making fun of me. No one knows I am pregnant, and I want to keep it that way."

We went back and forth for a few minutes. I screamed out in pain.

"If you don't get off that floor and get in the car, I am calling and NOW."

I obliged and got up. She took my hand and put me in the back seat of her car. I rolled from one side of the car to the other. It didn't hurt that much; it was just irritating. Mom started driving to Methodist Hospital. On the way I told her, "I need to push."

"No, Reign, you can't. We have to get to the interstate first. We have to get off on Capitol; we have to go to Methodist. We still have fifteen miles to go. You can't push, baby."

I pushed, and I told her, "My water just broke."

She made a quick turn and said, "We'll have to go to a closer hospital, Community East; it's two miles away."

I sat up in the car, and my son fell into my arms. I felt no pain. In fact, it felt good when he came out. All of the blood and goo came out all at once. *This is gross. Momma's gonna kill me when she sees the backseat of her car.*

My son was born in the backseat of Mom's maroon Nissan Sentra on October 11, 1995. She turned the heat on and began to pray. At that moment, my son opened his mouth and let out a scream that frightened me but made me laugh at the same time.

"Wow, little man, you sure are my son. Those lungs are no joke. It's okay, little man. Are you okay, baby? Hi, I'm your mom."

Mom continued to pray as we pulled into the hospital. She ran in and called for help. Three doctors opened the car door and looked at me as if I was a sideshow at the circus. There I was, legs spread-eagle, baby in my hands. All my business was out. It was cold, and they just stared.

"I am the doctor who mends broken bones. I don't do babies. But it looks like this one is already done," the fuzzy-haired man said.

He brought me a wheelchair and picked me up. I held my son in my arms. *My son ... I have a son.* After all the secrets and lies I had told, right now all that mattered was this moment. I looked into deep gray eyes and smiled.

"I may not have wanted you yet, but you are here, huh? You couldn't even wait until we made it to the hospital."

They put me in a room and took my son.

"What will you call him?" a short, pudgy woman asked. I had no idea. I didn't think he was coming so soon.

"Maybe we should call him Nissan or Sentra, since he was born in the back seat of one. No he wasn't conceived in one. I know what you are thinking."

I settled on Jamal. I thought it was a strong name. My mom loved it, and when Uncle Cleo came in, he did too. I realized Junior had no clue that his son had entered the world.

"Mom, can you call Junior and tell him I just had his son?"

She was reluctant but called him anyway. The pudgy lady washed Jamal up and gave him to me. He was so big, much bigger than Princess had been. I kissed him, and he purred in my arms. I took his finger, and he squeezed mine. *This kid is already strong.* We cuddled, and I fell asleep with him on my chest.

When I woke up, Junior was standing over me.

"Jamal? I think not, Reign. That shit is not going down. His name is Big Smooth III, just like mine. I am Junior and he will be the third. You must be out ya mind."

Mom was livid. "Reign, he was not even here for his son's birth, and he thinks he can get mad and change his name hours later."

It is not worth the fight. Mom doesn't get it. I spend all of my days fighting with Junior; I give up. I loved Big Smooth's grandfather, and he would be named after him.

I just went with it.

The family called, and no one could believe I had a baby.

"When were you pregnant?" Tomika was on the phone.

"I had to keep it a secret. I still wanted to sing and have my life. I didn't want anyone to know that I was pregnant again at such a young age."

"You could have trusted me. I thought we were friends."

"We are friends, Mika. I was ashamed; I'm nineteen with two children. I'm sorry, I gotta go."

The entire family came over to see the new baby. They all were amazed that I had been nine months pregnant and no one had a clue. Big Smooth was beautiful. He was a mix between my grandfather and Junior's grandmother. His eyes were gray, and when he was angry, they would turn green. He had jet-black curly hair. He was so light he could have passed for white. We made jokes and called him the milkman or the mailman's son. He was a wild baby who came out with a bit of an attitude. He always looked at us like we were crazy. He turned his nose up a lot, too. At church, he looked around as if to say, *What is this place?*

Big Smooth and Junior were real close. Junior would come home and hold him late into the night. He was proud to have a son. But having another baby just made things harder for us, and soon the happy family wouldn't be enough to keep us together.

After Big Smooth was born, Junior worked long hours. Daycare was too expensive, so I had no choice but to stay home. During the day, I would call Junior and bother him. I was lonely and bored being home with the kids. I tried desperately to please Junior. I always had dinner ready when he came home. I made desserts and cleaned the house. The children were always fed and asleep at night. I would get excited when I heard the hum of the car pulling into the driveway. But when Junior came in the door, he was often tired and irritated. He would pull out the bills and sigh.

One Valentine's Day, I was especially excited. I made a sign on the top of the stairs that looked like a restaurant. We had pork chops, mashed potatoes, greens, and rolls. I made the plates, set the table, and lit a candle. I bathed in scented bubble bath. I oiled my body down and slipped into a black one-piece cat suit. Although I was a mother of two, my body was still banging. My breasts were an ample 36, my waist was a small 34, and my booty was nice and round, although it was smaller than the rest of me. Junior used to love my body. I was confident that it would be a romantic night.

As he walked into the door, he called for me. "Reign, where you at, baby?"

I snuck out and moved my body into the candlelight. He smiled a wide grin. I turned on some music to set the mood. We ate our dinner in silence.

"Reign, turn down the music; it's irritating me."

I moved over to the stereo and huffed as I pushed the power button to off. Princess started to stir out of her sleep. I got up and went to check on her. When I came back into the kitchen, Junior was gone. He was in the bedroom sound asleep.

"Get up boy! It's Valentine's Day and you are gonna sleep?"

I jumped on top of him. Next thing I knew I was being choked and hit in the face. This time it was gonna be a two-way fight. I was determined to hurt him as much as he hurt me. I hit back and scratched. We tussled all over the bed and floor. After a while, we both became tired and gave up. We ended the night making love on the floor where Junior shed blood.

That fall, our singing group reunited to plan our next move. After a few disappointments over new opportunities and promised deals, the group began to have disagreements. We had a lot of personal issues and jealousy between us. Elisha was getting a lot of attention as far as her starting a solo career. We began name-calling, and one day we had a meeting and there was a full blowout.

Amber was put out of the group for her lack of ability to hold her own note. Shortly after, Elisha left the group, taking a huge amount of talent. Melissa left, stating she couldn't handle all of the drama. We were right back to just Tomika and me. Finally, after a few failed gigs, we fell out and split up as members and friends.

I joined two other groups and attempted to sing professionally. Finally, I gave up on singing in that aspect. *Women are catty and have issues. Someone is always jealous, pregnant, or trying to screw a manager or producer.* I got sick of the whole environment. *I'll save my singing for the car and shower.*

By this time, Junior and I had moved into a new apartment on the far east side of town. Junior was making more money, and I had a full-time job. For a while, things were pretty good and life was normal. There was work, kids, family, and sleep.

One day, Junior went bowling and stayed out late, as he usually did. I was sick of being lonely. As the song says, "Sick of being lonely while my man is out with his homies." I decided to call my long-time friend Joel. He was a man who had never liked Junior had and warned me about him when we were in high school. I had known Joel since I was eight years old. He didn't hesitate to come when I called him.

Joel was a great guy and easier to talk to than Junior. We talked music because we loved all types. He was a photographer and told me all about his hopes and dreams. He looked in on the children and commented on how beautiful they were and how big they had gotten. He had been there for me when I was pregnant with both children. He also associated with Junior but didn't trust him.

"My relationship is not going well. The only reason I am still with Junior is the children."

"Reign, you deserve so much better. I wish there was something I could do to make you happy."

He held me, and we kissed. I had wanted this for a while but never admitted it to myself. There was no stopping this moment. He lifted my shirt up over my head and played with my nipples. They became rock hard. He ate me with his kisses. I could feel his love for me pouring out of him. I had sex with Junior on a regular basis, but it was more like fucking or just 'doin' it' than sex. We would forcefully slam our genitals together, but this was soft, sweet, and passionate. As Joel tried to enter inside of me, I realized I was not as wet as normal. The mound in between my legs was not listening to what my heart said. I knew deep down that I loved this man. *Come on, work with me*, I told my body. *I've known Joel for years. What is going on?* My body was tense to the touch. I reached my hand down to touch his penis. *WOW!* This man, whom I had known for years, was packin'. My eyes widened, and he laughed.

"Boy, you got it like that?"

"That's yours if you want it."

He placed his fingers inside me and kissed me. Noticing my dryness, he grabbed my legs wide and devoured me with his tongue. My mind was somewhere else. *This is wrong. What am I doing? If I don't want to be with Junior, why not leave instead of cheating?* I forgot about Joel until he attempted to place his penis in my quivering body. He pushed his manhood around the lips of my vagina. It hurt badly, and each time he tried, I winced. *I'm trippin'*, I said to myself. *This is not Joel who stepped on my church shoes when we sang in the children's choir. This is not the boy who always liked me and I liked him too.* He tried to penetrate again, to no avail.

Frustrated, my mind started to wander. *Maybe this is not what God wants for us.* Finally we gave up, and the rest of the night he held me, and we talked and laughed. That felt much better. It felt natural for Joel and I to just be friends. Junior called to let me know he was on his way. It was two o'clock in the morning. Joel quickly left. All I needed was a friend to talk to who would listen, but I had gone too far with him.

I knew Junior was on his way home and would want sex. I quickly showered to erase any traces of another man. As I stood in the shower enveloped in warmth and suds, I closed my eyes and thought over my life. *What would have happened had I gone out with Joel? Why didn't I take his advice about Junior back in high school?* I crawled into bed and enjoyed what seemed like only minutes.

Junior came through the door and called for me. I faked like I was asleep so I wouldn't have to talk to him. He smelled of beer and Black & Mild cigarettes. He pushed and pulled me and told me, "Get up."

I lifted my head and asked, "What do you want? You were out all night. What you want from me now?"

He jumped on top of me and pushed down on my face. I kicked him off the bed and onto the floor. This time I would take my frustrations out on him. I kicked him until I couldn't see straight. He held onto his head and winced. I lay down feeling vindicated. Before I could get underneath the covers, he pounced on me again. He slammed my face into the pillow. I didn't feel a thing, but my adrenaline was pumping. I threw a set of keys at him. When he reached for me, I ran out of the house and into the night.

I raced through the complex feeling like some white woman in a horror movie. I heard his steps behind me.

"Bitch, don't run, or I'll kill you."

I never thought he would kill me, nor was I afraid. After all I had been through in my life, an overconfident little boy was not gonna scare me. I kept running and hid in the laundry room.

As I ducked under a drying table, questions ran through my mind. *Is this my life? This is what it has come to?* He came into the laundry room and grabbed me. He hugged me and apologized. I broke down, crying, and kissed him. That night we had sex. He fucked me like I was the dirtiest slut on the planet. It was nothing new; I had felt like that since I was nine. The next day I moved out of our apartment and the kids and I were back with my mother.

The last night Junior and I spent together, a child was conceived. I let him know I was pregnant a few months later. He didn't seem concerned at all. I was doing well and going to school while working. I didn't see him until late in my pregnancy. I was carrying his daughter, and she was due any day. I saw him at the skating rink, and he didn't even speak. He acted as if my swollen stomach meant nothing to him.

On Memorial Day, I felt a few pains in my stomach. I remember that day very well because the Indy 500 Race was supposed to begin. My back hurt, but that was really the only pain I suffered. Mom drove to the hospital, which was only a mile away.

"Ma'am, you are not dilated at all, and you are not really having contractions. Your back may be hurting because you are in the early stages. Go home and get some rest. She may be due in a few days."

We went back home, and I watched them postpone the race another day. It was raining so hard, they couldn't get the racetrack dry. I lay in bed and waited for my baby to arrive. The next day I woke up to lower-back pains and a headache. The pain was much worse than the day before, and I was throwing up. Once again, we went to the hospital, and they hooked me up to the monitors. The baby's heartbeat was fine. My blood pressure and other vitals were good. The baby still was not down far enough for them to keep me, and I was only dilated a few centimeters. This time, I walked around the hospital.

"Mom, I am not going home. This is crazy. I'm tired of being pregnant and ready to have this baby."

I walked around the hospital for thirty minutes and went back to the labor and delivery ward. The nurse was laughing when she saw me.

"Back again, huh." She smiled at me.

I got back into the stirrups and waited for another exam.

"Still not ready, sweetie. Why don't you go home and rest up. You will need it once the baby comes."

This time I decided to walk home and have Mom drive. I walked back home, past a Taco Bell, a Subway, and a China Buffet. I was tired when I got home, but the pain had stopped. I guess the doctors were right.

"OUCH!" I woke up with a backache and stomachache. I timed them.

"Momma, it's time. I am sure this time"

We went back to the hospital. This time there was another nurse on the floor, so there were no laughs. They put me in a wheelchair and prepped me. I was in pain, but not so much. I had been through this twice; this was nothing new for me.

"Reign, you are fully dilated. This baby is ready for takeoff."

Mom was standing over me, relaying to me what the nurses were saying. My head was swirling. I took a minute to call Junior and tell him his daughter was coming. Sophia answered and told me, "He's not home, but I will call him on his cell."

I, of course, didn't have the number.

Once again, it was me and Mom, Thelma and Louise. I looked into her eyes and thought, *My mom has always been there for me, no matter what. When I am right or wrong, it is me and Mom. Sometimes I think she does too much for me. When I look at her face sometimes I see age and wear. I know most of that is due to the pain she has watched me go through.* All of these thoughts went through my mind right before I heard one word.

"Push!"

I did, and in three pushes my daughter was born. She had so much hair, and her face looked like mine. She looked like a little Indian princess. She yawned and then took a big breath. She screamed at the top of her little lungs. I held her and said, "Babygirl, why didn't you want to come out? Why did it take you so long?"

She looked at me deeply like she knew something I didn't know. Mom came in, looked at her, and prayed for her. I named her after my great-grandmother. She was a sweet woman who didn't have a mean bone in her body. She took care of many people and fed others who didn't have much to eat.

"Yep that is what I will call you, Babygirl."

As I looked into my daughter's eyes, I was sad for her. I loved her, but her dad and I were not together. He didn't even think she was his. I lay back and thought to myself, *This child deserves a mother and a father.* Junior and his brother came up to the hospital right before I left. He picked Babygirl up and gave her a look over.

"Yeah, she's mine. She looks a lot like you, Reign. She also looks like Big Smooth and Princess. I am sorry I doubted you. Well, I have to run."

That was that, and he was gone. He spent all of twenty minutes with his new daughter and didn't even sign the birth certificate.

Mom and I waited an hour for doctor to release me. We were becoming impatient. Then we looked on the wall and saw the biggest roach I had ever seen. I was in the county hospital because Junior had taken me off his insurance. I was on Medicaid. I couldn't take it anymore. We grabbed Babygirl and left. As soon as we hit our front door, the phone rang. The hospital had the nerve to call my home and tell me they hadn't released me.

"I know. I released myself. Peace."

I hung up the phone and held my precious daughter in my arms.

The next few weeks I was so confused. My life was not in a good place. I would look at my daughter, and it seemed like she knew my thoughts from my soul. When I talked to her, she looked deeply into my eyes. It was like she knew what I was talking about.

"I'm so sorry; it's my fault Daddy doesn't want to be around."

Whenever I said sorry, she would snuggle up to me, like she forgave me. I asked her questions and watched her expressions. I kept asking Babygirl, "Why didn't you want to come out?"

She'd look at me sideways as if to say, "You know why."

I felt guilty for bringing her into a world that I no longer could control. Although my life had never been perfect, I had tried to keep control of things. I wanted to make my children happy. I wanted to make their dad love them. That was not my job. I couldn't make Junior love his children or me.

In the past, I had stayed with Junior because I thought having a father and mother was the perfect life for a child. Princess and Big Smooth had the opportunity to have Junior there for them, at least in some form. Babygirl had nothing, just Mom and me. But what I didn't know was that we were the best thing she could have. My family was the most supportive. They more than made up for Junior's absence. I still wasn't happy and knew I had to do something to better life for my children and me.

I sprang into action. I admitted that it was hard to take care of three children alone. I asked for help. I wanted Babygirl to have a mother and father around her. Princess and Big Smooth had the opportunity to have both parents; I felt Babygirl had a disadvantage by never seeing that. Uncle Cleo and Aunt Betty had her during the week while I was working. They nurtured her and showed so much love to her and each other. I knew Babygirl would feel that. Uncle Cleo fell in love with her. He treated her like his daughter. Nana also helped with Babygirl. She had boyfriend named Boyce; we called him Hey Baby, because he would come in the door and yell "HEY BABY!" They also helped take care of Babygirl during the week. They treated her like a daughter, too. She lived with my uncle, aunt, Nana, and Hey Baby during the week. I would call in the evening, and they would tell me what she was doing. The other children went to daycare while I worked. Babygirl got 24/7 care from the family.

I would spend time with Babygirl on the weekends. We were able to form the mother and child bond that we didn't have when she was first born. It may have been because I calmed down and forgave myself for bringing her into an unstable situation. The more confident I became, the more she latched onto me.

When she turned six months, I started keeping her during the week. Finally, I put her in daycare with the other children. During that time, Junior lost his cousin and best friend, Malik. He was having a rough time dealing with the loss. I called and tried to comfort him. Slowly, Junior started coming around. I told him what a tough time I was having raising three children alone. He understood and said he would help me. We reconciled and remembered why we had fallen in love in the first place. We eventually got back together. We were a family again. We were raising our three children. This time would be forever. It was now time to get married, for real, and stop playing house.

Junior and I made plans for the wedding. We wanted it to be huge. We had been together for so long we wanted to make it a wonderful event. Uncle Cleo and Aunt Betty helped to plan and pay for most of it. Mom got the invitations and thank-you cards. Dad and Momma Lisa did the reception for us.

We had seven bridesmaids and groomsmen. Princess was the flower girl, and Big Smooth the ring bearer. Yep, it was a ghetto-fabulous event with our kids in the wedding. We were married by

Junior's Uncle James. He was an ordained minister and was always supportive of us in all that we did. Junior's Aunt Benita and cousin Jerrica sang songs at the ceremony.

Finally, it was time to take the vows. I was glad it was over. Everything was perfect for about ten minutes. As we made our way downstairs to have cake and ice cream, Junior started telling me his finger was hurting. I looked at the finger I had placed the ring on, and it was swollen and red. By the time we cut the cake he was wincing in pain and agony. The ring would not come off, and it was obvious the blood was not circulating.

"My damn finger is turning blue," Junior shouted.

"Please don't cuss in a church. What is wrong with you?"

I looked at him and rolled my eyes. Someone called the fire department, and in moments they were there. To me it was funny everyone in the church was cracking up, including the firemen. They cut the ring off his finger, and we took some pictures. They told us that was a first for all of them. Just another event to add to the circus that was my life. Junior and I argued as we cut the cake. *What have I just done?* I thought to myself

We left the reception and went to a hotel my brother-in-law had paid for as a gift. I forced myself to sleep with Junior. *This is what a wife is supposed to do, especially on her wedding night, right?* After the long day and arguing, I just wanted to go to sleep. The lovemaking was short lived, and I quickly dozed off into La La land.

As I slept, I dreamt about something that happened earlier that day. On the way to the church, my mom had said, "Reign, are you sure you want to do this?"

"I think so." She then told me we could just drive off to Cincinnati and be out of there. I thought she was joking. I considered it but opted for my fairytale wedding instead.

"I hate this house! Who lives in their mother's house? This is insane! Why would you marry me and we have to live here in this dump?"

Once again, it was the same story. I was in a situation I didn't want to be in, but it was my own fault. I thought it would be a fairytale life; unfortunately, my Prince Charming was having his own separate happily ever after.

We were living in Sophia's old house. I thought we would at least get a nice apartment. The week we moved in, the water heater went out, and my father-in-law had to buy another one for twelve hundred dollars. The house included a family of ants, roaches, mice, and rats. Junior would put steel wool in the wall to keep the mice out, but they always made their way into the house. They ran in packs of twos and threes. One day I was lying down on the couch, and I heard a mouse crying for his life. I went into the kitchen. *Look at Mickey Mouse dying in the mousetrap.* He was clinging to life. It was awful.

Then, one evening, we smelled something stinky in the house. We looked into the trashcan and checked the garbage disposal. We could not figure out what the smell was. Junior lifted the couch, and there was a dead rat under the couch with gnats flying above.

Finally, my father-in-law said he would pay pest control to come out. My father-in-law was always helping us and paying for something. The man from the company came out. The worst part was a closet. He opened it, and I told him it always smelled horrible. Sophia told me it was the old clothes from the seventies stinking. That was not the case. When the exterminator looked into the closet, there were several dead mice and rats above the closet, with rat droppings everywhere.

You had to plunge the sink to wash dishes, and the smell was bad. The one small bathroom was always stopped up, and the tub the same. *This house is a health code violation. This is where I am supposed to live?*

I cleaned the floors with bleach daily, which never helped, because the dirt was years old and embedded in the floor. The seventies carpet was beyond raggedy. The couch had holes in it, and you could see the cotton in the cushions. I guessed it had once been leather, but it wasn't anymore. Junior's friends had used it to bone chicks on a regular basis. My children were sitting on the same couch.

"I'm leaving this house; it's unsafe for me and my children."

"You can't leave because rent is due tomorrow, and my mom needs her money."

"Rent, nigga' for a junky, holes-literally-in-the-walls house. Hell naw, I ain't paying jack. My kids are being chased by mice and have roaches for pets."

"Girl, the house ain't that bad; you just running your mouth. I mean, what do you want from me? We can't afford a house yet. For now, we have to stay here, and we have to pay my momma some rent. She has to pay her mortgage, and since we are here, we are paying."

I packed my stuff and left with my children. This was the beginning of me running from the marriage when things went bad.

A few days later, Junior called me at Mom's house.

"Baby, come home. I decided I would buy you a house. I will do anything to make you happy. If you want to leave my mom's house and move into our own, we can do that."

Those were the words I had waited so long to hear. I hung up the phone and waited to hear Junior pull up to my mom's. We quickly signed up for a home ownership class and began the process of buying our first home.

"Happy New Year's, baby." Junior kissed me. It was our first night in our new home. "We are homeowners, baby," I screamed out into the sky. We moved in on December 31, 1999. Everyone in the media was saying the world was going to end. They said the computers would go down and the banks would freeze all assets. Nothing happened. Junior and I ate cheese and drank wine until the wee hours of the morning. The past was behind us, and we were looking forward to our new life together. Things were well for quite a while. The children were great in their new school, and our marriage was thriving, but then everything came to a screeching halt.

"What the heck is that, Princess?"

I stared at the elbow-like bone sticking out of her side. I pushed and pulled it, and it sank back into her side. There was some small mass above her hipbone. I wasn't sure what it was, but I was going to find out.

"Junior, we need to call Dr. Yancy. Something is wrong with Princess."

He sulked into the room. "What now, Reign? What is the big emergency?"

I pointed to the small bump on her side.

"She probably fell on the playground; you are so dramatic, damn!"

"Well, you do what you want; I am taking her."

"What are you going to tell them? My daughter was playing on Crooked Creek's play yard and she fell, help?"

He walked out of the door for a basketball game and stuck his head back in.

"Well, you better take a cab because I am not taking you."

"Pull the bell Princess so we can get off this bus," I said as we headed to the doctor's office. Princess and I always had a great relationship. We have been close since the womb. I would read to her when I was pregnant. She heard me laugh, but she also heard and felt the pain I went through while pregnant with her. At seven years old, she was smart, funny, and very innocent. She was my little sweetheart. But she had never seen what I had seen in life; I tried to show her only happiness and good things. When Junior and I fought, I smiled like things were fine. I held back tears for her happiness. So when she asked me what we were going to the doctor for, I told her she needed to be checked out and acted as if it were normal.

"Ma'am, I am not sure what this is. You will have to go to Methodist to have them X- ray the mass."

The next day, Junior and I went to the hospital to have her checked out. The room was eerily quiet and cold. No one spoke as they took the X-rays. They put us in a room, and we waited a long time. When I saw the man's face, I knew bad news was coming. I hated Junior for not believing me. I knew something was wrong with Princess. The doctor told us that the lump on her side was a tumor. He said, "It will need to come out, and the surgeon will give you more information tomorrow. It is urgent that Princess go into surgery in the morning."

A day later, we were in surgery. My Princess, whom I gave back to God at three months, was hooked up to machines and given morphine. We all laughed at how she looked while under the influence. Her eyes were glassy, and she was telling us how funny we looked to her. Junior and I held hands and prayed. We became so close in those moments. Whatever we argued about seemed very small. All we could do was be there for our daughter, together.

"Please wait in the family room and have your family come back, Reign." I went and gathered everyone together. The doctor, the surgeon, and members of the grief staff came in to talk with us. They began to tell us how the surgery had gone. The kidney had been removed, and it was cancerous. It was enlarged three times the size. Had I done nothing, it might have gotten worse and spread throughout her precious body. They told us about the chemotherapy and radiation she would undergo. I heard nothing past that. I saw her lips moving, but no words came out. I felt like I would lose consciousness. My limbs went limp. *Did she just say chemo? What does that mean? Princess doesn't have cancer. What's happening here?* My mind was racing with everything she was saying, everything I wanted to believe, and every horrible scenario I could imagine.

I saw the faces of my family members begin to change. I looked at Aunt Rhonda, who had just gone through the loss of her mom to breast cancer. I locked eyes with Junior, who wore a blank stare.

Somehow it was his fault. *Maybe it was the abuse I endured while pregnant. Maybe it was the stress and arguing that did it.* I somehow caught my train of thought and listened to what was going on. The surgeon gave us the post-operation instructions and left.

The grief staff handed me a stack of paperwork. They told me what the future would hold. They were just words to me that meant nothing. *My baby will be fine. She has to be. There are only three things I have ever done right; they are Princess, Big Smooth, and Babygirl. I have to fix this and fix it now.*

The next month or so was a maze of chemo appointments, radiation treatments, hospitalizations, family, and friends. We lived at the hospital. I took a leave from my job. Junior would work, and as soon as he was done, he would come to the hospital and see Princess. We had a room there; one of us would sleep with her, and the other would sleep in the room. Sometimes I went home, showered, changed clothes, and left again.

Every day, I was moving a hundred miles per hour. My only concern and drive was to heal my child. I didn't like the idea of her only having one kidney. Earlier that year, we had bought our first computer. The first research I ever did was on cancer and kidneys. The cancer was called Wilms tumor kidney cancer. It was somewhat rare and had a high remission rate.

The chemo and radiation were going okay, but there were many other issues. Princess was sick all of the time. Not due to the chemo but just ill. She was in pain for the first few months. Each time we went to the hospital, they kept her. She would be home a few weeks and then admitted into the hospital again.

One day, we were leaving for clinic and Princess was feeling very bad. Most times, she was very mild, quiet, and polite. This particular day, I was getting her into the car. She held on to the car door and yelled at the top of her lungs, "I am not going to the hospital. No more doctors, no hospitals. I am sick of this. I don't want cancer anymore. I hate this!"

I carefully pulled her legs into the car, and Mom helped me calm her down.

After that day, the pain became less and less. The clinic visits were becoming normal. All of the doctors and specialists loved Princess and made me feel at home. Dr. Hock and his staff were amazing. She returned to school to cheers and applause. We were getting back into the swing of life.

I had to finally make sure that I made time to spend with Big Smooth and Babygirl. We went to dinner at Arni's Restaurant and had a ball. We talked about Princess and how we felt about her illness. They asked questions; I answered them. I tried to explain what was happening and that things would be fine. Convincing myself would be the hard part.

"Your hair is gonna be so cute, Princess. Do you want it like Babygirl's?"

I loosened the ponytail scrunchie and let down her beautiful mane. This year was the first time we had allowed her to straighten her hair and wear it in pretty curls. I began to comb, and she was silent. As I combed and ran my fingers through her hair, it came out in my hands. I sat there silently and tried to hold back tears.

"You okay, Momma? I tried to hide it from you. I didn't want you to be sad. It's okay, Momma, the doctor told us that would happen."

My seven-year-old daughter put her arm around me and smiled.

"Momma, I am still Princess. Now I have a fade like Big Smooth and Daddy."

Thank you, God, I thought. They say a child shall lead them. This small, sweet wonder was so strong and full of life. I took the hair out of the comb and put it in a bag. The rest of it filled up two huge bags.

"So, miss lady, what do you want to do about your hair?"

She rolled her eyes and said, "Nothing, it makes my head feel cool with no hair. I like it."

Momma Lisa, Sophia, and I bought all kinds of scarves. Momma

Lisa bought so many cute colors adorned with jewelry, and Princess loved them. She would match them with whatever she was wearing that day. We bought her hats too, but the scarves were her style.

One day, we were at the local Apostolic church and it was late and hot. The preacher was all worked up and doing his thing. The next thing I knew Princess had snatched off that scarf and said, "Ohhh, Momma! My head is sweating, and I am hungry too."

I laughed so hard. I was worried about how she would feel about losing her hair. All along, she was comfortable in her own skin and her own head.

I got the idea to cut my hair off in support of Princess. I mentioned it to Junior while eating dinner.

"You are not cutting your hair, Reign. What kind of bullshit is that?" Junior grabbed his plate of food and punished the bread.

"I want to do it for Princess. She is bald; why can't I be?"

I felt this was a meaningless argument. Just like all of them.

"That is dumb. You don't have cancer. Or do you want it?"

I sat down at the table across from him, defeated. "Junior, why does it matter to you? I am doing this for our daughter."

I secretly wished he would choke on the rolls.

"Ain't no woman of mine gonna be bald headed. I picked you because you are sexy. You have slanted eyes, long hair, big breasts, and you're light skinned. Just be happy with that. That's all you are. If you get rid of your hair, you ain't shit."

Wow! I went over that in my head. *All he thinks of me as is some trophy for him to brag about. Look, my wife had three kids, check her out. This is all I am to him. I have no feelings, no ideas, and no brain. My only purpose is to be something for him to look at and, when that gets old, someone to abuse. I should divorce him, and then cut my hair.*

Dealing with Princess's health was a never-ending roller-coaster ride. That frustration, along with the lack of sleep, made for more disagreements. By this time, we were spending the night during

Princess's hospital stays. One morning, I was trying to wake Junior. He didn't hear me knocking on the door of the room. I banged harder and pounded on the wood. The door to the room was locked, and I didn't have a way to get inside. I then went back to check on Princess.

After an hour, I went back to the door and knocked. I gave up and went to pick up breakfast for Princess and me. When I came back from the café, I could hear Junior calling me from her room. When I entered the room, he got in my face and yelled at me. He spit when he talked, and it got in my eye. I warned him to leave me alone.

I went back to the room and fed Princess. We watched some TV and talked a bit. Junior came in the room and pointed to the hallway. I followed him outside.

"Look, Junior, don't start no bullshit in this hospital. Can we just act normal in front of these white people?" I put my hand in his face.

"I don't want to hear nothing you have to say." He grabbed my finger and asked, "What is your problem?" He got back in my face and said, "Listen to me!"

I walked away, and he grabbed my arm. The nurses and doctors looked over, and he let go. I went back into the room with Princess, thinking he would walk away. He came in behind me and began to yell again. I was used to this kind of behavior. It was the way our relationship had been for almost eight years. I thought he would at least be cool with our daughter in a hospital bed next to us. I was trying to see the good in him but couldn't see past all of the hurt and pain.

Since we were at the hospital often, Mom thought Junior and I needed to get out more. She gave us some tickets to the Easter Passion play *Upon This Rock*. I thought that was a good idea, and maybe we could take our minds off what we were going through. We got dressed up in our Sunday best. I had on a lime-green ball gown with shoes to match. He had a nice white suit with a green bowtie and handkerchief. We were excited about the night ahead.

The play was nice and very intimate. It told of the life and death of Jesus Christ. I felt it was important and enjoyed being there. I had not been to this production since I was a small child and had not been out with my husband in months. I looked over at him to see his reaction to the play, but he was sound asleep.

On the way home I asked, "What did you think about the play? Did you like it?"

"I got some good Z's and counted five hundred sheep. That mess was boring and depressing."

I was angry and hurt. Here Mom was trying to do something nice, and, as usual, Junior had messed it up.

We rode the rest of the way home in silence. I paid attention to the windshield wipers going back and forth. I sat close to the door and looked out of the window.

"Do you want to go do it?"

I agreed, and we pulled up to the house.

Junior's family was at our house. Since Princess was at the hospital a lot, most of his family would stay there with the little kids. We walked in the door, and my home was a mess. There were plates all over the house; shoes were all over the place, a total disaster. They were tearing my home apart. We had only lived there four months.

Junior followed me around. "Why are you mad? Stop cleaning up. The house doesn't look that bad, dang. You act like this is a palace. You ain't all that. Plus this is my house. If my family wants to hang out here they have every right to."

I began to pack my things.

"Yep, and I have the right to leave."

As I packed my bags, my mind began to race. *I am so tired. It has been months of appointments, doctors, ups and downs. My day consists of waking up, getting breakfast for the kids, and sending them off to school. I try to work some hours waiting tables at lunchtime. I come home, make dinner for the family, and leave again for my second job. At nights, Princess is usually feeling bad. I spend lots of nights caring for her and trying to ease her pain. I am so tired. I need something.*

I also spent a lot of time praying but didn't know if I had faith that God could hear me. My past had taught me that faith is a weak-minded moral. If God had wanted to answer my prayers, my daughter would have never gotten sick and my marriage would not be falling apart. I still prayed every morning and every evening.

When I got home from the play, all I wanted was peace and quiet in my home. Junior's family didn't have a clue about peace, and they sure didn't give a damn about me. I called Mom at the hospital and told her I would be up there in a few hours. I packed my stuff and walked toward the door. Junior told me to come in the bedroom so we could talk. I followed him back there, and he shut the door.

"What do you want?" I asked. He began to kiss me. He took my shirt off, pushed my panties to the side, and stuck his penis inside. Five minutes later, he weakened and fell on the bed. He asked me was I ready to go. I grabbed my stuff and we left.

I got back to the hospital and showered. I let the hot water hit my back and massage my shoulders. I tried to relax and get everything out of my mind. All I could think about was my daughter. *If she does make it out of this situation, will she be able to deal with the divorce that I know is going to take place? Can I stay with someone I hate for the kids' sake? I have done it for years; why stop now?*

"You guys need to either be quiet or leave."

The nurse raised her voice at Junior's family. Princess was doing better but still being watched at the hospital. She was fine until his family visited, loud-talking and making a fuss. The nurse came in and said, "Every time one of you comes in Princess's blood pressure goes sky high."

I knew their intentions were good, but for Princess's sake, they would need to calm down.

Finally, everyone left, and I had some time alone with her. I kissed and hugged her. She asked me where I had been, like always. When Mom and I would leave the room, she would chastise us when we came back. The morphine made her so bossy. One day, we came up from getting lunch. Her face was turned into a mean scowl.

"Where have you been?" She was so mad.

Mom laughed. "We were hungry Princess."

This was a different side of my mild-mannered child. Another day, we went through some tapes to see what she wanted to watch on the VCR. She yelled at me because I put the wrong one in the holder. She asked to look at the box and see which one she wanted to watch. She never allowed any repeats and only watched new movies.

Another time, I couldn't keep myself from laughing. She had a rough time going to the bathroom. It hurt her to even walk. The nurse on duty was a heavyset man who looked like the Incredible Hulk.

He said, "You need to walk to the bathroom instead of using the bedpan."

"No!" She said and crossed her arms.

"Come on and try, sweetheart. If you do, I will give you a treat when you are done."

The man really tried hard to be patient. Next thing we knew, my forty-pound seven-year-old yelled, "No, I will not get up. No, I will not go to the bathroom, and I don't want a treat. I am not a dog."

"Will you try for mommy?"

I tried to raise her out of bed. She snatched her arm away. We tried again. This time she stood up and looked at the nurse like she would hit him. It was so out of character for her. Princess had never thrown a temper tantrum, even as a toddler. But here she was looking a 310-pound man in the face. Finally, Mom, the nurse, and I got her to the toilet. She was fine and had no pain.

The chemo and radiation lasted six months. At the end, there was one more surgery. It was a small procedure to remove the port. They insert a tube to allow the chemicals to flow. When the chemo and radiation is done, the port can be removed. The surgery was scheduled for a few weeks out.

Junior and I were still separated, and the children were splitting time between the two of us. The day of the surgery, I was at Mom's house with the little ones. Junior had Princess with him. I told him to meet Mom and me at the hospital for the procedure. We got there at seven forty-five in the morning. The surgery was at eight. Junior wasn't there yet. At eight ten, he arrived and rushed Princess over to us. She was admitted into outpatient surgery. The nurse asked, "What has Princess had to eat this morning or last night?"

The answer was supposed to be nothing. But Junior had given her yogurt that morning. The surgery was postponed. Thoughts of hurting him filled my head.

"You gave her yogurt? I mean, how dumb are you? You knew about the surgery, and everyone knows you can't eat the morning of a procedure. You are such an idiot."

Mom stood between us and rubbed my shoulders.

"Calm down, Reign, it's rescheduled, and next time *we* will make sure she doesn't eat before her surgery."

"We will take her to school," I told him as we left him standing in the waiting room.

"Hey, big girl, it's your last day."

I hugged Princess tightly. Big Smooth and Babygirl laughed and squealed in delight. All of the people at the hospital were happy as they waved goodbye. No more radiation or chemo; we would finally be back to normal life.

"Now you must have scans like this once every six months until you are twelve years old, alright."

Princess gave him a high five. "Super!"

My eyes filled with tears; we had made it. My girl was gonna be okay. It was time to move on with our lives. We would get past this. Princess was my survivor. She had shown us all what real strength was.

The nice nurse came into the room and smiled from ear to ear. She told us about a program called the Make-A-Wish Foundation. Princess would be able to do anything or go anywhere she wanted.

"You can take your family."

The nurse held her hand and said, "Princess, what is your wish? Do you want Britney Spears? How about to ride a horse? Anything you wish is yours. Make a wish."

Princess's eyes were wide as half-dollars.

"I want Mickey Mouse. I want to go to Disney World."

We scheduled the trip for six months out and left the doctor's office.

We were settling into life after cancer. For a few months, things were wonderful, and then our financial situation changed. I was working two jobs and making good money. I was working at the Spaghetti Factory in the day and Conseco Fieldhouse on game nights. I began putting money away for a rainy day, or a day when I would leave the marriage. Junior began to question where my half of the mortgage was. Not once did I pay any bills. The only responsibility I had was food and the kids' needs.

We were doing our usual nightly routine of bathing the kids. One of us would wash them, and the other would dry. After that, we would pray with them and then begin to talk about grownup business.

"You need to at least pay a bill."

"Junior, I understand I need to help to pay the bills, but why is it my responsibility to take care of your mother? My mom has been by herself for years, and she pays her own bills, goes to school, and works. Why would a grown woman need help from her son? Does she not know we have three small children?"

He tried to butt in, but I wouldn't let him. I cut him off when he tried to speak.

"Dang, when I first met you, you were so much fun. You seemed mature, but not only are you a momma's boy; you are her husband too. You are still the man of her house. I need you to be the man of our house and take care of us first. If we have extra, then we can help your mom."

"I am not a momma's boy. You are jealous of my mom, just like you have always been. I am the man of this house. I take care of you. What bills around here do you pay?"

It became so heated that we were screaming over each other, and the kids were in the middle yelling, too.

"This grown woman, who moved out of town, then back to town, has no job, and wants her son to bail her out. Once again the roles are reversed."

He walked away, but I followed behind, still ranting.

"Junior, this is some bullshit. We are trying to save money. How can we save when your fifty-year-old momma is in our pocket? Then you let her bring her couch in here, and we have two couches in the same room. Who has a beige couch and an all-white couch in the same room? The white couch is more like gray. How ghetto can we get?"

"You know what, Reign? You can leave. My momma can have what she wants. I will give her money when I want. I make all of the money, so you need to shut up. If she wants to bring her couch in here, she can. Why are you so damn jealous?"

We were up in each other's faces. If Big Smooth had not pushed him away from me, I am sure it would have been another full-on fight. The kids were hitting us and screaming for us to stop. *This was insane. It was time for an intervention.*

We decided that we couldn't solve our problems alone; we needed some help to gather the broken fragments of our life, so I scheduled an appointment with a therapist.

"The appointment is at five, Junior. Is that cool?" I prepared dinner for the family.

"Sure, baby, that's fine. I want to work on us."

Secretly I didn't care about working on us. All I wanted to do was make sure my children were stable and happy. I didn't care if I didn't love him. He could beat my ass every night. I could just see other guys. In my mind, I would stay married to this man until my children were eighteen. I had to make the marriage work for them. They deserved their mom and dad. That was what I was planning to do.

We pulled up to the Victorian Home on the Butler University campus. I was nervous walking inside. As I filled out paperwork, I thought to myself, *Glad I have some acting experience. It's show time, Reign.* I acted concerned as the therapist introduced herself.

"Hello, Reign and Junior, I'm pleased to be able to help you restore your marriage to what it once was. Now, tell me, what do you want from me? What can I help you with?" She was looking right at me. My mind was blank. Junior started and mentioned the money issues we had. He told her that I didn't want to help by contributing to the household finances. I said something about how I wanted to keep my money and made up something about wanting to save for the future. Deep inside I knew I wanted to have some money for the day I left him. When that day would come, no one knew. We talked about him choosing his family over the children and me. To this day, I don't remember what happened in that session. All I really remember is that the co-pay was twenty dollars.

I had one thing on my mind: the day this marriage would be over so I could move on with the man who had my attention at the time, Rico. Rico was a guy I knew from work. He would always give me compliments and made me feel attractive.

We began to ride home from work together. We use to talk and laugh on the way home. He had a girlfriend he was living with. I respected her at the time, but that would soon change.

One day at work, I was upset from struggling with Junior. Rico listened to me.

"Why are you with that fat muthafucka? Baby, you deserve better. You're a sweetheart, and look at you."

"He's the father of my children. I ain't goin' nowhere. I appreciate you listening, though. But it's no use, 'cause he ain't gonna change and I ain't leavin.'"

"Why stay with someone who doesn't love you? Don't you think the kids will see that it's all bullshit? Don't you want a man in your life who wants to be with you?

I started to speak, and he grabbed my face and kissed me right there at work.

That night I waited three hours for Junior to pick me up from work. I called Rico, who picked up on the first ring.

"Junior never came to pick me up."

He was there in ten minutes.

"Baby, if I was your man, you would never wait a minute for me to get you. You see how fast I got here?"

We talked on the way home and decided to stop by his apartment for a while.

I was so tired when we got back to Rico's apartment. We played my favorite old-school group, the Isley Brothers. I lay in his bed, and he came up behind me, grabbed me, and hugged me. Instantly, I was moist and excited. I had not felt wanted or needed by anyone in ages. Rico tore open a condom with his teeth and slid it on. I had not used a condom in years. Rico made love to me so sweet and slow. It was the first time I had relaxed while having sex. This man whom I had only known for a year acted like he knew my body so well. However, I knew it was only that way because I was needy and lonely.

The next morning I called Mom.

"Junior came by last night asking if I had seen you. He claimed he drove around downtown all night and couldn't find you. Where were you?"

I lied and said, "I stayed at a friend's house." I knew she knew what I was doing, because Momma always knows.

Junior knew I was with another man. He had to know. I had never stayed out all night anywhere. He knew I wasn't at my mom's. Where else could I have been? Sure enough, he asked me where I had been. I told him at a friend's house. We never discussed it after that.

Rico and I slept together after every event at the fieldhouse. One day his girlfriend took me home, and I was on the phone with him the whole way. He had gone to Chicago to see his son. *How crazy is this? I am in the car with the girlfriend of the man I am sleeping with, while on the phone with her man.*

I started to forget who I was. *I am not this person.* I would look in the mirror and hate my reflection. *Why am I married? I hate my life. I am doing this for my kids, but will this really benefit them? What kind of woman commits adultery and does it within days of each other?* The sex became less and less with Junior and me. That was strange, because as a wife I felt that cooking, cleaning, raising the kids, and having sex was my duty. I did it because I felt it was right. *What did it matter now?* I rationalized it in my head. I would stop messing with Junior and only sleep with Rico. In my mind, this was the only way I could keep my marriage together.

Rico went back to Chicago for a while, but we kept in touch over the phone. Most times, he would ask how I was doing or how Princess's health was.

"Hey, Reign, my girlfriend and I broke it off. She couldn't deal with me being back and forth to Chicago to see my son."

"That's crazy. Are you talking to anyone right now?"

"The real question is when are you divorcing Junior?"

"You know the answer to that, Rico. I am not leaving him until the kids are out of the house. That doesn't mean we can't kick it though."

"Nah, I ain't feelin' that. Holla at me when you done playing games."

He hung up without saying goodbye. I wouldn't talk to Rico for another six months.

Junior and I began to watch a lot of porn around this time. It was one of the ways we kept an interest in one another. I would close my eyes and pretend he was Mr. Marcus, dark chocolate skin and all. At first, we watched heterosexual pornography. We soon became bored with that and started watching girl-on-girl, group-sex, and more risqué pornography. This opened the door to a completely different spirit in our marriage.

One day, I walked up to Junior and kissed his neck.

"Baby, let's go out tonight. My dad says he will watch the kids for us. Let's get a room and hang out."

"Cool, Reign, let's do that."

We decided we would go to the spot we had used to go to in high school. We went to the Budgetel on the east side of Indianapolis.

When we got to the hotel, we had a plan. We'd call an escort and have her come over and stimulate our minds. I thought that since I wasn't being satisfied by Junior, maybe watching another woman with him would excite me. Watching the porn had me curious, and I wanted to try some of that. I called the number and told the woman what we were into. Thirty minutes later I opened the door and a brown-skinned sista with almond-shaped eyes stood at the door.

"Hey there, pretty lady," she said, looking me up and down.

"Um, hello." I was shaking, and a warm feeling came over my entire body.

"Did you call for an escort, sweetie?"

She must have been around twenty-five. She had skin the color of those Brach's caramel candies with the plastic wrapper. Her hair was light brown and looked to be a weave. It was in an updo ponytail. She had lots of makeup on but looked to be naturally pretty. She smiled with a set of full lips and very white teeth. She was tall for a woman, maybe around five foot eight. I laughed to myself. *She is taller than Junior. Wonder if she will run when she sees him.*

She took my hand and walked into the room. Junior took one look at her and stood at attention. She laughed and sat in the chair.

"So, what ya'll tryna do?"

"Um, whatever you want to do," I said softly. I kept my eyes on her. She put her soft hands on my face. A chill went up my spine. I was confused. *Wow!* My idea was to enjoy watching Junior with another woman. I wanted to eventually lead him into the arms of another woman. We could be roommates. My thoughts came back to the moment as she planted a soft kiss on my cheek.

I wish I could get rid of Junior's wack ass. She looked at me like I was wanted and desired. That is all I had needed in the last few months. Rico provided that to a certain extent. Realistically, that was because I needed a distraction from my situation, and Rico was in a bad relationship too.

"You are very pretty and have beautiful skin and cheekbones."

I was about to say thank you when I remembered she hadn't told me her name. "What's your name? You never did tell us."

"It's Ebony. I am sorry, beautiful. What is your name?"

I told her my name and introduced Junior. We all sat on the queen-size bed. She said she had never been with a couple before. *I wish we were not a couple.* She sat on Junior's lap and danced on top of him. Slowly she grinded her body on top of his. I sat quietly, taking it all in. I watched her silhouette dance around the room. She smiled at me as she danced. I could smell her perfume in the air, mixed with mine. I watched Junior's face. He was pleased. She then moved over to me, but I didn't want her to. I wanted to watch what she would do to Junior. I was scared if she came over to me, I wouldn't want her to leave. I shook my head no and moved her back over toward him.

She began to peel her clothes off piece by piece. She started with her shoes and threw them near the door. She then removed her skin-tight pants. She had legs for days. Like an acrobat, she gyrated until her panties were on the bed. I tried to keep my legs still but couldn't. *What is this feeling that has come over me?* Deep inside I wanted to feel nothing. I wanted to see if I could watch them together like I wasn't even there. This was my test to see if I could deal with Junior being with another woman. *Hell, she can move in and be his concubine if she wants to.*

I felt something strong, and I knew it was a longing to be with her. I wanted Junior to feel something from this experience, but it was me trying to keep my cool. She made her way to my side of the bed. I helped her get out of her shirt. Two very healthy breasts popped out and bounced uncontrollably. She was fully nude, and I liked it. She moved around me like there was music in the air. Junior obliged and turned on the small clock radio. She danced for another thirty minutes, touching and teasing me. I forgot that Junior was in the room.

I danced with her, and our bodies met in the middle. We held hands and danced. I was having a ball. I hadn't experienced so much fun in years. We kissed, and a huge stream went down my legs and made a puddle on the comforter. I had had enough and needed to regain my composure and get my head right. I ran into the bathroom and took a quick shower. While the cold water took control of my body, I tried to work on my mind. *What has gotten into me? What would my family think about what I am doing? Why am I doing this? Is this what it has come to? I am really enjoying this, but why?*

"You okay, Reign?"

Junior smiled and licked his lips. I almost threw up. Why did I set this up? He had just ruined my entire night. I should have come alone. I don't want to save my marriage. I want to be loved, wanted, and made love to. The rest of the night we spent talking and laughing.

Ebony was a mother of two. She was in nursing school. Her children's dad had left her and had not provided any financial support for his children. We talked about everything from family to food and everything in between. Junior fell asleep, but Ebony and I talked until five in the morning.

I poured my heart out and shared my secret with her.

"We are not a happy, healthy couple who just want to explore. I am miserable. I have three children whom I love dearly. I just feel trapped. I hired you to make love to my husband. I wanted to see if I could handle that. I also wanted to see how he reacted. If he wants another woman he can have one."

"Are you serious? You guys seem so cool. Fooled me."

"I just want to be roommates. I want us to be in the same house together with the kids."

"Are you serious? You don't mean that. He seems like a nice guy, but whatever happens, I will leave you my number. Call me if you need to talk, sweet pea"

I hugged her tight as if she was my best friend. I paid her, and she left. Then I was back with him, and I felt as empty as I had felt every night before.

The hotel room meetings became a habit with us. We began to initiate random meetings with strippers and escorts. He didn't put a gun to my head, but I didn't want to be there. What he didn't get was that he could have done it alone. I had no desire to be with him in any sexual way. I enjoyed the presence of the women if they were my type, but I missed the attention from Rico. I tried to call him, but he would ask if I was still married, and when I answered, he'd hang up.

On our anniversary, we made special plans to have dinner and went to one of the nicer hotels. I booked the room and invited Kasia to meet us at the hotel. Kasia was a bartender who worked at the local BW3's. We met at the bar and talked when she finished work. We hung out, drank, and ate wings. I drank on a daily basis, and she was my drinking buddy. I told her all of the things I did for Junior and what he put me through. At the end of the night, we kissed like the end of a date. Most nights, Junior picked me up after my date with Kasia. I was very confused about our friendship, relationship, or whatever it was. One thing I did know: I was attracted to her.

I still didn't consider myself bisexual, since I had never been sexually intimate with a woman. I had only kissed, held hands, and, of course, talked. *I'm not sure what gay people do. But I surely ain't one of those.* I liked Kasia; we got along real well. She knew of the troubles Junior and I were having.

The plans were made. Junior and I had dinner at Red Lobster and made our way downtown. I quickly showered and put on something real sexy. Junior kept on the jeans and the T-shirt he had worn all day. I went downstairs to grab some ice and passed Kasia in the hallway.

We grabbed the ice and entered the room. We talked a bit and watched a little TV. Then I told her to quit playing and get down to business. I grabbed her arm and pulled her close to Junior. She retreated and grabbed me. The next forty-five minutes proved to be one of the most passionate moments in my young life.

I was spent after Kasia released me onto the bed. I realized that Junior had been sitting in a chair in the corner for the past forty-five minutes. He had not participated in any of the acts that we had shared. He was only a voyeur. This hadn't been part of my plan. I wasn't supposed to have been turned out in the process.

After that, things changed. Junior started acted funny and weird. One evening, I wrote him a letter.

Dear Junior,

You know I love you right? (Bad news always starts off this way, huh) We both love the children. But this marriage is not working at all. I want us to be stable for the kids. So I am proposing that we become roommates. I do not want a sexual relationship with you. I don't want to cook for you. We don't need to go out or even fake it anymore. We can split the bills and raise the children. You can see who you want to see. I will date as well. I think this is best for the children. They are what matters and the best part of both of us.

Friends forever, Reign

To my surprise, he didn't feel the same way.

"Reign, we are not friends. I am your husband, and you are my wife. We can't be roommates. What kind of shit is that? I thought we were working on things. What happened to that?"

"Junior, we keep going back and forth. We are beating a dead horse, and neither one of us is happy. All we do is argue and fight. We are both unhappy and bitter."

Junior and I began to fight more. I decided that from now on I would fight him whenever I became upset. It worked for him, so why not for me? We began to argue and fight daily about any and everything. Each time we argued, I would threaten divorce.

Once we went to a party and he wouldn't dance with me, so I slapped him in front of the whole club. I use to black out when we fought. Most times, I didn't feel a thing. Fighting became a rush and a way of life for me. If we were not fighting, we were sexing like crazy while making up. I would say I was divorcing him, and hours later lay in a pool of semen.

Junior's brother was in town for the weekend. They were about to go out, and I would be left with the kids. *This time it's not going down.*

"Where are you guys going, Junior?"

"Why? You ain't going, and no one wants you there."

"Well, I hope where you going allows kids, 'cause you taking them. Brianne and I are going out."

"I ain't taking them kids nowhere. You act like I can't go nowhere with my own brother."

"You can go where you want; just take your children with you! You always out as it is. If you knew you were going out tonight, you should have stayed in last weekend, and the weekend before."

"How 'bout I'm going. See you later."

They drove off, and I began calling his phone. I dialed the number over and over. Still no answer. After calling many times, I gave up and called Brianne.

"I guess we are not going out, 'cause Junior left me with the kids."

"What's new, girl? He always does that mess. Well, we can hit the mall tomorrow if you want to."

"Okay, I'll holla at you later."

I looked at the clock; it was nine minutes after midnight. Junior walked in the door and turned on the TV.

"So, where have you been?"

"With my brother. Why?"

"I know who you were with. I said, Where have you been? Was it that important that you had to be gone all night?"

"I guess so, since I was. I was bowlin' and clownin' with my friends."

"Aww yeah?"

I got in his face and pointed at his forehead. He slapped me in the face.

"Get your hands outta my face, girl."

I put my hands back in his face. This time he hit me, and I hit him back. We tussled all over the living room. He flipped me over the couch and charged at me. I grabbed a hold of the huge aquarium and brought it to the ground. Oscar fish and goldfish were all over the carpet. There was water all over the floor and couch. Junior took one look and walked out the door. I could hear him from inside.

"I'm goin' over my dad's house, and I ain't comin' back. You can clean this shit up."

Now what?

I called Uncle Cleo and told him what happened. He arrived with Brendan. The look in their eyes when they walked through the door was priceless. Uncle Cleo spoke first.

"What the … ?"

Fish flopped all over the carpet, some dying; some holding on. I found a net, and Uncle Cleo got most of the fish. We found a pot and put some fresh water in it. Brendan looked scared and stared at his dad and me.

"Well, boy, help us. These fish ain't gonna do nothing to you."

"But, Dad, most of these fish are dead. Let's just put 'em in a trash bag."

"Reign, what happened?" Uncle Cleo sat on the couch.

"Junior and I got in a fight. I am not sure how the tank was broken. I'm sorry you guys had to come over."

"Well, you are gonna have to get this water up or the carpet will mold."

I called Junior all night at his dad's house. I left several messages, but he never answered the phone.

The next day, he came home, and we made up. We both took off work and went to the movies and lunch. We borrowed a wet/dry vacuum and cleaned the carpet. Later that week, the babysitter came by and saw the tank gone and the fish in a pot. She never said a word. It was just another part of the dysfunction that was my life.

On September 11, 2001, I formed a new outlook on life. Planes hit the Twin Towers and the Pentagon. Life was too short to be miserable, and I had been in constant pain for the past eight years. *How much can one woman take?* While I stayed in a dead-end marriage, life for others was much worse. Some people couldn't find their loved ones. Mothers would never see their children again. I started to contemplate; maybe I was jumping the gun. My life was not that bad. Maybe I just needed to learn how to save my marriage.

A week after the tragedy, I had another bout of depression and post-traumatic stress syndrome. The same feelings resurfaced as when I was first diagnosed in 1986. All of the time my daughter was sick, we were strong. We stuck together and put all the arguing and fighting on the back burner. The cancer was over, but the pain for me was just starting. We were there for our daughter, the other children, and our family, but just like every crisis in my life, just when I thought it was over, it came back.

I spent a lot of time watching the September 11 news coverage. I switched channels repeatedly. I paid attention to the towers as they fell. I became obsessed with the coverage of the crisis. I began to think it was my fault. *What could I have done to help this situation? Hell, I couldn't even help my own child while she was ill. I would just watch her in pain and pray. Prayer doesn't work. If it does, why are all of these people dead?* This kept me embroiled in more darkness and anger. I was delusional about a tragedy happening thousands of miles away from me.

I was in bed with an ear infection, and the medicine was not working. I was staying in bed for days, not eating, just sleeping. Sophia, Junior, and the kids were in the front room watching movies and eating. Junior had become accustomed to making dinner and getting the children ready for school. I was sinking deeper into the dark familiar hole. I had been here before, but it had been years.

My body ached, and I would rock back and forth. I replayed the past six months in my head. I could see Princess at the doctor's office being diagnosed with cancer.

I remembered Mom and me at the chemo treatments. Princess was so strong; she acted as if cancer was nothing to her. She ate cancer up and spit it out. Everything happened so fast I didn't have time to process it. I never thought of my daughter dying. I didn't have time to see how real it was to me. I took immediate action. From March to October, I cared for her. Now was the time I needed someone to care for me.

"You are not depressed; you are just lazy. Black people don't have the luxury of being depressed."

Junior yelled at me and took the blankets off my face.

"Take a bath, you nasty ho."

I tried to move but couldn't. It hurt to open my eyes.

"I'm calling your mom to come and get you."

I begged him not to. "She has her own life, Junior. Don't bother her."

Thirty minutes later my mom came. "What's wrong?"

I had no clue. "My ear hurts, I feel tired all of the time, and my body aches."

She took me to Methodist Hospital, where they ran a battery of tests.

"I ain't crazy if that is what ya'll are gonna tell me."

The doctor's found nothing wrong with me. I went to Mom's house and stayed in bed for another week. I called and talked to the children that weekend. At that point, my children were my only reason for living. The only part of my life that was happy and beautiful was them. I decided to go home no matter how I felt.

I slid my key in the door and turned off the alarm. As usual, Junior was snoring and didn't know I was in the house. I hugged and kissed my babies while they slept. They felt so good and warm. I put my mouth in their hair. I missed them so much. I had to get better. *Why couldn't I just get happy like most people?* Most of my family and friends dealt with things by drinking and smoking their troubles away. Those things didn't work for me.

I walked into my bedroom in the dark and laid on Junior's back. He sat up straight in bed.

"Leave, Reign."

"I'm sorry I acted the way I did. I am better, see," I smiled.

"You should be glad I don't throw you out of this window. Do you know how dumb you made me look? You were supposed to sing at Granny's wedding."

"Junior, I'm sorry; please forgive me."

He got up and went to the bathroom. I sat next to the door and explained what was going on.

"Yeah, right. You are screwing some nigga'. Who is it?"

I tried once again to tell him how I had been feeling. He wouldn't listen.

"Depressed, my ass. What you are is lazy!"

I had never been lazy. Most times, I was going ninety-five miles per hour, but when I wasn't, I was like dead weight. I tried to explain to him how I felt about what had happened to our daughter.

"Get over it; it's over. Everyone else is over it. Why can't you be?"

I didn't have an answer for that. I just knew that I was still in pain. Not physical pain, but emotional and mental. Every event in my life went through my head. I couldn't stop the thoughts. On a daily basis, my mind raced from D cumming inside me, to me being hit by a car, to the abuse between Junior and me, to our daughter being sick. I felt like a failure, but I couldn't fail this time. I had loved Junior for eight years. I could not let him go.

I was roused from my thoughts by a door hitting my head. I had fallen asleep lying outside the bathroom door.

"Reign, you need to leave. It's over."

He walked into the kitchen, and I held on to his legs. He couldn't walk.

"I won't leave. I love you, Junior." He shook me off.

"Remember what you said back in the day. You said we would never break up unless I was in a body bag. Remember that, babe?"

"That was high school, Reign. It's over, but you know I will fuck you one more time. Tighten up and lock up on it for me."

He kicked me in the head. On the floor, he parted my legs and rammed his penis inside of me. A sharp pain pierced my side, and I twisted out of his reach.

"Well, if you ain't giving up no ass, you can leave, bitch."

Instantly, I busted him in the face. All of the pain I had ever felt in my life triggered my mind and came out of my hands. I gouged his eyes, scratched his ears and mouth. I bit him in the neck and back. He punched me hard in the face and blacked both of my eyes. I felt nothing, but all at once, I had my energy back. I was renewed; I felt wicked and possessed by the devil.

"I am calling the police on your ass, Reign."

I ran outside into the dark. I knew the neighbor and asked, "Can I use your phone to call a cab?"

"Girl, don't come over here with all of that drama. Ya'll are made for each other."

I went back into the house, and Junior was on the phone.

"Your mom is on the way to get you."

When I got to Mom's house and saw my face, I knew it was over. One of us had to end this, and if it had to me, so be it. If we stayed together, someone would be dead. My children didn't need one dead parent and the other in jail. We had forced things for too long. We hated each other. I needed help, and Junior would never be able to provide the help I needed. At best, I needed to heal the old wounds that had haunted me for the past sixteen years. I left the kids with Junior and fled to my mother's house.

"Momma, I don't want to go to that girl's wedding. What if D is there?"

I played with Babygirl's hair. She smiled up at me and pulled on the phone cord.

"Well, Reign, if you don't want to go, you don't have to."

I hesitated and thought to myself, *I'm a grown woman now. I am twenty-three years old and I have children to care for. I hope I do see him, so I can look him in his eye and ask him how he could do the things he did to a child. I hope he says something to me; maybe I will shout out what he did in front of everyone.*

As we exited the car, D's sister was walking into the church. Just being that close to where the abuse took place made me shiver. The church was just a block away from Aunt Peaches's apartment, and I could see it from the church.

"What am I thinking?" I said under my breath. I stared at the Bell's Chapel sign and dragged myself into the church.

The wedding was beautiful. The bride and groom looked great. I remembered my wedding day. My mind started to drift back to that day in June when Junior and I were so happy. I shook it off and tried to enjoy the rest of the ceremony. We headed downstairs to the basement, where the reception was held. I felt D's presence before I saw him.

I froze, paralyzed in fear. I looked up at him, and his face was blank. As he took his place at a table, I noticed a lady with her head down. I also saw two little boys who looked like him. *Thank the Lord he has boys. But what does that mean? Boys can be molested and raped just as girls are.* They seemed fine and were running around like normal kids.

I tried to peek at the lady, but she kept her head down. When she did look up, her face was sunken, and there were dark circles under her eyes. Aunt Peaches came over and told me that was D's wife and sons. D never said a word to me; he just stared at me like he saw a ghost. I was glad he never came near me. I wanted to scream at the crowd and tell them to take those boys away from him, but that would have messed up the wedding. Instead, I kept my eyes on his kids and wife. A twinge of jealousy came over me. *Why do I care? Why do I still want to be with him? Why would I want to be her? She is pitiful. He is not my boyfriend. What is wrong with me?*

I paid attention to them when they interacted. She never looked at him when he spoke to her. She turned her head to the side and narrowed her eyes but never looked at anyone directly. I said a short prayer for D's family and hoped God heard me. He never answered my prayers, but maybe he could help those boys. On second thought, he wasn't there for me as a kid, so I erased that prayer.

Junior and I separated for good. The day our divorce was final, Brianne and I went to the tattoo parlor.

"I have a great idea, B."

"What's that?"

"I'ma get a tattoo with Rico's name on it, just to show him it's over with Junior and me."

"You sure you wanna do that? Girl, a tattoo is final."

"Yeah, I'm sure I love that nigga' and he love me. He already got a tattoo of my whole face on his arm. It's my turn."

"Aight, I'll take you, but I ain't gettin' no tattoo."

"Rico with a heart around it, there ya go." The tattoo artist held the mirror behind me.

"Wow, that didn't hurt one bit. It was annoying but no pain."

Brianne was shocked. "It didn't hurt! Your face didn't say that."

"It burned more than anything."

"You did it, Reign. How do you feel? You gone tell Rico?

"Girl, I'm 'bout to call him now."

I looked at the tat. *I got a sexy back already, and this sets it off. Rico is gonna be all over me when he sees this.*

"Ooh, baby, that's tight."

"I knew you would like it."

"Most def, but I got you on my arm; I got all of you. Let me lick that spot."

He began to lick my back, my arm, and worked down to my breast. He nibbled on one and caressed the other. He made his way to my stomach and took a trip downtown, where he licked me softly.

"Rico, this feels so good. I am your woman now. Finally, it's me and you, baby."

He raised up and wiped his mouth with his shirt. "Reign, baby, just because you got a divorce doesn't mean we gon' be together. You want me now, but you didn't want me then. I am scared, Reign. What happens when you get sick of me and play me? You been using me; what happens when you're through?"

He got up, grabbed his hat, and walked out the door, hard-on and all. I quickly pulled up my pants and grabbed my bags. I slammed the hotel door and didn't even take the key. I saw him get into the elevator and took the stairs. In the hotel lobby, I tried to grab him.

"Get off me, Reign. This is how it has to be. We can be friends, but I can't be your man."

"I did this for you. I got this tattoo for you. I divorced my husband because of you. My kids are in a broken situation because of your black ass. This is how you do me? After all the shit you said. I left him and you still trippin'."

"Reign, you didn't leave Junior because of me. I hope you left him because he wasn't a good husband. He beat your ass. He mentally abused you. He was a lousy man who didn't have nothing to give his kids. I have been giving you money for them for a minute. If you left him because of me, you done fucked up. Later, babe."

I stood there looking like a fool. Some of the guests and people at the front desk just stood there watching.

Junior and I were sharing the children, and one day he didn't bring them for their visit. I didn't bother to call and see where the children were. I just climbed into the bed and slept for months. I didn't want to see the children, nor did I want them to see me. I went into the deepest, darkest depression of my life. I had never felt so alone. No one from the church was there. All of my friends were there for Junior and not me. Mom was the only one who knew what I was going through. My daughter had been diagnosed with cancer, my marriage had fallen apart, and I had not seen my children in months.

"I am not strong enough to handle this," I cried out to my mother.

"Yes you are, Reign. I know what you are going through. You feel like someone has died, like you have lost something." She rubbed my shoulders.

Some days I would wake up and try to call my children, but Junior wouldn't allow me to speak to them. After a few weeks, he changed the phone number. My mom would try to call just so we could hear their voices. I tried to schedule times to see them, but he wouldn't show. I decided that since I couldn't control my life, I would just waste away. I wouldn't take care of myself; I would simply sleep through the day.

I did not get out of bed much and would not eat. Uncle Cleo would come to the door with Long's donuts just to get me out of bed. I would grab the white box and run back to bed to eat alone. He would walk around the house, pray for me, and call my name. One day he yelled at the top of his lungs, "Reign, I will not let you die! I love you!"

All of the neighbors came out and looked at him.

"I don't care if these people look at me, and I will be back tomorrow."

I lay in the bed and cried. When I wasn't crying, I was sleeping. Mom tried her best to take care of me, but I didn't want to be taken care of. I wanted to die. I went to a hotel, took a bottle of No Doze and a fifth of gin, and drank it all. I then went back to Mom's and waited to die.

When I woke up, I was angry and upset. Once again, Mom was standing over me, and I was in a hospital hooked up to machines. "Why am I here? I am supposed to be dead; I can't even do that right."

Mom and Dad were there, and they told me they would not let me die. After a month, I was given the antidepressant Paxil and sent home. The first thing I did was cut off all my hair. I had one inch of hair. No more long hair to please a man. It felt so good. I was my own woman. I didn't have to please anyone. Junior was not in my life anymore. After nine years, I was free. I was done dealing with men for good. Now I had to get my babies back.

Reality

Reality Checks In

I DON'T REMEMBER THE EXACT DATE, but it was an unusually warm day in November 1990. The sun sparkled amazingly that day. I remember thinking about how I couldn't wait to get out of my Junior Reserve Officers' Training Corps uniform and about all the homework I had to complete. I wondered what Mom was going to cook for dinner. I walked up the long sidewalk to our housing project townhome, unlocked the door, and stepped inside to total chaos. Sampson, our puppy, greeted me, and apparently he'd spent the day tearing up everything in the apartment.

"Damn dog! Get yo' ass in your room!" I yelled at him as I dropped my book bag by the steps and headed to our neighbor's apartment. I knocked on the door. Miss Anna came to the door and looked at me over her glasses. "Miss Anna, do you mind if I use your phone, please?" She was a weird lady with a 'juicy' Jheri curl, thick glasses, and a nervous tick. She was also the twins' mother. "Sure, come on in."

I stepped into her apartment, just beside the door, and she brought the phone to me. She stood next to me as I dialed. I stared her down with a bend in my brow. The look I gave her must have made her read my mind, because she went into another room. A friendly voice came over the phone and asked my name. I gave her my identifying information, and she placed me on hold. The doctor had told me that morning that the test was just to make sure I was in the total clear. Everything should be fine; this was just a formality at this point. I figured I had nothing to worry about. The nurse came back on the line and said, "Congratulations!"

"For what?"

"You're pregnant."

"What?"

"You weren't expecting that?"

I screamed, "No, No!" and hung up the phone.

Reality Check #1: Having unprotected sex can and will result in pregnancy, even if you are fourteen.

My periods had never been regular, so when I didn't have one, it didn't bother me. Earlier that year, my mother had put me on birth control. I guess I hadn't taken them correctly. I know there were a few days I forgot.

A baby? I was in shock as I walked to my apartment, closed the door, and slid down against it. I sat there with my face in my hands until my little brothers came home. They walked in, said hello, and made a beeline for the kitchen. I eventually went upstairs and changed into an old pair of jeans and a sweatshirt. I looked at myself in the mirror and gazed at my stomach. *Not flat, but I don't look pregnant. I don't feel any different. My breasts are bigger, but they don't hurt.* I had just attributed that to the fact that the women on my father's side of the family were all busty, and figured that was all that had happened to me. I saw my mother's car drive past my bedroom window, and my heart leapt into my throat. *How will this affect her?* I conjured all the bravery I had in my body, ran down the stairs, and met her at her car.

"Ma, I called and got the results of the test. They said ..." I gulped in air, and tears ran from my eyes. "I'm pregnant."

"You're what?" She answered. Her eyes pierced right through me. She was so angry that she didn't say anything. She walked past me into the kitchen. My heart was heavy because I knew the news had disappointed her.

That night, the phone rang off the hook. My cousin Charise called me.

"What are you doing?" she asked with an edge in her voice.

"Nothing," I said, barely audible.

"Reality, what were you thinking? You know you are not old enough for all that."

"I don't know. I don't know. I didn't think it could happen, ya know."

"Betcha know now."

"Yeah. I'll call you back." I hung up the phone. Talking to her made it a true reality.

The whole family was disappointed with me. I called Darrell to tell him, and although he didn't deny it, he was not really interested in knowing about it. We talked for a few minutes and got off the phone.

Reality Check #2: Just because you get pregnant by somebody doesn't mean they will automatically fall in love with you and want to be with you. Usually, it's the exact opposite.

A few weeks later, I went to the doctor again and found out I was about five months pregnant. I was too far into the pregnancy to have an abortion, and I didn't want to put the baby up for adoption. My mother didn't speak to me for a month. I felt isolated, alone, and scared.

It was hard getting used to the idea. When I'd see Darrell in school, he would tell me, "You don't look like you are pregnant." I didn't think I looked pregnant either, but I was, and I had to deal with that reality. I went to school every day, but I started having morning sickness. People started talking bad about me. One particular girl told me, "You ain't gonna be shit. What can you do? You're fourteen and pregnant!"

I snapped back at her, "Shut the fuck up! You don't know nothin' about me. If I wasn't pregnant, I'd kick your ass!"

I still participated in gym; I used the leg weights and did a lot of walking around the track. I was still active in the JROTC. Besides the morning sickness, I felt great, and nothing had changed but my stomach size.

During my pregnancy, I fell on ice. I went to the emergency room, and there was a nurse there telling me, "You really shouldn't be in this position. You should be out somewhere hanging with your friends, but instead you are in the hospital going through what a grown woman should. You just a baby having a baby that you can't take care of."

I cried like an infant because her words really hurt my feelings and made me wish things were different. It was true that I didn't have a clue about having a baby at fourteen. She didn't have to rub it in and keep reminding me that I was in a truly fucked-up situation. I wanted to tell her to mind her damn business, but how could I, when my mother was right there, nodding her head in agreement with her?

Mom was sick of the projects, so in January 1991, the middle of my freshman year, we moved from the projects to another apartment complex. We moved on the coldest day in January. I got my own room again, but this time it was much smaller. I didn't have anything for my baby, nor did I have the money to buy anything. Darrell dropped completely out of the picture, but Todd was around, somewhat. My cousin Sasha told him about the pregnancy, and he assumed the responsibility of taking care of the unborn child. He surprised me when he took me shopping and started buying things for the baby and me. Even though he did do some things, he kept his distance from me—partially because my mother threatened to kill him, and partially because he was having another child with another teenage girl.

When Mom enrolled me into the new high school, I learned that the administration didn't want me to attend there. They wanted to send me to a day adult program at a school on the other side of town. I refused to go. I babysat all the time, and I didn't think a school where they showed me how to take care of a baby was where I needed to be. I also had my mother to help.

I was very angry during the pregnancy. I was suspended from school because a teacher put her hands on me and I told her I would kick her ass. It was cold in her classroom, and I wore my coat. The class was in the basement, and my locker was on the third floor. She tried to make me take my coat to my locker, and I refused, so she grabbed me. Mom did nothing to her. I was mad at Mom. She should've had my back.

In mid-January, my doctor put me on bed rest and I couldn't go to school anymore anyway. I figured the administration felt that I wouldn't be back. I'd lie around much of the day, doing nothing. I was fourteen years old, seven months pregnant, and depressed about my growing belly. I became more afraid every day. I would feel the baby move inside me, and cry. I would try to think up names for the baby, but that made me even more depressed. I truly did not want the responsibility. I didn't want to go through it, but it was too late for me to do anything about it.

Thinking about giving birth made me cry because I felt it wasn't fair that this could happen to me. There were times I prayed that I would miscarry. I pleaded with God not to allow this to happen. I told Him that I had learned my lesson. I begged Him to make it stop, often screaming out, "It's not fair!" I was a good student, and I was missing out on life. I woke up every morning and stood in the door as the other kids were getting on the bus, and I watched them get off in the afternoon, wishing I was one of them. It was January, almost February; my due date was April 11. February crept through, and my birthday followed in March. It wasn't a bad birthday, but not extravagant, either.

Todd bought me a gold bracelet for my birthday. Mom made me a nice dinner: ham, greens, mac 'n' cheese, and cornbread. Turning fifteen should have been a happy thing, and I was happy, temporarily. I wished that I wasn't having a baby within the next three weeks. I was angry because I couldn't go anywhere for my birthday, and I tried to will the baby away.

Four days later, as I sat in church, I felt a pain in my side. I brushed it off as gas. I felt about three of those pains during the two-and-a-half-hour church service. I didn't tell Mom, because I didn't think there was anything to tell. After we got home from church, I walked down to an adjacent apartment complex where my cousin Sasha lived. She cooked my favorite food, fried chicken. I hung out at Sasha's house, still feeling pains but not paying them any attention. That is, until we were standing in her kitchen, laughing and talking. I was eating a wing, and one really hard pain hit me. I doubled over, "Ouch."

Sasha stopped laughing and asked, "What's wrong?"

"I just had a pain, but I'm fine." She immediately drove me home.

When I got home, I told my mother that I was having pains. She gave me Tylenol, and I went to bed. I tried to sleep, but the irritating pains kept coming. I got scared because I thought something might be wrong with the baby, so I woke my mother up. We went downstairs, and she propped me up in a chair. My mother, tired and drained, went to work. She told my brothers to call her when the pains were five minutes apart. They called her immediately, as I was crying and squeezing their hands to the breaking point. She came back home and picked me up, and we went to the hospital.

Once there, I was rushed up to the 'Mommy' ward and hooked up to a baby monitor. The doctor asked me, "Would you like an epidural?"

"Yes, please."

"Your mom is going to have to sign for it."

Mom hesitated for a second. "I ought to not do it."

Aunt Janet said, "Girl, you know she can't handle that. Go 'head and give her some relief."

Thank goodness my Aunt Janet was there to have my back. I probably would have gone into shock had I not gotten the epidural.

Four hours after my arrival at the hospital, I gave birth to a small, but healthy, boy. Aunt Janet held my leg as I pushed while there was no one else in the room. The doctor ran in just as my baby slid onto the bed. Mom, who had gone to change into scrubs to prepare to go to the delivery room, changed back out of the scrubs. She said she had heard him cry in the bathroom and had automatically known that it was her grandchild. The doctor whisked him away from the bed. A nurse brought him back about fifteen minutes later. My body shook so bad that I couldn't hold him. Mom scooped him up and kissed him. She wanted to name him Lamar, but I asserted myself and said no.

I named him Prince. My feelings for him changed the moment I held him in my arms. I thanked God he hadn't let me have a miscarriage. *Thank You, God, for blessing me with this little person that is my responsibility.* I knew that God would lead me to where I needed to be and that I would eventually make it with my son. I held him in my arms that first night and cried. I cried so hard, I dry heaved. I prayed over him, and I held him really close. I became a mother that day, not just because I gave birth but because my mind grew each moment I held him. I could no longer be selfish. I had to get it done.

Life with Prince was challenging because he cried all the time. Not just a normal baby cry, I'm talking Mariah Carey, Whitney Houston, ear-piercing crying. I got so frustrated, I would cry with him. Many times, I would let him cry and separate myself from him because I would get dangerously angry when he wouldn't be quiet. Thank God for my mother, or I probably would have been in jail, seriously. Not only was the stress of being a mother upon me, but depression was there as well. There were times I would look at my son and feel anger boil in me like him being here was his fault. I would cry continuously when no one was home. I even thought of suicide and planned how I would do it. I loved my son, but I couldn't deal with the pressures of motherhood.

I planned on going back to school once Prince was six weeks old. However, I had gallstones, and that would keep me from going back as planned. The doctor said that he couldn't believe that I had gall-stones. After all, I wasn't 'fair, fat, and forty.' A few days before I was to have an ultrasound to assess the damage my gall bladder was causing me, I got sick. Really sick. Prince was only four weeks old.

We were in church, and I felt the familiar pain that happened shortly after I ate something. This time was different because right when the pain started, I was nauseous. I ran to the bathroom and threw up all over the stall. Mom ushered me to the car, figuring the air would do me some good. I threw up even more outside, but this wasn't ordinary sick: it was unusually bitter and yellowish-green. Mom took me to the hospital immediately. Aunt Clara took Prince and my brothers to her house.

We sat in the emergency room for about an hour before I went to the back to be seen. Mom raised hell for the doctors to find out exactly what was wrong with me. They ran a few blood tests. After the results came back, they immediately admitted me to the hospital.

My enzyme level was so high that the doctors were amazed that I was still conscious. They stopped me from both drinking and eating. An ultrasound was done, and it determined that my gall bladder was full of stones and I had pancreatitis. Since this was so rare in a person of my age, the doctors figured that the pregnancy had sped the condition along. I started having the symptoms late into my pregnancy.

I was in the hospital for a week before the surgery could be performed. My enzyme level had to go down before surgery could be done safely. I was scared and thought a lot about death. I pulled through all right, but my recovery was slow. Before I could leave the hospital, I had to have a bowel movement. Three weeks went by, and I still hadn't had one. I went without food for a little over a month. I only saw Prince once during my hospital stay. I cried because I didn't want him to go home. I wanted him to be with me, but it was impossible for me to take care of a baby when I had an IV in my arm.

The day finally arrived for me to go home. I had lost about 75 pounds, and the last semester at school. The illness stopped my plans of returning when Prince was six weeks old. I withdrew but had every intention of going back.

My dad came to visit shortly after I was released from the hospital. He brought my Aunt Bridget with him. He stayed about an hour or so, then he left. He came back a few weeks later and stayed for a week. He met Todd before he left. He didn't say anything derogatory to him; he just shook his hand.

That summer, Todd would come over every morning after Mom went to work. The majority of the time, he came over and slept on the couch. We would have sex every so often, but at the time, he took good care of Prince. He came over and saw him daily, bought him more stuff than he needed, and made sure he had diapers and formula. Prince really didn't want for anything much.

One time, he came over and left his friend in the car passed out. Todd was in the house about three hours before his friend came to the door drenched in sweat. He walked over to where Todd was sleeping and smacked his head on the floor. I laughed. Later that day, Todd put hot sauce and powder in his friend's hand and tickled him. When he smacked himself, I laughed again.

Everything was good, until Todd found out that I was talking to boys on the phone. The main person I talked to was my friend from the sixth grade, but there were a few more. My mother's boyfriend's daughters, my 'stepsisters,' had boyfriends, and sometimes the boyfriend had a friend. Nothing was real serious, but Todd was upset. I couldn't understand why. He had a girlfriend.

"Look, Reality, I can take care of you and my son. If you want me to do that, you can't be talking to no niggas on the phone. Just me."

"Um, you can just take care of Prince. My daddy lives in Memphis. I can take care of myself."

"Think about it. I can take care of my son, but you think about that. I'll be back."

He came back about a week later talking the same thing. I repeated myself, and things changed instantly. He didn't want to have anything to do with either of us.

He would tell me he was going to come and pick up Prince and wouldn't show up. One time, my stepsisters and I decided we were going to the SoulFest, a yearly carnival in the city right before the Indiana Black Expo. Everyone in the city would be at Washington Park that weekend. The cars, hootchies, kids, grandparents, everybody. I stayed in the house the majority of the time, so I thought it would be fun. Prince needed some diapers, so I called Todd.

"The baby need some diapers," I said.

"I'll bring them later on today."

"Well, what time? I'm going to the park, and I'm taking him with me. I wanna make sure somebody is here."

"I know you are not taking my son to that park. People shoot out there. You betta not take him out there."

"Um, do you want to come get him?"

"No."

"Well then, he's going with me. Are you bringing the diapers or not?"

"Yeah," he said and hung up on me. Thirty minutes later, he walked to my door, opened it, and threw the diapers inside. I shook my head and laughed at him. *So immature, and he's a grown man. He's just mad 'cause he can't tell me what to do. I ain't gonna bow down to him like those hoes.* We left the house, went to the park, and had a great time. Prince enjoyed all the sights and sounds.

In fall 1991, I began my sophomore year of high school. Technically, I was a freshman, but I was determined to graduate on time. Getting good grades was very easy for me. Before Prince, they were just letters, but in my sophomore year, they became my ticket to a better life for us.

When I went to get my schedule, I noticed that I had all freshman classes. I had passed the majority of them in my first semester, so I wondered why I had no sophomore classes. I went to the Guidance office to inquire about my schedule.

"I was just wondering why I don't have any sophomore classes on my schedule."

The guidance counselor told me, "You are not going to graduate with your class; you've missed a semester of school and are too far behind."

"I will catch up and graduate on time. I don't have a choice."

"When you drop out of school for a semester, you may just want to get your GED. You are not going to walk with your class. I'm not changing your schedule."

I stood up and walked out her office, and told her, "You got me fucked up. My class is '94; that's the class I'm walkin' with!"

When I got home, I told Mom. She went up to the school, and they changed my schedule to reflect the classes I needed to graduate. Each semester, Mom would call the counselor or come up to the school to make sure my schedule was changed to include the classes I had missed, along with the classes I needed to take. Each semester of my sophomore year, I had two English, two Math, Spanish, and Science classes. My day rounded out with Health and a half-credit elective.

I was on welfare for a year before I got a job. I worked, went to school, and took care of my son. I smoked marijuana occasionally. I had crushes on various boys and still gave myself away knowing full well they didn't care or give a damn about me.

There were a slew of rumors about me. While recovering from the gall bladder issue, I had found out I was allergic to the chemical that makes cherries red. This same chemical is found in laxatives. We wouldn't discover this until after many trips to the emergency room. My lips would swell and blister, and I would have blisters all over my body. The blisters left dark marks on me, including around my lips. I was so embarrassed at my appearance. I got talked about … bad.

One guy said to me, "I bet you can suck a good dick, can't you." He said it right in front of the class. I wasn't skilled in playing the dozens. But I had one thing working in my favor; he was just ugly.

So I said, "You would love to know, wouldn't you? I'm sorry, because even if I did suck dick, and yours was the last on Earth, I wouldn't suck it. Lumpy-faced bastard. What kind of grades do you get? Yeah, dumb muthafucka. Talking about sucking dick, yo' ass need to learn how to read."

Needless to say, he shut up and never spoke to me again.

I will never forget one person in my Geometry class who was really nice to me. He was white and fine as hell. Kevin looked just like Brian Austin Green from the original *90210*, but a little smaller. The boy had mad flavor. He dressed in the latest Cross Colors outfits, and he always smelled good. He would stand in the hall and wait for me to come to class. He had a hug for me every day.

Kevin also helped me with my Geometry. He was patient with me and would smile at me all the time. He never seemed fake or phony, and I really liked him. I just couldn't get past the fact that he was white. *My family would kill me. My dad would disown me.*

I dated Shawn, a really geeky guy. He was about ten pounds soaking

141

wet, but he had his own car and was nice to me. We didn't have a lot of money, but we went on a few dates to the movies. He liked Prince, and my family thought he was alright. Charise said, "He looks like Pee-Wee Herman."

"Yeah, I know." This was true.

He was such a good listener. I would call or page him and he would come running. He was a friend to me, a shoulder. We had sex, and he was good at that, too. Everything seemed to go good, but Shawn had his own bed of issues to deal with. He needed me as much as I needed him, but I was unavailable to him because of his nerdish appearance. I thought he made me look desperate. He didn't understand why I couldn't be there for him. I never explained; I was afraid I would hurt his feelings.

We were at my apartment one day, standing in the kitchen. We argued, and before I knew it, he grabbed a knife and held it to his chest.

"Reality, I'll kill myself."

"Whoa, Shawn, you don't want to do that."

"Why not? Who loves me? You don't."

"I do. I do. Put the knife down. It's not worth it. I'm not worth it."

Shawn put the knife down on the counter but held the handle. I walked over to him and hugged him. He let go of the knife.

"You know you have to go."

"Yeah."

I never spoke to him again.

Not long after I broke up with Shawn, I got a letter telling me that I had an abnormal Pap smear. A few weeks later, I had a procedure called a colposcopy, which is procedure that uses a scope to magnify the cervix to view abnormal cells. During the procedure, a biopsy of my cervix was performed. It was determined that the abnormal cells on my cervix could be precancer. Shortly after, I had a cryosurgery, which is a procedure where the cells of the cervix are frozen off. I was sixteen and facing cervical cancer. Subsequent Pap smears came back normal, so I was okay. Even though I went through all of that, I didn't stop dating.

I met Gregg at the skating rink. He was older, and he looked cute in the darkness of the skating rink, but when I saw him outside of that, he was just ugly. His lips were big and always wet. I could tell he wanted to screw me off the top, but it wasn't about to happen. He had a really good job, but he was stingy.

One time, my stepsister, Shonny, was over, and Gregg had a friend he wanted her to meet. We were supposed to go on a date that afternoon, but they didn't show up until later that night. Gregg knocked on the door.

"You are late. Why don't we just go get something to eat?"

"What?"

"Damn, somewhere."

He took us to Taco Bell and was angry when the bill was seven dollars. I laughed at him and took my food.

A few weeks later, he came to get me. I was supposed to go meet his parents, but instead he took me to a hotel room. I took Prince with me. Once we were there, he tried kissing me. *Ewwww, this is so gross!* I told him I had left something in his car.

I went outside to find something to make him take me home, so I looked in his glove compartment, and there was a picture of another female who was the same age as I was. I grabbed the picture and walked back toward the room. *Start an argument and go home.* I smiled. I put on my best angry face.

"Who the fuck is this?"

"Um ..."

"Naw, nigga, take me home."

"But I just paid for this room."

"Good, stay the night. Take me home, now."

We got in his car, and he took me home. I was so relieved. Mom said, "That was quick."

"Yeah, I know. His parents are nice."

My Wants, My Wishes

August 15, 1993

I want a certain man for me
To fill my life with ecstasy
To hold me close and hold me tight
Someone to hold me through the night
You're the only one man I want in my life
Someday I even hope to be your wife
If one plus one equals two
Then why can't love equal me plus you?
I love the way you make me feel
I hope someday our love can be real
I really want you to love me
'Cause my love goes deeper than the eye can see
I wish your love could be the same
'Cause when you hurt me who's to blame?
I wish you would return that love to me
So open your eyes, look and see
All the things I can give you
And most of all, my love would be true

During my junior year, I dated Mr. Popularity. I liked him for that reason. He was a cool person, but I knew to keep him at a certain distance. He had a girlfriend, so I knew a commitment would be out of the question. We went to the movies a few times and hung out.

One night, after a date, he came to my apartment. Everyone was asleep. Prince wasn't home. We were watching TV, and we begin to kiss. He kissed me deeply, and we lay on the floor. He was caressing me, and things were getting heated—that is, until Mom came downstairs.

We were fully clothed, but she saw him on top of me.

"What the hell?"

"Momma! I'm protected. It's okay."

"Get the hell out of my house! Reality, what the hell are you thinking?"

"It's not that deep."

Angry, she stomped up the steps. I went to my room like nothing had happened. The next day, his girlfriend approached me. "You dating my man?"

"Check ya man, not me."

"You fucking him?"

"No."

She walked away. She was the first person to insinuate that I was fucking him. It baffled me.

His cousin mentioned it to me. "I did not have sex with him. What is he talking about?" I decided I would ask him. There was a problem; I didn't know where he was. I looked for him at school all day, and I didn't run into him. I called him. I didn't see him for a while after that. Hmm.

Reality Check #3: Having a baby as a teen automatically labels you as easy, so be careful when dating; especially if you date Mr. Popularities with girlfriends.

I put guys on the back burner. They were too much trouble. I was on target with school, though. I got a job at Hardee's.

Hardee's proved to be very interesting. Everyone was cool, but when Glenn started, shit hit the fan. He was tall and slender and had a nice smile. He was extremely funny, and we worked well together. It wasn't long before we exchanged numbers.

Glenn was the classic young pimp. He went to a township school and played basketball. He was another Mr. Popularity, just from another school. He acted really interested in me. He asked me to come over. I spent the night at Charise's, who had her own apartment at the time. She drove me to his house.

The house was massive. It had four floors: a basement, main floor, bedrooms, and an attic, which was like a small apartment. I really thought we were gonna chill out for a while, but he jumped right in.

I held him off for a while, repeatedly said no. The more I said no, the more he pushed. Eventually, I gave in. *He's trying so hard. Maybe he really wants to be with me.*

When we got back to work, Glenn ignored me. I didn't understand.
"What's up?"
"Oh, hi."
He turned away from me. I ran to the bathroom. A co-worker saw the exchange. "Reality, you okay?"
"Yeah."
"Look, honey, it's alright. You thought it would make him like you, huh?"
"Yeah."
"It won't. Don't you let him see you cry, and don't you be upset. They come and go."

Reality Check #4: Sex does not start, nor does it maintain, a relationship. It's simply sex.

I walked from the stall, washed my face, and finished my shift. Unfortunately, that wouldn't be the end of Glenn. He started picking with me every day at work.
"Leave me alone, Glenn."
"Why, you big, you bad?" He threw something at me and laughed.
"Okay. I got you."
I continued my shift as usual, but when I found him at a vulnerable moment, I threw some food at him. He got angry. I ran to the back of the kitchen.
"You play too damn much!"
"You started it." He pushed me. *Yes, exactly.*
I drew my hand back and slapped the *shit* out of him. It was so loud that the manager came running to the back.
"What the hell is going on?"
Glenn tackled me to the floor, but I went down swinging. I fell into some bread trays and hurt my back. I jumped up, but the manager stood in my way. I really didn't care; I'd got exactly what I wanted. A nice hard slap in the face and embarrassment for him. *Revenge is sweet.* I quit Hardee's not too long after that.

I was envious of anyone that had a relationship or seemed happy. I fantasized about someone truly giving me the love I wanted. I wanted a boyfriend so badly, and I really didn't understand why. I just wanted to feel love. I loved my son, I loved my family, and I knew they loved me, but their love was not enough. I wanted a boyfriend, a man.

Cedric was the darkest, sexiest dude I had ever seen. I didn't hide the fact that I was diggin' him. I knew he had a girlfriend, but I just couldn't see myself without him. He was almost six feet, had really dark brown skin, and had some sexy lips. He had a good body, and I wanted him, bad.

Cedric was the first person I really pursued. He crushed me when he wouldn't go beyond a friendship. He rode my bus, and we had a class together, so seeing him every day was hard. He was really sweet to me, but I didn't take a hint. It didn't help that I felt his arms around me. He hugged me every now and then.

One day, I was coming from the bathroom, and he was leaving our classroom. I saw that as my chance. I walked up to him and tried to kiss him. I just had to feel those lips. I got to touch them with mine, but that was it. He pulled me away. I was embarrassed, but after that, he gave me his phone number. I gave him a picture of me, and that was our relationship. We spoke to each other and talked on the phone, but nothing really came out of it. We were friends.

My senior year was one of my proudest. I would graduate from high school. I had a job and took care of Prince. Even with all my accomplishments, I could never get the relationship thing right. In essence, I was just plain desperate.

One day, as I took my son to play in the park of our apartment complex, I met a guy named Jeremy. He was there with Chad, one of the guys that rode my bus from school that I was cool with. Jeremy was really tall and lanky, wore glasses, and was very cute. I had never seen him before, but we were considered an item in just four days.

I had just turned eighteen when I met Jeremy, and he was fifteen, straight jailbait for me. My heart had been longing for stimulating conversation. I like to talk, and I like to talk about things that matter in the world. I don't know what really did it for me with him back then, but he was my first real love. I was the laughing stock of my apartment complex and my family. I was a senior, had a three-year-old, and was dating somebody who couldn't even get a job. He always wanted to get a job to help me out but couldn't due to his age.

I graduated from high school in June 1994. Mom, Aunt Suzie, Grandma, Charise, Aunt Janet, and Leon, Charise's brother, all attended my graduation. Prince was in the front row, cheering me on. When we left the stage after the ceremony, Prince ran up to me, hugged me tight, and said, "Mommy, you so pretty, I so happy." However, there was an empty seat in the auditorium and the cafeteria, the one for my dad.

I had talked to him earlier that day, but I had to call him. I sent him a graduation invitation about a month prior to my ceremony, but he gave me some lame excuse as to why he couldn't come. Later that night, I cried because my father didn't care enough to make the trip to see me accomplish something so big. Jeremy held me close and said, "You'll be okay. You made it."

When Jeremy turned sixteen that August, he did get a job at a local restaurant. He would give me over half his tips and bring food to Prince and me constantly. I could depend on him when Prince's dad wouldn't give me anything. We did a lot of things together, like hang out, smoke weed, go to movies and parties, listen to music, eat dinner, all of the things that no one else had done with me. He would cook for me and was very romantic. He bought me rings (very tiny, but still nice). I truly thought that I had hit the jackpot because he treated me better than older guys.

I was scheduled to have my tonsils taken out late August. About two weeks before, I had to have lab work done. On the day of my surgery, I was in the hospital gown waiting to be wheeled into the operating room. The anesthesiologist came in.

"Ma'am, I'm sorry, but we can't do the surgery today."

"Why not?"

"You're pregnant."

"What? It can't be."

"Well, the test came back positive."

"What if I said I wanted to have the procedure anyway? Would you still do it? I'm not keeping this baby."

"I'm sorry, but we can't. You are going to have to reschedule."

The news shook me to my core.

I was eighteen, still living with my mother, working on baby number two, and unbelievably devastated that I would have to tell my mother that I was pregnant, again. Mom was visibly upset. We left the hospital and drove toward home. We pulled into the gas station across the street from Jeremy's apartment. I jumped out of the car, grabbed Prince out of his car seat, and ran across the street. I frantically knocked on the door. Jeremy answered the door with a confused look on his face.

"What you doing here? Surgery done already?" he joked. I looked at him. He got serious.

"Reality, what's wrong?"

"Lemme in," I whispered. I started crying.

"Come on in. What's the matter?"

"Uh, uh, I'm pregnant," I sobbed.

He sat down in the chair, stunned. "You sure?"

"That's why I can't have my surgery."

"Damn," he blurted out, "Well, it's okay."

I glared at him. "Okay? I don't think so. How the hell can this be okay? Remember, I planned on starting community college in a few weeks. You don't even have a high school diploma."

"Reality, I won't let anything happen to you or Prince."

"What the hell can you do? I can't do this. I'm having an abortion."

"Reality, don't do it. Please don't kill my baby."

"I don't think we could have a choice. I can't do that. I can't have another kid. It's not time."

"According to you?" he asked. "I had something to do with that, too." In essence, he was too calm for me. I stayed there until his mother got home from work, and we told her about the pregnancy. She seemed slightly amused, but for the most part she was cool about it. "I'll support you in whatever you want to do," was all she said.

My mother threatened to kick me and Prince out on the streets. I didn't want that. I told her that I would get an abortion, and she and Jeremy's mother gave us the money for it, and Jeremy reluctantly gave some as well. Of course, I didn't have any money to put in.

Even though he had given me money for the abortion, he constantly tried to talk me out of getting it. I still saw no other way around it. I made the appointment. He was reluctant but supported my decision and went with me. Aunt Clara drove us to the clinic.

The counselor at the abortion facility knew that I really didn't want to have the abortion. The whole session, from sign-in to checkout, was only supposed to take about four hours, but it took us all day. I finally said I was ready for the procedure. Jeremy sat in the waiting room.

I felt a little dilation. It felt like someone was pricking me on the in-side. Then I heard the machine and felt some suction as the vacuum inhaled my unborn fetus. It was over. I was no longer pregnant. I was in the room for about twenty minutes.

I was sent away with a bag of antibiotics and pain medication. Aunt Clara picked us up. Jeremy didn't speak to me the whole ride home. It was as if he was in a deep trance, in another time and dimension. We were dropped off at my house. Jeremy constantly looked at the pamphlet he had been given by the anti-abortion protesters. Tears flowed down his face like small streams. He got out of the car, turned away, and walked home. *Damn, I feel horrible. I know that I have killed his spirit and that things may never be the same again between us. What other alternative did I have? How will the relationship be able to survive this? I am certainly not going to deal with the pain of the decision that I have just made again. I'm getting Depo.*

Taken Away …

October 1994

I see your face a thousand times
At night, I feel, I hear your whines
When I wake to see what's wrong
It's nothing but my sad song

The love I felt when I first knew
Was refreshing as an early morning dew
The hate I had for myself when you were gone
Had damaged me, for I feel alone

This empty feeling in my soul
No longer permits me to be whole
I have nightmares where I see your face
I have put you in another place

In the months that have passed
My heart is in an iron cast
Although it has be a while
I still long for your smile

You were a human being
You could have grown up to sing
You could have had an excellent life
Someone's husband, or somebody's wife

But I have taken you away.

I went to my OBGYN to get the Depo shot and talked to him about how I was feeling. I was sad all the time and wondering if the abortion was a mistake. All of the hurt, confusion, and sorrow had built up in me for so long that I used the OBGYN doctor to get them out of me. I broke down in his office. The doctor prescribed Prozac for my depression. That didn't sit too well with my mother, who thought that I should have been 'over it.' Mom made me toss my pills because I 'didn't need them.'

Jeremy still came around, but he would barely touch me. Even though we had what seemed like a huge age gap at the time, my relationship with Jeremy was relatively okay. We fought a few times, but we always seemed to get back together, until I found out he had cheated on me.

He was walking with another girl, and my mother and I drove past them. We saw them kissing right there in the street, as if he was putting on a show. Another time, I actually saw the same girl walk into his house. I ran over there and banged on the door. He didn't answer.

Jeremy and I dated for a year, and I naturally grew close to his immediate and extended family. His cousins Pat and Carisa in particular. They stayed in the same apartment complex as we did but shared a unit with his grandmother, their children, and Pat's boyfriend, Carl. Carl had a female cousin, Sherry, that would visit on occasion, and Jeremy took up with her, too. Sherry and I both went to his house to confront him. The confrontation was uneventful because the both of us were still screwing around with him afterwards.

A few weeks later, Jeremy and I broke up, but we continued to see each other off and on. I knew that he really didn't want to be near me. Nothing was ever the same between us, and I knew it was my fault. One day, I felt angry about how the relationship was. I was angry about him cheating on me and the abortion. I called him over, argued with him, and hit him in the mouth, and we broke up for good. No more back and forth, hanging out, or sleeping together. I decided that a simple breakup just wasn't enough satisfaction. Something more dramatic was brewing in my head. Now it was time for my big payback.

Even while Jeremy and I were together and happy, I always had an eye on Carl. There was something mysterious and sexy about him, and I was always curious about what it would be like to be with him. I'm not exactly sure what it was, because physically he wasn't my type, and he was the exact opposite of Jeremy. He was shorter and much smaller, but he was dark like milk chocolate, and he had the cutest eyes and smile. His personality was amazing. He was hilarious, laidback, and just a real cool guy. We started talking one day and found out that we had some of the same interests, the biggest one being smoking weed. The other was mixed tapes.

Carl and I became really cool, and we were together all of the time. At first, he was like a big cousin to me. He was ten years older and always talked to me. He helped me understand things about myself and about Jeremy. Carl's girlfriend, Pat, thought it was cool that we all got along. I was over to their house every day, sometimes all day. The day of Pat's daughter's birthday, that all changed.

The birthday party was a family get-together. Pat, Carl, and their Grandma Joanne barbequed and cooked a lot of food. There were kids everywhere. In the midst of all those people, Carl kissed me lightly on the lips. It stunned me so much that I left. I was digging on him a little anyway, but I felt guilty.

I told Pat that she had better keep a close eye on him. I didn't tell her everything. I knew what he was doing behind her back. Carl would come over my house in another female's car. He would call me from his mistress's house and bring me sacks of weed. It got to the point that he would call me on the phone while Pat was sitting right in his face. I told her a few times she needed to watch him. She trusted him so much, it was heart wrenching, but I didn't push. I got in on the action.

Pat would always talk about how good Carl was in bed. I often wondered why she did that. Telling me what he did only intrigued me more about him. If he was so much the bomb like she would tell me, then I was curious to see exactly what it was that he was doing that made her brag on him. I knew he wouldn't have a problem with showing me exactly what he could do, and the fact that it was a secret turned me on even more.

Reality Check #5: Never *ever* tell another female everything that goes on in your bedroom. Doing so may result in some infidelity, both in the friendship and in the relationship.

Carl's father was out of town. He, Pat, their kids, Prince, and I went to his house. I spent the night. During the night, Carl snuck into my room, and it was all she wrote. *Carl is the bomb.* Having sex with him drew us closer together. He would come over at night, and we would walk around the neighborhood and talk about everything. He knew that I liked him a lot, and I knew that he was playing around. In front of everybody else, we were just the boyfriend and ex-girlfriend of two family members. No one really had a clue. Pat's mother had suspicions, but she couldn't prove it.

One night, Carl came over. When he showed up at my door, the look on his face told me something was wrong. I had just made it home from being with my friend Roy.

"Wassup?" I asked him as he stepped inside.

"Won't you come and walk to the gas station with me. I need to talk."

I said okay and grabbed my keys. We walked down the street.

"Reality, man, I don't know what I'm doing," he said to me. "I love Pat. But she wants me to be a stay-at-home muthafucka, man. That's not me."

"Have you told her that?"

"Yeah, but I don't understand why she wants to keep me in the house."

"Maybe another chick?" I mused. He laughed.

We talked all the way to the store and back. What we didn't know was that Jeremy spotted us. Carl walked me home and took off toward his apartment. About three minutes after I walked through my door, Jeremy and Pat flew around the corner.

"Reality, were you just standing out here talking to Carl? Did you kiss him?" Jeremy screamed at me.

Not one to ever be caught up, I looked at him funny and said, "Boy, please. I just got back from hanging with Roy. What are you talking about?"

"I just saw ya'll walking down the street."

"Couldn't have. I just got back from the west side."

"Reality, whatever."

"You trying to get my man?" Pat countered.

"Carl? Girl, please," I laughed. "Don't think so."

"Yeah, okay. We'll find out," she said, as she turned around. They walked off.

I went inside, and the phone rang. It was Carl.

"Did they leave yet?"

"Should be walking in the door right now."

"Okay. What did you say?"

"Don't worry about it. It wasn't about you."

"Aight, I'll get back at you," he laughed.

"Okay," I said, and hung up the phone.

A few days later, Carl came over with a bag of weed and a new tape. He popped it in my tape player and fired up the dubie. We got busy on the floor. I could see my mother turning the corner. Carl ran to the bathroom, as I quickly put on my clothes.

"What are you doing?" she asked suspiciously.

"Nothing." Right as Carl walked out the bathroom.

"Who are you?" she asked.

"Marvin," he said, and I almost died of laughter. "Uh, Reality, I'll call you later."

"Okay, Marv. Holla at you then," I responded, stifling a giggle. He walked out the door. My mother was suspicious. She didn't actually catch us in the act, but she knew. I know she did. It was written all over her face. She just shook her head at me. I shrugged my shoulders. I had to admit, the shit was wrong, but it was so fun. That's when I learned that I really didn't give a fuck about nobody's feelings. I was always getting hurt, and, dammit, I didn't care if I hurt someone else.

My first car was a 1987 burgundy, two-door Plymouth Horizon. I absolutely loved it. I loved the freedom that it gave me. I could go where I wanted whenever I wanted. I packed my and Prince's clothes in the trunk, and we stayed between my mom's house and Charise's apartment. I was going to community college and working part time at KFC, where Charise was the manager, making six dollars and fifty cents an hour. I filled out applications for public housing. A few months later, I received a call telling me that I was approved for an apartment and signed my lease.

Prince and I moved in to the Weyerbacher, notorious for drugs, hos, and old people. It was an old hospital, and the building we lived in was the old nurses' quarters. It was a loft on the top floor. Small, but okay for Prince and me.

Pat started calling me all of a sudden. I knew something was up. She was too friendly. Then one day, she just went off on me.

"I know you fucked my man," she said through the phone.

"How do you know that?" I asked.

"He told my cousin Dom, and Dom told me. You probably felt the tongue and everything," she accused.

"Maybe," I retorted. "But I tried to tell you about him. I told you,"

"I started to come up to your job and beat your ass," she yelled at me.

"Oh," I replied, "Gotta let a ho be a ho, I guess. I tried to tell ya."

"Yeah, bitch. It's all good," she said and hung up the phone.

I shrugged my shoulders, didn't think twice about it.

We lived by ourselves at first. Charise moved in a few months later. Our house was known as 'party house central.' A few months later a guy named Donald, whom I had just started dating, moved in with us. Around the same time, we befriended a bunch of dudes using a few apartments as their hot spots. We had fun all the time. Being grown and on my own was a thrill.

Donald looked like Charlie Brown. We worked at KFC together, and he was very funny. I ignored the fact that the sex between Donald and me was just okay. I was more in love with the idea of being free to have 'in-house' sex whenever I wanted it. While I was working at KFC and living with Donald, I had a KFC fling on the side named Billy. I guess you could say I was the KFC whore. Billy and Donald didn't like each other, which made things a little more interesting.

One day, I got a call from my Aunt Janet. I went to Charise's house for breakfast. Apparently, she had been calling me all morning.

"Reality, there's been an accident."

"With who?"

"Your mother."

"What happened?"

"She was in an accident. She's pretty broken up."

"Come and get me on the way to the hospital."

Aunt Clara picked me and Charise up, and we went to the hospital. I was allowed in the back where Mom was. The sight frightened me. Although she was covered, I could tell her injuries were bad.

"Babydoll, I need for you to call my job. And make sure them boys eat."

I knew she was gonna be fine.

She was in a head-on collision. Her car was totaled; the dashboard was in her lap. Every bone from her hip to her foot was broken. There was talk that she would never fully regain strength to walk again. I was crushed. She went to surgery that night. Many more surgeries would follow. I went to see her almost every day while she was in the hospital, and I visited her daily when she went home.

She had a hospital bed in her front room, and my aunt stayed with her. My mother's recovery was slow but steady. Eventually, she was able to walk again. She was the only person I knew that could drive with a cast on her foot.

Shortly after her accident, I graduated from community college. Mom couldn't attend, of course, but Charise, Donald, and Prince were there. Again, another empty seat; my dad wasn't there. Again, I sent him an invitation, and he paid it no attention. I brushed it off that time. *Hell, I made it through without his help.*

Dad came to visit a few months later. I was happy to see him, but it quickly turned to disgust. My father, a wannabe Muslim, liked to talk about being Muslim, but didn't live by the values. He wanted me to be involved.

"Um, Daddy, I don't want to be a Muslim. I don't agree with some of their teachings. It's not my thing."

"You just dumb. I shoulda known you would be that stupid. You don't listen."

"I'm not dumb, Daddy. I disagree with you."

"I know I shouldn't have let you come up here. You brainwashed. Just dumb. I'm leaving."

"Bye."

Soon after that, I learned that he paid for my cousin to go to a four-year college. It crushed me because, originally, I had wanted to do that. He knew I had a kid and that I was struggling, but he didn't offer me a dime. *That's okay, I'ma show him.*

Donald and I would fight all of the time, and most of the time it became physical. At first, I would take it. Soon after I graduated, I put him out. He tried to get back with me, but I wasn't having it. One morning, I was tired after a night of working and Prince's early morning school bus. He tried to take my son's shoes and more things that he had had no hand in buying. I clicked and had what I like to call a 'Tina Turner moment'; I kicked his ass. I had him hanging out the sixth-story window. I threw him and a mattress down the steps, hit him in the head with perfume bottles, and did various other violent things. He had picked the wrong day. He called the police, who silently laughed at him because he had two black eyes. I was summoned to court and faced jail time for battery. The sentence could carry two years in prison.

Donald was staying with Charise's brother, Leon, in the same building, a few floors down. Everybody that we hung out with knew when we were together and when we broke up. Our friend LD come over and saw the summons to court. He eyed it from an angle, then he picked it up.

"What's this? Reality, what did you do?"

"That nigga picked the wrong day."

He laughed and said, "I gotta go get Dude and 'nem." He left the apartment. A few minutes later, LD and the whole clique came to the apartment. They all laughed and made fun of Donald. I laughed, too, because the whole situation was ridiculous. Somebody broke out the weed, and we had a smoke-fest.

The first time I went to court, they booked me, took my mug shot and fingerprints, and put me in a holding cell for about an hour or so. I went before the judge and was released on my own recognizance. I didn't realize that by showing up to court, I had actually turned myself in. I could have gone to jail that day.

Oh my God! I can't believe this shit! How in the hell am I getting charged when this muthafucka is the one who went upside my head? I couldn't believe it. I didn't know how I had gotten into this situation. It was so similar to what I had witnessed my mother going through when I was a child; the only difference is I had fought back.

Billy went with me to other court proceedings. My lawyer had the charges against me dropped. Apparently, Donald wouldn't show up to court.

Reality Check #6: Don't play with the law. It can come back and haunt you.

Billy and I started out cool, but I found out that he was sneaky. I learned that he talked about me to other people, and I cut him off. However, the boy had a penis so big that I'd use him just for that.

Billy almost got me locked up. Even though I had my own car, one day he drove to my house and took me to work. We drove all on the west side of town, just hanging out. He dropped me off at work, and as soon as I walked through the doors, the police swarmed the parking lot, and Billy took off down the street. The car that he had said was his aunt's was actually stolen.

One witness said, "I saw him with a young lady who was wearing a black shirt." Of course, that young lady was me. I hid in the manager's office and listened as she told the police, "No, sir, there is no one here that fits that description. Whoever she saw could've went in the bathroom and left already." I dodged the law by the grace of God.

I met a guy named Nate, who was five years older and had his own place on the west side of town. We always talked on the phone but didn't do much else. We decided I would come visit him and just stay the night.

The first night, Nate was cool. We had dinner and watched TV in his bed. He didn't try anything with me, and I was okay with that. He held me as we went to sleep. I woke up the next morning, and he took me to work. About a week later, I drove to his apartment.

This time, one thing led to another, and we had sex. I felt funny afterwards, and I didn't know why. Instead of staying the night, I went home. Nate and I continued to talk and hang out. One day, I went over to his house just before he was supposed to go to work. I had on a T-shirt, some short shorts, and some sandals. I was perched in his bed, watching TV, when he came in the room from the shower. I just lay there.

He walked over to me and lay on top of me. I tried to push him off, but he grabbed my hands. He forced a kiss on me, and I tried to turn my head.

"Girl, you know you want it. Stop fighting."

"Nate, I don't want to do this."

He moved my shorts and panties over while holding my hands above my head. I tried to move, but his weight was too much. I could barely breathe. The next thing I knew, he was inside me. I tried to scream, but the look he gave me scared the shit out of me. I lay silent until he finished. He got up, and I ran out the apartment crying. I cried on the way home.

I can't believe I was raped. Oh my God, who would believe me? I was at his house in his bed. No one would believe that he just took it. I walked into my apartment, took a long hot shower, and went to bed. I couldn't sleep for a while. I didn't tell anyone about the ordeal. I thought it was my fault. About a year later, I told Charise. She was piping mad because I hadn't said anything earlier. By that time, Nate was history.

Reality Check #7: No means no. Period. If you say no, then no one has a right to make you have sex with them, no matter where you are or what you are wearing.

Independent living turned me into a bona fide weedhead. I smoked in the morning. I smoked in the afternoon. I smoked before I went to bed. I was always high. Smoking weed allowed me to 'forget' about any problem or situation I had no control over. I didn't stress about anything. To get over any bad thing, I would get high. It was my outlet.

Reality Check #8: Getting high does not resolve any problem. You are going to have to deal with the problem eventually.

One day, I decided I would try some other stuff. Actually, I didn't know it was other stuff until after I hit it.

Reality Check #9: Not knowing what you are smoking or taking can subject you to an addiction you don't want.

At first, I had a weird sensation in my mouth. I was high, like I had smoked some weed, but my mouth was numb. I didn't know how to handle it at first. I kinda liked the high, and it made the high from weed last longer.

I started smoking the primos just as much as I smoked the weed. It made me feel nice and relaxed, but I also had a boost of energy.

We moved into another apartment complex. Billy came to visit one day. I guess I couldn't let it go. We had the best sex that we had ever had and didn't use a condom. About three days later, I felt uncomfortable and I was in a lot of pain. I went to the hospital at three in the morning. I was tested. I had contracted gonorrhea, and the shit was no joke. I got a shot in my thigh that stiffened my whole leg. I had to throw away my underwear. I paged him about ten to fifteen times before he called back.

"Yeah, babe. What's up?" he asked.

"Where the hell are you? I need to talk to you."

"I just left church. Why?"

"You nasty dick muthafucka! You burned me, you son of a bitch!"

"What? I'm sorry."

"Take your nasty ass to the doctor. Don't call me no more, you bastard!"

I was pissed, and I vowed never to have sex without a condom.

Reality Check #10: Not all that looks good or feels good is good.

I got a letter in the mail saying that I had a car in the police impound and that I had to come and get it out. The only car that was in my name I drove, so I didn't understand. A light bulb lit up: Donald had my information and had bought a car in my name.

I knew about his new girlfriend. She tracked me down and talked to me about him. She didn't mention the car, or anything else besides the way he treated her. She also thought he was messing around with a transvestite. I just wanted to know about the car.

I got a credit report, and, sure enough, there was a car in my name. I tried to contact anyone who would listen, but no one would even give me information about it. This was something on my credit and in my name. I was livid, but there wasn't anything I could do.

Reality Check #11: Be aware of where you put your sensitive information. Make sure it's hidden pretty well. Someone could use it and ruin your whole life.

Prince stayed with my mother the majority of the time because I worked second shift. Rather than have him get up at eleven thirty at night to come home, my mother kept him so that he could go to school. I was still very much involved in his life, but I partied every day of the week. Charise and I worked at a warehouse and had to be at work at two p.m. Monday through Friday. We usually slept until one p.m., and our ride would pick us up at one forty-five to take us to work. There were days we would call our crew of cousins and friends to see if they were smoking, drinking, and having company. If so, and if we felt the urge, we would leave work at lunchtime to go hang out. I saw nothing wrong with my lifestyle, because even though we were always high and out partying, our bills were paid, we had food, our hair and nails were done, and we went shopping almost every week. Prince didn't want for anything.

I was twenty-one, and I felt like partying would probably take its toll on me. Smoking primos was getting to my conscience. I think it's because we were getting high so much that I felt I could have been labeled a dope fiend. I knew how disappointed my mother would be if she ever found out. I started to think about the direction of my life. I was finally free from my mother, and partially free from my kid. I couldn't let it go. I was having too much fun.

We went to great lengths to keep our crack smoking a secret amongst us. It was our own little pact. We felt that no one knew about it, and we wanted to keep it that way. Smoking crack was stigmatized, and we knew that our families would talk and be disappointed in us. That furthered my conscience messing with me.

One day, I went to my cousin Faye's house. Our dope girl was coming through, so I went to party with the rest of the crew, which consisted of my cousin Sasha, Faye, and our beautician, Leah. Charise stayed at home.

The dope girl walked in, and everyone put up their money. We made small talk for a few minutes, and she left. We divided the crack and the weed on the counter, whipped out the cigarette wrapping paper, TOPS, and started rolling and having a smoking session, as usual.

We were rolling joints, laughing, and talking. I didn't know that Sasha had told her younger brother to come over so she could braid his hair. She neglected to tell him not to come right then, but he did. When he knocked on the door, it sent me into a complete panic attack. All the while, I was high off weed and crack.

My heart raced fast and blood rushed through my veins so powerfully that all I could see was red. I thought I would have a heart attack and die. My thoughts raced fervently: *What if my mother finds out?*

They are gonna be so mad at me. Why did I start this? God, please don't take me. What about Prince? Could he live without me? Would CPS take my son? I am a bad mother. College-educated people don't smoke crack. Why did I start? Am I a crackhead?

The thoughts made me jump up, put my coat on, and run across the apartment complex toward my apartment. Sasha called Charise and let her know I was on my way there, so Charise was at the door when I walked in. She met me at the door, took one look at me, and called 911. I was hyperventilating, my lips had turned blue, and I was on the verge of passing out. I tried to fool the paramedics, but they already knew I was high on something. Faye and Charise met me at the hospital, and after two hours I was released. I know the doctors ran some tests on me, but I'm not sure what. No one ever came by the house or called.

The panic attack scared me so bad I didn't ever want to risk going through that again. I tried to get high just off weed after that, but it would send me into a panic attack too. For about six months, I wasn't right at all. I was in and out of the emergency room, not knowing what was going on. I started smoking cigarettes heavily to calm my nerves. I was extremely paranoid about everything. Life had taken me through a tailspin off one high.

Reality Check #12: If you are embarrassed or ashamed to be doing something, don't do it.

I started hanging back from my old friends and family a little, just to give me some breathing room to get myself back together. That's when I started hanging with Betty. I felt that since I wasn't doing the same things as my inner circle, I would hang out with people who didn't do those things.

Reality Check #13: Watch whom you call a friend, and don't be afraid to let the friendship go when things start to seem a little funny.

Betty was a cool person. She worked at the same warehouse where

Charise and I worked. That's where I met her. That's also where I met her friend Dingbat. I never liked Dingbat.

Dingbat thought she was the shit. She had her nose in the air and poked her chest out for attention. I figured she thought that if her breasts were up front and center, men would notice her. She wasn't an ugly person on the outside, but she let her conceit make her an ugly person on the inside. To top it all off, she was a complete airhead.

Betty was as silly and goofy as I was. We talked about many things, and she would take Charise and me home after work. It wasn't too long after that we started hanging out.

I've always been the type of person that if I don't like someone, then I just don't like them, and there's nothing or no one can make me like them. Betty tried to get me to like all her friends. Some I did, and others I had a problem with. Betty also thought she was prettier than I was and had more sex appeal. We would go out to the clubs, and it seemed as if Betty tried to take attention off me. I never understood why, because I was the biggest girl in the whole group. Usually men looked past me anyway. At first, I didn't really pay attention to what was going on. I would see a guy look at me, and I would smile. If Betty caught wind of it, she would approach the dude before I could even start my flirting. She would get his number and then come back to me.

"I can get any dude I want," she would say. "I just got his number, but I'm not even gonna call him." It shocked me at first, because a real friend wouldn't do that.

Reality Check #14: Be careful whom you trust. If someone could stab you in the back over something as petty as jumping in the face of any man you might be interested in, you've gotta beware.

Things went on like that for quite some time. I felt horrible about it and noticed the obvious differences of going out with her versus my old crew. I didn't want to go back to hanging with my drug crew, and I wanted to believe that Betty and I were close. I started talking to her about things that I never told anyone else. I confided in her about my depressive moods and about a lot of things in my past. I later found out that she had divulged all the things that I had confided in her about to at least one person. Even still, I didn't stop being her friend.

In August 1998, Charise, our friend Cara, and I went to the movies to see *Halloween: H20*. There was this guy standing in line at the concession stand as I walked to another line. I know I stood out because I was wearing a red camouflage tank minidress, black sandals, a weave ponytail, and big silver earrings. I was ghetto-fabulous.

I felt him stare a hole in me, and it made me a little uneasy. He wasn't handsome, but I noticed that he had a nice build. As it turned out, he went to see the same movie as we did.

As we walked out of the theatre, I heard a deep voice from behind say, "Excuse me, miss lady."

I turned around and noticed it was the guy who had stared a hole in me. I replied, "Yeah," as I walked to the car. He followed me.

"Can I get your name?"

"Reality."

"Well, Reality, it's nice to me you. My name is Tony."

"Mmm hmm."

"Do you have a number where I can reach you?"

"Sure."

I gave him my pager number and drove off in my 1985 burgundy Park Avenue. I had a date to get to.

He was persistent. He paged me a few times before I'd even called him back. Tony wasn't my type. He told me that he had had an accident as a teenager, and his kidneys didn't work. He was on dialysis. I didn't really understand the severity of his condition, but he seemed cool enough to talk to. Plus, the soft spot in me felt a little sorry for him. He had been dealt a raw deal.

Our first date was probably one of the best dates I'd ever had. We went to a place that was an arcade for adults, equipped with a gerbil tube. I felt like a big kid, and I laughed the entire time. Afterwards, we had a bite to eat at Denny's, the only sit-down restaurant in that area that was open at that time of night. He had good conversation, he was nice, and it was obvious he was digging me.

Tony would take me anywhere I wanted to go and even paid a few of my bills. At times, he would come over to my apartment and just sit, for the most part, as if he enjoyed being in my presence. He was a quiet guy, real reserved. I continued to see him, but I wasn't too serious. I really didn't like him like that, because he wasn't what I wanted; he just wasn't my type. I had two or three others on the side. One day, one guy I really wanted to get with came over while Tony was there. I told Tony he had to leave, and it was obvious that his feelings were hurt. I was like, "Fuck it," but I did apologize to him shortly after that.

One night, I drank Hennessy heavily. During that time, Tony and I really weren't speaking. According to him, I paged him and told him to come over. I woke up the next morning, and he was right beside me. I felt sick to my stomach, and attributed it to my overdrinking the night before. I got up and went to work, only to return home a few hours later due to my vomiting.

A few weeks later, I realized I hadn't come on my period. I called in to work and went to a pregnancy center for a test, and it was positive. I was stunned. *This could not be happening again.*

Reality Check #15: Be careful when you drink. No matter what, don't get so out of it that you can't remember what you did. You could end up pregnant.

It was not a serious relationship. I was supposed to be having fun. I didn't like the father well enough to have a baby by him. We hung out, he gave me things I needed as far as money, and I enjoyed having sex with him. I didn't expect to get pregnant, so I told him that I was having an abortion. He didn't agree with it, so he wouldn't give my any money toward it. I asked my mother for it, and she gave it to me, again. I made the appointment. I went for the consult, paid the down-payment, and scheduled the procedure.

Charise went with me to have the abortion. I was nervous, and scared. I didn't want another baby right then, but I got to thinking, *What if it's my girl? Would God forgive me? How could I get caught like this again?* Déjà vu set in, and all the old feelings I had felt when I had the first abortion flooded my brain and my heart. I cried on the table. I saw the utensils they were going to use, and I freaked out. I believe God spoke to me and told me not to do it. I jumped off the table, put my clothes on, and walked out the clinic without checking out. Charise, a little angry at my decision, said, "Don't cry now."

Reality Check #16: Abortion is not always the answer.

I was devastated, because I knew that having this baby would take the little life I did have away. I had to grow up … again.

Dream

Sixteen and Grown

WHEN I STARTED HIGH SCHOOL, I immediately formed two singing groups. The first was with my best friend from the sixth grade, Jada. We met Kim, who had just moved three houses down from me. We had a lot in common and quickly bonded. Kim also liked to sing, and the group was started. There was a new girl to the school named O'Leta. I heard through the grapevine that she had powerhouse vocals. One day, I approached her when I saw her in the lunch room. "Hey, are you O'Leta?"

"Yeah"

I chuckled to myself, *She has a funny accent. Oh Lord, I hope she don't sing all country.* "Do you sing?"

"Yeah, I do." She was smiling but had a confused look on her face. I knew she was thinking, *How do you know who I am, and how did you know I could sing?*

"Well, me and two of my friends are starting a singing group. Do you want to be in it too?"

"Yeah, sure, that sounds like fun!"

"Okay, cool! We are going to have practice at my house Friday after school. Here's my number if you have any questions."

"Okay, thanks!" she said in her weird accent. I went back to our lunch table and beamed, "She's in! She's real nice too, but she sure does talk weird!"

O'Leta's mother dropped her off Friday for practice. She came in, and we all formally introduced ourselves. "Hey, I'm Dream."

"Kim"

"And I'm Jada."

"Hi, I'm O'Leta."

"Hey," we all chimed back.

"So, you are new to North Central, right?"

"Yeah, me and my family just moved from Racine."

"Where is Racine?"

"In Wisconsin."

"Oh, okay, I've never met anyone from Racine. So can we hear you sing something?" I asked her.

"Yeah, I just did a pageant and I sang 'Wind Beneath My Wings.' Do ya'll know that song?"

"Of course, we know that song. We love Bette Midler."

"Okay, good, are you ready?"

"Mmm hmm." We all sat in a circle waiting for her to sing.

"It must have been cold there in my shadow, to never have sunlight on your face ..." I was amazed.

This girl can sang! I thought to myself. I glanced over at Kim and Jada, and I knew they were thinking the same thing.

We started singing songs off the radio. There was a new song that had just come out called "Don't Know Nothin'" by a girl group named For Real. It was an a cappella song, and our harmonies shined through. We sang our song everywhere we went—in the school hallways, for our parents; we would even call people on the phone when we were having rehearsal to sing for them. Kim had just gotten a part-time job at Krispy Kreme; we'd drive there and sing for them and all of their customers. We were the Inseparable, Fantastic Four. If all four of us weren't together, we were in pairs. We sang in all the talent and fashions shows in school and for different functions around the city. We had a really great time.

We named our group DaSangaz. We grew very close and considered ourselves to be sisters. We'd call each other's mom Mom, and we adopted each other's families. One night, Kevia came home and told me, "Ooooo Dream, we were in Wal-Mart and Mamma was flirting with this man. He gave her his number, and they are going on a date tonight."

"What! No, not our mamma."

"Kevia, quit tryin' to trick us," O'Leta said. "You know your mamma ain't goin' on a date."

"Are you going on a date, for real, in real life?" I asked Mom.

"Yeah, I guess I am," she answered.

"Oh my God, where are you going to go? This is weird. I haven't seen you with anybody since you and Dad broke up. I'm excited."

"Yeah, I told myself I would never be with another man until my kids were out of the house. Every man I met hurt my children. I just can't have that."

Hmm, I never thought about it like that. Tisha's dad hurt her; my dad hurt all of us. I want her to have fun and enjoy her life, but she's right. Men do hurt children.

I was sad for her; I wanted her to enjoy her life, but I didn't want to get hurt. "Are you nervous?"

"No, not really; it's just dinner, then I'm coming back home."

I went back and talked to Jada, Kim, and O'Leta. "Hey, we should go to the restaurant too and get a seat in the back where we can spy on him, behind a fake tree or something. If he tries to pull something slick, we can jump out the bushes and yell, 'Hey! Back up off my mamma!'" We rolled on the floor laughing hysterically. It was funny, but in the back of my mind I was serious. I wanted to protect my mother, just how she vowed to protect me.

I started liking boys my sophomore year, but for the most part it seemed as if none of them liked me. I envied the pretty cheerleaders, whose boyfriends would meet them at their lockers and escort them to class. I would fantasize that my boyfriend was the star athlete. I daydreamed that he would give me passionate kisses as he held me tight, while everyone watched. I felt ugly and awkward. I was skinny, but I had big breasts. They weren't big in size; they just looked to be really big because I was so skinny.

A guy named William and I started dating. I didn't like him; I thought he was ugly, but I liked the idea of having a boyfriend in school. We would walk down the hall holding hands. He'd kiss me and tell me he loved me. I'd tell him I loved him too. We shared our childhood experiences. He had been beaten by his father and watched his mother be abused by him too. He also sold drugs. I was just with him to be with him. He had a car and could drive me places that I wanted to go. I don't even remember us going on dates. We were in the gospel choir together. I don't know how well he could sing, but he was a good piano player.

William also wrote songs, which was right up my alley, since I had been writing poetry and songs since I was a young child. We formed a group with Kim, a girl who was in the gospel choir with us. I don't even remember why William and I broke up, or who broke up with whom, but we will still practiced with the group.

We were at my house getting ready for practice. I told him, "I think you should make a change in the song; on this part you should …" The next thing I knew, I was in the air. He picked me up and threw me across the room, and my head almost hit the ceiling fan, which was on. Keenan and I were the only ones there, and we fought him back. I wouldn't say we won, but he knew he wasn't going to be able to hit on me. Surprisingly, I had no scratches and no pain either.

A friend from church named Rodney told me he had someone he wanted me to meet. We decided to meet in front of my friend Tiffany's house. It was getting dark outside, but I could see very well. *Oooooooo, that boy is so fine. Man oh man.* I was fifteen and instantly blinded by his height and build. *Oh my Lord, he has hazel eyes. Mmm, those are kissable lips. My boy did a good job with this hook up!* I already knew Rodney, and another guy introduced himself as Ricky. The one who caught my eye introduced himself as Pretty Boy. "Eeeeeeerrrrrr, pump the brakes. You're fine and all, but I am not about to call you Pretty Boy! What's your real name?"

"Allen." He answered with a snickering laugh. We exchanged phone numbers and started dating. We went to rival high schools. We'd joke with each other about our schools. His school was in the 'hood and was what I considered ghetto. He thought mine was bourgeois and white.

Allen and I got along great and had a lot in common. He was an aspiring rapper, and I wanted to sing. We were a match made in heaven. The annual Guy Black Star Quest Talent Show approached. Guy Black was the most popular R&B radio personality in Indianapolis. You would always see him out hosting various events, but everyone looked forward to the Guy Black Star Quest Talent Show. There were judges, some famous, some not so famous. Everyone would come to see the newest talent. Allen and one of his friends had written a rap song. They asked me to go to the studio with them to record the hook. We would all enter the talent show together as a group. I had been in the talent show every year for the past three years and knew the routine. I was excited because this was my first time being in the studio. He wanted to buy T-shirts with our stage names on them. "What do you want your name to be, Dream?"

"Dream."

"No, you need a stage name, your alias."

"I know what you mean, boy! My stage name is Dream. I am my music, and music is me! Dream is my name."

"Okay, I'm gonna give you a name."

"You can't just give me a name!"

"Yes I can; you're my girl. I am Pretty, he is Black, and you are gonna be Ace."

"Ace?"

"Yeah, you are my Ace, so I'ma call you Ace."

I gazed into his hazel eyes and thought to myself, *He's trying to do the Jedi mind trick on me!*

"Whatever. I'm Dream Ace! Since this is your song, I'll be Ace for a day. But tomorrow it's back to Dream." I laughed.

The day of the talent show, all of our friends and family came out to show support. We didn't win the contest; we placed third, but we had a lot of fun.

As Allen and I grew closer, he would try to persuade me to have sex with him. "If you just give me some, then I promise I won't sell drugs no more." I hated that he sold drugs. I didn't want him to get arrested, but I knew he wouldn't stop just because we had sex, so I didn't. I saw Allen as a wannabe thug, but he was really too sweet to be a thug. His family was cool, and he had more freedom than I did. Every time I went to his house, his mother, Angela, would have me sing for her. She had her favorite selections of "Amazing Grace," "Precious Lord," or "His Eye Is on the Sparrow." Allen had an older sister named Delta, who had the cutest baby girl, named Rasheeda.

One summer day, Allen invited me to a family BBQ over his father's house. I met his cousin Junior and his girlfriend Reign. They had a daughter named Princess, who had the cutest, chunkiest cheeks. I soon lost focus of Princess when I met Allen's father, Big Al. All I could say was "Whew!" *Oh my God! He was a darker version of Allen!* Reign and I joked about how fine this older man was as we ate BBQ and played with Princess.

I just knew we would be together forever. He was my first true love. He never said or hinted it, but that's how my mind envisioned us. I really couldn't see past our *now* moment. I was one hundred and ten percent head over heels down and dirty in love.

We would hang out anywhere, doing everything or nothing; it didn't matter. Our favorite spot was the toy isle in Wal-Mart. We would find all the toys that made noise and make them all go off at the same time and just laugh as the shoppers and employees looked around to see "What the devil is all that racket!"

We didn't have sex until we had been together for six months. The first few times we did, it hurt too badly, and I made him back off for a few months. After I got used to it, we would have sex on a regular basis. I enjoyed it, although I really don't know why. I can't recall any moments of pure bliss. He was all I knew, so of course it was great. We always used condoms. No exceptions. That is until one day … out of nowhere I got this 'bright idea.' "I want to know what it feels like for you to come inside of me." Of course he said "Okay." As long as he was getting some, I'm sure he really didn't care. I already knew about the birds and the bees and about STDs, but for whatever reason I figured,

That's them, the people in the books and on TV. It only happens to the people in the documentaries or the people that come to the school and have some type of program or presentation. Never in my mind did I think pregnancy or STDs could or would happen to me.

We had our spot in his mom's red Dodge Shadow. We'd park behind the dumpster in the lot of the school I went to kindergarten at. We'd turn on R. Kelly's "12 Play" tape extended single, hop in the back seat, and it was on. R. Kelly would be singing his butt off. "My mind is telling me no. But my body, my body's tellin' me yes. Baby I-I-I don't wanna hurt nobody, but there is something that I must confeeeeeeeeeeeessssssssssss. Yeah. I don't see nothin' wrong with a little bump and grind." All of that sexiness just heightened my 'I'm grown' complex. I was a little disappointed that when he came inside of me, I felt nothing different from when we used a condom. There was no gush of warmth, no overwhelming feelings of euphoria, fireworks, dramatic scenes, or moans and groans like in the porn videos. It simply was what it was, finished! He smiled as if he had accomplished something as significant as climbing Mount Everest or capturing Rome. I just smiled. I wasn't upset, just curious and thrown off as to why it didn't feel any different. *Why do people say that it's so much better without a condom, when you really can't tell the difference?* Since I felt nothing different, we used condoms every time after that. None of this changed my feelings for him; I was still in love. He was my man, and I was his woman.

I was on cloud nine. I had a real boyfriend that I was truly in love with. We had sex at any opportunity we could. Even though he didn't go to my school, he was very popular, and most people in my school knew him. It was the end of my junior year, and auditions were coming up for the highest choir in school, Counterpoints. The choir was known across the nation because they had won many competitions and held the number one position for the past five years. I set to learn and perfect my audition piece. Unlike most things you audition for, Counterpoints didn't display a list to let you know who the lucky winners were. Instead, you were kidnapped in the middle of the night by Counterpoint seniors who wouldn't be there the next year. No one but the seniors knew what day they would do the kidnapping. It was considered an honor and a privilege to be accepted into this choir. It was like a sorority or fraternity.

One Saturday night, I got out of the shower and was about to go to sleep. My mother told me, "You need to put some pants or something on."

"Why?" I asked. I was confused, because I always wore a T-shirt and underwear to bed. It was hot outside, and we didn't have central air.

"Just do it, okay." She sounded annoyed. I was too tired to argue; I put on some pants, but I took them off before I went to sleep. I awoke startled; someone had jumped into my bed and was straddled across me. I couldn't get up. Another face had duct tape and taped my mouth and blindfolded me. I punched and kicked, trying to get the two assailants off of me, but I couldn't. I started to calm down as they tied my arms behind my back. It was two familiar female voices laughing and joking at how hard I was fighting.

"Welcome to Counterpoints, Dream!" they chimed.

"Ahhhhh," I screamed from behind the tape. *That's why mom wanted me to wear pants to bed. Oops!*

"Where are some pants we can put on her before we take her outside?" I overheard one girl asking my mother.

"She doesn't have any pants on?" Mom answered.

"No, ma'am," they laughed.

"Dream, you just don't listen, do ya? I told you to put some pants on. Now all of North Central can see your underwear." We all laughed as Mom helped them find some pants and put them on me. They guided me out to the car and took the tape from over my mouth. "Say hello to your new choir member Dream."

"Dream, you made it too?" I heard a male voice yell.

"Franklin, is that you? Oh my God, we made it, we made it."

The door closed, and we drove off. We talked and laughed. I told of how my mother had told me to put on some pants but it had been too hot for that. Kendra and Maya drove some ways and stopped the car.

"Get out!"

Franklin and I were still tied up, but got out.

"Okay, follow our voices."

We tried to follow their voices as we stumbled down a small slope.

"Am I gonna run into any trees?" I asked.

"Don't worry about it, just follow my voice!"

I eventually found them, and they took off my blindfold. "This is the last test of being a Counterpoint. You must drink this special formulized drink to prove that you want to be in," Maya said as she handed Franklin and me squirt bottles.

"Well, what kind of drink is it?" I asked

"Just drink it!" Franklin and I took a gulp and spit it out.

"Ugh! What is this?"

Kendra laughed hysterically, "It's ten different kinds of Kool-Aid mixed with Sprite. Isn't it yummy?" They giggled.

"Ya'll woke me up for this?" We fell in the grass laughing.

We got back in the car and drove off again. We ended up at a big house. I didn't know whose house it was. There were a lot of cars outside, and, as we walked in, I realized it was the whole 1995–96 Counterpoints choir. Everyone was laughing and exchanging their kidnapping stories. It was five a.m., and there was enough breakfast cooked to feed an army. One of the parents volunteered their home for the final meeting place for the kidnapping. We got to learn a little about each other and were all ready to start our summer rehearsals in a few months.

While I stuck true to my unspoken vow of monogamy, Allen was being Mr. Playa, Playa, Rapper, Upper Classman, Football Player Mr. Pretty Boy himself at his own school. I found out that he had cheated on me with someone I thought was my friend and whom I had classes with. She would smile in my face and act as a friend, all the while sleeping with my man.

Diary Entry

December 29, 1994

I've grown up a lot since I last wrote in you. I can't believe I'm actually writing you. I'm 16 years old, almost 17! I don't need to write in my diary! The last time I wrote you I had just lost my virginity. Now I kind of regret it. Now I'm in love. Can you believe it? Me, Dream, the girl who's had bad experiences with every male she ever came in contact with, and I've had sex 12 times and counting! His name is Allen Ray Carter and we're just alike. I don't know why I'm so hooked on him because I was hooked even before we started having sex. There are only 3 things I don't like about him. I mean don't get me wrong; everybody has their own little problems, but these are real bad. First of all he smokes weed a lot. Secondly he drinks, not as much as he smokes, but too much. I can understand every once in a while for a celebration or something, I just don't want him to end up like Granddad, who doesn't know how to keep in touch with his family and loved ones, and always drives drunk; and I've only seen him 3 times. Lastly he sells drugs. He told me that if I let him fuck me in the ass he'd stop, but I'd have to do it 3 times for him to stop everything. I won't be able to enjoy him after all of that because I'd be dead! Mom likes Allen though. She didn't like him for a while because she caught us naked in my bed in the middle of the night. He had come through my window, but now she likes him which is good, but her and everybody else in my family swears up and down that I'm gonna end up pregnant. Which might be true, but I doubt it. We did it yesterday without a condom. Whoa! Was that good! If I do end up pregnant and have a baby girl I'm gonna name her Destiny Morae Carter. Allen is kinda being a role model to Keenan. That's what he needs right now. He's hittin' puberty; I just hope he doesn't teach him any of his bad habits. He better not! I'd kick his ass! But he's the only man who comes around here anymore, 'cuz our faggot daddy didn't come around for birthdays or Christmas this year. Not that I wanted anything from him, but now he stopped fakin' like he cared. I think he has another family, though, 'cuz a couple of Halloweens ago I was manning a booth at church and these BeBe kids were hangin' all over him callin' him daddy and shit. Not that I care if he has another family, but damn take care of

*me first. I was there first, his flesh and blood and the spitting image of
him, but it's okay though, that's why sometimes I wish I had a baby so
I could show the Muthafucka how much I hate him 'cuz I wouldn't let
him near my child, male or female! For one because of what he did to
me. Two because he's only around when he feels like it. Other than that
he doesn't give a damn. So now I'm working on changing myself. Not
personality, but never again will I let another nigga trample over me.
I've always been too nice; just because someone asked I went ahead and
gave them something or let them abuse me and use me. Not because I
wanted to but because I was raised to make sure everybody around you
was happy and fuck me if I wasn't. But all of that is about to change as
soon as I get myself together again. But Allen is cool people. I just hope
he doesn't leave again. That hurt. It took me next to forever to learn
to trust him then he broke my heart. I don't even know why he left. I
cried once though. Damn I've got it bad. I was mad at myself for lovin'
a nigga so much I would cry. Hopefully we'll last. I've got good feelings
about him. I've been so patient with him and Lord knows that I have no
patience. So I guess you could say that I am maturing. Yuck! But I'll be
alright. Nothing can possibly happen to me that I can't handle. All week
I've just been seeing my life and all that I've been through and it kind of
gives me the blues. I think Allen can tell. He's done a good job in keeping
me cheered up. He's like a male version of my best friend; a best friend
who is just like me (nasty and everything), who I can tell my innermost
feelings to. It's just so hard to let it all out. I hope he doesn't think I don't
trust him because it's just that I don't want to hurt anymore.*

About two months after our one time of having unprotected sex, I
woke one morning with an aching stomach. I was what I know now to
be dry-heaving, but at the time I had no idea what dry heaves were. I
told my mom, "I can't go to school today. I feel like I have to throw up
and it won't come up." She completely went off on me.

"If you think that you can stay home every time you get sick you
ain't never gonna graduate! You are pregnant and that is no excuse
for you to not go to school."

This threw me so far off my guard. I had no idea what she was talking about and why she was saying it. I had just had my period. I still

had my six-pack stomach. What in the world was she talking about? I sucked it up, got ready for school, and got on the bus. A few days later, that little voice in the back of my mind told me to take a pregnancy test. I had a friend who worked at Target buy me a pregnancy test because I was too embarrassed to buy it myself. She brought me the E.P.T. test. I went into the bathroom and read the directions three times before I squatted over the toilet and peed on the stick. As the color changed to say "pregnant," I threw up. It was as if there were flashing neon lights on the stick with the brightest fluorescent bulbs screaming, *Your mother was right. Yes, you are pregnant, pregnant, pregnant,* followed by a wicked, sinister laugh. I sat on the toilet in total disbelief. *How in the world did this happen to me? This only happens to other people. I can't believe it happened to me.* My thoughts raced; random things flowed into my brain. *My mom is going to kill me. I need to eliminate this problem.* I called Allen on the phone: "Um, I just took a test and, um, I'm pregnant." I tried to hold back my tears but couldn't.

"Uh really? Wow, well, what do you want to do?"

"I don't think we have many options. I'm gonna have to get an abortion so my mom doesn't kill me. I'm not ready to be a mother! I've got to make some calls, I'll call you back."

I had a friend who used abortion as a form of birth control. I didn't necessarily agree with that, but I needed to do something quick. I would have the abortion and literally never have sex again. I never really thought of abortion as killing a life. To me it was just not being pregnant anymore. I knew there was a lot of controversy about it, but I didn't really understand the depths of it. At school I talked to a few of my closest friends. "I'm going to go to Planned Parenthood to get some birth control pills."

"What's the purpose of the pills if you are already pregnant?" one friend asked.

"If I take the pill it would not let the baby survive." I knew it was to prevent pregnancy, but I also thought that if I took the pill, the baby would abort itself.

Prom time for both schools approached. I told Allen the color and theme of my prom so we could coordinate. "In the Mood." I bought the non-refundable tickets and waited for him to give me the information for his. I knew that his prom was before mine, but he still hadn't given me any information about it. I was so in love and naive I didn't think anything of it. One week before my prom, I asked him, "So, when is your prom, again?"

"It was two weeks ago."

"Two weeks ago? Did you go?"

"Yeah, I went."

"With who?"

"I already had a date, and we already went."

"You already had a date! What's that supposed to mean? What about my prom?"

"I'm not going to your prom because I already went to mine."

I hung up the phone. I can't believe this shit! This nigga done knocked me up and taken another girl to his prom! I hate him! My life can't get any worse! I had to decide what to do next. My mother had already started making my prom dress, and I had already bought the tickets. *I don't want to be a loser and go by myself. Everyone in school either already has a date or I don't want to go with the ones who don't have a date. I can't force Allen to go. Who can I take to the prom?* I called a friend who was a freshman in college to see if he would take me to my prom. He agreed, so that part was handled. I really just wanted my picture taken in my prom dress to say that I had gone, and then to go home. I was already distraught about being pregnant and everything, and now I didn't even have a prom date. I went to prom and had an okay time. I showed my face and took pictures, but my mind was really elsewhere. *What am I going to do?*

I asked Tisha to loan me the money so that I could get an abortion. She's always been very religious, always preached to me about everything. I should've known she'd say no, but then again, like I said, I really didn't understand, nor had I ever thought about abortion in its entirety. I ended up getting money for the abortion from two friends. We were teens and they had part time jobs; one fifty or two hundred dollars was a lot to come by and to ask for. I had no idea how I would pay the money back; I had a part-time job making five dollars an hour, and I only worked about fifteen hours a week. Allen didn't have a job, and he didn't even try to help me get any of the money together. I did the research and had all of the information I needed secretly mailed to me at my house. I scheduled the abortion. I only talked to him to give him the info for the abortion. There was only one place in Indianapolis where a minor could get an abortion without parental consent. I called him a few days before the abortion was to take place and asked him to come over and have sex with me to 'loosen me up' so that the abortion wouldn't hurt. Of course, he agreed, even though we weren't on speaking terms. There was no big falling out or cussing match; we just stopped talking. Of course, this time we had unprotected sex because it really didn't matter. What more could happen? I hadn't been with anyone else, and I was already pregnant. What more could happen? The whole episode was boring, meaningless, and only fun on his side. I laid there lifeless, feeling stupid and wondering why in the hell I had invited him over. He got up and put his clothes back on. No kiss, no hugs. I lay motionless, still half-dressed, on my mother's couch. My only glimpse of hope and happiness was that he had on dress clothes and told me he had been out looking for a job.

One of my friends who gave me some of the money for the abortion drove us to the abortion clinic. There were double-locked doors with a security guard outside and one inside. *Man is it really that deep?* I thought to myself. Allen and I sat in the lobby waiting for my name to be called. We didn't say a word to each other. The nurse finally called my name. I walked into the room alone. I thought the abortion would happen right then and there, but the nurse put some of this warm gel on my stomach and spread it all around. Then she pushed on my stomach with some plastic-looking thing, and on this screen right next to me you could see this image. It looked like a baby, and you could also hear this steady beat. She told me, "That is your baby, and it has a strong heartbeat. You are about four-and-a-half months pregnant, not one or two like you thought. If you still want to have an abortion, you will have to pay more money."

I didn't have the money that I had borrowed, let alone more money. My life seemed over. I couldn't see past that day. I didn't even see the rest of the story—having the baby, working to take care of the baby, finishing school, none of that. I was just afraid of how badly my mother was going to kill me when I went home and told her that I was pregnant. To me it seemed like I would be pregnant for the rest of my life. As we walked out of the clinic, there was a bowl full of free condoms. Allen grabbed a bunch of them and stuffed them in his pockets while giggling. I didn't see the humor in it. How could he laugh and be so carefree about any of the events that had taken place on this day?

I went home, closed the door to my room, sat on the floor, and cried. Just when I thought I couldn't cry anymore, I cried even more and even harder. My singing career that I just knew I was going to have was now over. All of my hopes and dreams, everything was over. I wouldn't be able to do any more talent shows by myself or with O'Leta, Kim, and Jada. That same afternoon I felt the baby move for the first time, which only made me cry some more. I wrote my mother a letter. I told her that I was pregnant by Allen, but I wasn't going to get an abortion, and I still planned on finishing school and going to college. I put the letter up under her door while she slept. I didn't go to sleep that night. I had to stay awake because I knew when she read it, she would come in my room and literally kill me! She came into my room early in the morning kind of giggling to herself, with the letter in her hand. She said, "I knew you were pregnant! I thought you weren't going to tell me until you went into labor. Abortion is not an option. We don't believe in abortions. You have two options. You can get a job and raise the baby on your own or give the baby up for adoption. Those are your only two options. You make the decision on what you want to do. You need to get prenatal care. You can go and get Medicaid. That will pay for all of your medical expenses." That was the extent of our conversation. We really didn't talk about it after that, but she made sure that I ate balanced meals.

I set up an appointment for prenatal care. I was shocked because I had the option to choose which doctor I wanted to have. There were some male doctors and some female, but I chose a woman by the name of Dr. Amanda Lewis. She just had a look about her that was so calming, and I knew for sure that I didn't want a male doctor. She laid me down on the table and talked me through the procedure. "Bring your bottom all the way to the end of the table. Open your legs, relax, now I'm inserting the ..." My mind started to wander again. I had a flashback, and went to myself in the third grade, when I had my first Pap smear. Apparently I was tense. Her voice brought me back to the present time.

"Okay, relax, relax. It will go quicker if you just relax." I took a deep breath.

Damn! She finished and had some long cotton swabs that she smeared into a dish. "I'm going to go and run a few tests and I'll be right back." I sat and waited. *I didn't know they gave you Pap smears while you were pregnant. That is so gross! What if they hurt the baby's head?*

She came back again and performed an ultrasound. I had just had one a few weeks prior, and I couldn't see the difference. I couldn't even tell which part was which.

"See that right there? That's the arm; there's a leg. It's a little too early to tell if it's a boy or a girl yet, though. The baby has a very strong heartbeat." She wiped the jelly off of my stomach. "Okay, I'm going to go check the results, and I'll be right back. You can go ahead and get dressed." I put my clothes on in a hurry. *How embarrassing would it be for her to open the door and I'm still not dressed. I guess it really doesn't matter. She was just all up in my stuff.*

A few minutes later she walked back into the room. "Okay, I'm going to write you a few prescriptions. One is for prenatal vitamins. Make sure you take them every day. The second is for Chlamydia."

"Cla who? What is that?"

"That is a sexually transmitted disease. The symptoms are hard to detect in women, but the male usually knows that something is wrong."

"Wow, well, will it hurt the baby?"

"No, take this medicine until it's all gone, then come and see me in two weeks, and I'll retest you to make sure it's gone."

"Will the medicine hurt the baby?"

"No, the baby will be fine, but you are going to have to tell the people that you had sex with that you have Chlamydia."

"It's only one person. I can't believe this!" I knew exactly when he gave it to me. It was when we had sex to loosen me up before I was going to have an abortion. I didn't even think to use a condom, because I was already pregnant. I was more in a daze than angry. I couldn't believe everything that was happening to me back to back.

I called Allen when I got home. "I just left from my first doctor's appointment and found out that you gave me Chlamydia."

"Oh, okay."

"That's all you have to say?"

"What do you want me to say?" I hung up the phone. I am never going to talk to that nigga again! I should've gotten in his ass. *Who else have you been with? You had symptoms and still didn't warn me or bother to use a condom?* I had so many things to say to him, but I just couldn't, or didn't. I was embarrassed, alone, and overwhelmed.

Since I had decided to keep the baby, I knew I would have to call my new choir teacher, Mrs. Williams, before Counterpoints started their summer practice schedule. I didn't know how I would still be allowed to be in the choir, being pregnant. It was a show choir, with lots of very intense lifting and dancing. My heart pounded as the phone rang and I anticipated her answer before I even asked.

No, you can't be a part of the choir. We will have to give your spot to someone else. Too bad this is your senior year; I guess you won't get to be a Counterpoint. I immediately recognized her voice when she answered, "Hello."

"Hi, Mrs. Williams, this is Dream."

"Hi, sweetie, are you ready for our summer rehearsals? I'm so excited; we've got a lot of great things coming up this year."

"Well, that's why I'm calling you." I felt the tears begin to well in my eyes. When I had auditioned, she had told me that she'd had her eye on me since I was a freshman and did my first solo. She was so proud that I auditioned.

"I don't think that I can be in Counterpoints."

"Oh no, Dream. Why?"

"Well, I just found out that I'm pregnant."

"Oh, I see. Well, I wouldn't say that you can't be in the choir. It's not the end of the world because you are pregnant. You have a beautiful voice and are a great addition to the choir. I think you should stay, but it's up to you."

"I want to stay, Mrs. Williams, I really want to. I just don't know how it can work."

"You let me worry about that. We will make it work, okay? I'll see you in a few weeks for practice. Thanks for calling and giving me the heads-up."

"Okay, thanks, Mrs. Williams. I'll see you then." I had my reservations, but I was more than pleased with her response. I would get to be a Counterpoint after all.

That summer I went to the mandatory six-hours-a-day Counterpoint practice. I learned all of the parts and dances, but no one was allowed to lift me, so I would have to stand out front or on the side and do something different. I wanted to be one hundred percent involved but knew that I couldn't. I was just happy to be around others who were very talented and had a lot of drive like me. After Counterpoint rehearsal I started summer school. I wanted to get as many credits in as possible, because I didn't know how my year would go, since I would soon be a mother.

There were only a handful of friends that knew I was pregnant. One of them was a girl named Elisha. We had piano lab together, and she would always rub on my stomach and wait for the baby to kick.

I threw up consistently. I threw up when I ate food, saw food, thought about food. When I went to the bathroom, I could smell all the cleaning agents and everything the cleaning agents didn't clean. I was miserable and hungry all of the time! I was still in denial. Two of my closest friends were males, and I definitely didn't want to tell them. We were changing classes one day during summer school, and one of them, Timothy, pulled me to the side and asked me, "Dream, are you pregnant?" My body just got hot all over. My first thought was, *Oh no! Now people can really tell. These big shirts and jackets in class aren't hiding this growing belly.*

"Yes," I answered.

"Why didn't you say anything?"

"I don't know." I was still in denial, and if I admitted it to myself then it would be true. As long as I didn't admit it to myself, it was all a bad dream, and eventually I would wake up, but now I had said it out loud to someone who had no idea and it was true. School let out for the summer. Allen graduated and had made plans to go to Vincennes University in southern Indiana. I took no part in his graduation activities, nor was I invited to. We didn't talk, but every once in a while I called him, and he still hadn't told his family. Every time we spoke he swore he would tell them.

The bus to go to summer school was at the middle school. I had to walk to the middle school every morning, then back home after school let out. It was a two-and-a-half-mile hike each way, but it felt more like ten miles. I saw Allen in a car with his cousin talking to all of the other kids that got off the bus. He saw me but didn't say one word. Then he watched me as I walked my two-and-a-half-mile hike back home in the hot sun with my six-month-sized belly. I was steaming mad physically and emotionally all the way home. *How dare he see me and still let me walk home while I'm pregnant with his child.* I really couldn't believe that he would do me like that when just a few months prior we were inseparable and so in love. I thought to myself, *How did I end up here?* It was ninety degrees outside, I was boiling mad at him, and this sun and my belly were not getting along. I was so upset I couldn't even cry anymore. I really just didn't understand. It seemed like overnight my stomach grew. It felt like I woke up one morning and had swallowed a watermelon. Not only was my stomach the size of a watermelon, but I had the line marks like a watermelon too. There were stretch marks on my stomach, sides, back, and breasts. I'd look in the mirror and say, *Oh my God, what's wrong with my body? Will these ugly lines go away?* There would be no more sexy body and no more six pack. I had been teased before for being too skinny, but the way my body was looking, I thought that no one would ever want to look at me again.

I got my driver's license. I had to get it right away because I didn't know how I was going to get to school and get my baby to daycare. We couldn't ride on the school bus. There was a center on the school campus where you could take classes for a trade, and they also had a daycare there. You could pay them twenty dollars a week to watch your child while you were in school. It was right on our campus, so that worked out perfectly and was something that I could afford. As my due date approached, my guidance counselor set it up for me to do home school. I basically would read my books on my own and teach myself. I had to come up to the school to take my tests, but that way I wouldn't miss any school and could graduate on time. I had to come to the school once a week to pick up my class assignments and turn in the assignments I had already done. It sounded like as good of a plan as it could get, but I was still walking in a daze. Allen still hadn't told his family. Mom was only there for me to give me the basic info that I had no idea about. Other than that, I was on my own. I couldn't afford any maternity clothes, so I wore 2XL T-shirts and shorts, and pants with elastic waists. Sometimes I would even wear the big shirts and leave my jeans unbuttoned and unzipped. The shirt would cover that part, so no one could tell (I hoped). I really was all belly. I was already producing milk, and I always wore a jacket in class: for one, it was freezing inside the school; two, I would leak milk and it would be all on my shirt, but the jacket covered it up so no one knew about it. I was embarrassed and didn't know how to remedy the problem, so I just dealt with it.

Diary Entry

August 27, 1995

Dear Diary,

I am 6 months pregnant, by Allen of course. We broke up in March. I knew he was playing on me, but that's not why I broke up with him. He didn't have time for a relationship. He went to day & night school every day so he was too tired for a relationship. I wouldn't have let him keep playing on me either, but the love was fading. I found out he was playing me because he forgot my birthday. I called him and asked him how old I was, he said 16, I said no 17! Thanks for remembering my birthday! and hung up. I weigh 117 now! I've gained 12 pounds. Today I found out that my best friend Kim is pregnant. She just left for college. I'm hoping she doesn't have an abortion, so we'll just have to wait and see. Allen left for college too. He goes to Vincennes. Can you believe he didn't call or visit me before he left? No I don't want him back, but we're still cool, and I believe I deserve more respect than that. Ever since prom (which he stood me up a week before) I've had this whole different view about him. I don't even know what it is I saw in him. Every time he comes around I just have this real evil mood swing. Even when I saw him bald in a tank top with a tan over the summer I didn't get excited. When I look into his eyes that used to be so gorgeous it's just like looking someone in the eye, nothing special. The love just isn't there anymore. I know deep in my heart that I still love him and I always will, but there's no feeling. When he hugs me I'm just like get off of me! I know he loves me too (deep down), but he's probably scared of commitment. Yeah we were together for a little over a year, but every time something serious came up there he goes trippin'. Right now I definitely don't want him, maybe after he gets older and a little more mature.

I was eight months pregnant, and I asked a friend of mine to throw me a baby shower. I told her I would help with the costs if needed. (Yes, I had to ask someone to throw me a baby shower. How desperate was that?) Since Allen still hadn't told his family and was off at college still living his life, I sent his mother an invitation to the shower. She called me and said, "Congratulations I had no idea! Who's the father?"

"Allen."

"Allen who?"

"Allen Carter, your son!" She was obviously caught off guard.

"What! Are you serious? How far along are you? Are you okay? I can't believe that boy didn't tell me!"

"Yeah, Angela, I'm due in a month. I kept telling him to tell you guys, but he never did. Hold on. I'll call him on three-way." I tried to hide my excitement because I knew Angela would not be gentle on him. The phone rang, and he picked up on the first ring.

"Hello."

"Allen, why didn't you tell me that girl was pregnant?" Angela yelled.

"Huh, um well, I didn't want you to not let me go to school."

"Oh, so it's okay for her not to go to school because she's pregnant, but not for you?"

"Mamma, I'm sorry!"

"Don't sorry mamma me, boy! I am so mad at you right now, and it's not because of the baby. You just left her here alone and pregnant with no help or game plan. We've missed the whole pregnancy because you are only thinking about yourself! You are coming home this weekend, and we are going to have a family meeting!"

"Okay, mom. I'm sorry. Okay."

"I'm hanging up now," Angela said, "but we will settle this, this weekend." I could hear her continuing to fuss as she hung up the phone.

"Why did you tell my mamma?"

"Well, I gave you eight months to tell her, but you haven't told her yet, so I did what I had to do!" I felt like five hundred pounds of weight had been lifted off of me.

We made amends for the most part with just that conversation. Just the fact that they knew was such an uplifting experience for me. We talked all night and he told me, "Dream, I never wanted you to have an abortion. I was just scared."

"I didn't want to have an abortion either! I was scared and was only doing it because that's what you said you wanted me to do."

Angela and her daughter Delta came to the baby shower with tons of clothes. I was carrying a baby boy. The next time Allen came home, we started to mend our relationship more, and I guess you could say we were boyfriend and girlfriend again.

We discussed what we would name our son. He wanted him to be named after him and his father. I disagreed, because I believe that names carry weight, and his father was a drug addict, and there were things about even Allen that I did not want my child to carry on. I came up with Christian Anthony. He claimed that was too 'white.' He wanted to name him Divine Allen as a second option. He was so conceited and stuck on himself that he was talking about himself as being divine. His mother and I both knocked that off the list, but I agreed to Jordan Allen Carter.

I worked my part-time job and went to school as normal. I planned on doing both until I felt pain and couldn't go anymore. I felt better about the whole situation because I no longer felt so alone. Things weren't perfect, but things were looking up. Aunt Yvonne had been giving me birthing classes, as she always did for everyone in our family. One night, she was over at the house, and my oldest sister was there as well. I had my weekly doctor's appointment the next morning.

"Dream, I don't think that you should drive to your doctor's appointment tomorrow. You look like that baby is about to drop, and I don't want you to go into labor while you're driving and have an accident," Mom said.

"I'll take her in the morning. After that we can go do a little shopping and get everything else we need for the baby," Tisha replied.

It was fall break, so we were out of school Thursday and Friday. Allen was due to be home that weekend but decided not to come until the following weekend. Tisha was joking, saying, "When you go into labor your hair is going to be all over your head. You are going to be kicking and screaming and acting a fool!" Aunt Yvonne in her always-so-soothing voice gently said, "No, she's not. She's going to look just like she does now."

That night, I woke up because I felt something wet in my underwear. I went to the bathroom and wiped myself, changed my underwear, and went back to bed. There was no blood or anything, so I didn't think anything of it. Not too long after that I felt wet again, but this time I put on a maxi-pad. I woke up Tisha and asked, "What does it feel like when your water breaks?"

"There will be a big gush of fluid that comes out that you can't stop or control like if you were peeing." I didn't tell her that I had already been up and put on a pad, because uncontrollable rushing water wasn't my symptom. I figured it was just my baby and my hormones making me more 'moist' than usual. We awoke the next morning and went to my nine a.m. doctor's appointment. Tisha had her youngest child with her at the time, Angel, who was just six months old. When I saw my doctor, I was laughing and joking and telling her how at first I thought my water had broken the night before, but it hadn't. She checked me out, and to my surprise it had and was breaking. It didn't have a complete break; it was just slowly seeping out. She hooked me up to a machine to check if I was having any contractions, and to both our surprise my contractions were five minutes apart. I was in active labor. Once again, I was still in denial. I had things to do that day; I wasn't feeling any pain, and I still wasn't convinced that my water was breaking. So in my mind there was no way that I was giving birth that day.

Labor is supposed to be painful, and you are supposed to hardly make it to the hospital on time. That was not my scenario. The doctor went through the doors to the waiting area and told my sister that I was in active labor and I had to go to the hospital and she would meet us there. Tisha was so mad at me. "You cow! Are you serious? Well, you are going to have to call somebody to be with you. I didn't want to be part of the whole birthing process. I was just driving you to the doctor. Breathe, girl, breathe! Woo ooo wooooooo woo ooo woooooooo,"

"Don't worry. I'm not really in labor. Something is wrong with her machine, and as soon as I get to the hospital and recheck it, they'll see, and then we can go." She dropped me off at the entrance while she parked the car. It seemed that there were absolutely no parking spots, almost like she parked in the last spot in the last row. She walked swiftly back to the building carrying Angel in her car seat. She got to the door and was fussing at me. "Why are you standing there? Why didn't you go and get admitted?"

"Because I'm not in labor!"

We went to the admittance desk. A man named Ricardo took all of my information. He tried to make me sit in a wheelchair so he could take me to the birthing area, which was upstairs from the emergency room. Ricardo was getting on my nerves; there was nothing wrong with me. I had no pain. They still hadn't convinced me that I was really in labor, so I yelled, "Ricardo, get from behind me with that wheelchair!" He followed me with the wheelchair down the hall into the elevator and down another hall, until I got to the waiting room. All of the birthing rooms were full, but it didn't make a difference to me, because I was cool. *No pain and no baby today.* I've been known to play jokes on people, and when it was time for me to call Allen to tell him I was in the hospital, he didn't believe me, so Tisha had to get on the phone and make him believe. Mom and Aunt Yvonne showed up, and my mother was in disbelief that I couldn't feel any pain. She said, "When I was pregnant with you I was in labor for …"

The doctors induced my labor because I still wasn't feeling any contractions. The doctor said that she wanted me to feel them so I would know when to push. I thought, *Why would you make me feel pain? Just tell me when to push.* We were still waiting to see if Allen was going to make it before the baby came, and I went to sleep. When I woke up and there were still no labor pains, they induced labor again. I felt some contractions, but not the full contractions. I could only feel the climax of the contractions, not the buildup or the breakdown of the contractions. The only way that I was prepared for the contractions was by looking on the monitor and watching them come.

I was so stunned with each contraction that I kept trying to get out of the hospital bed. My mom kept asking me, "Where are you going?"

"I just want to go home!" A nurse came in to check to see how far dilated I was. She walked in the room putting on her gloves. "Can you just wait a minute? I'm having a contraction."

"I just need to check to see how far dilated you are."

"I understand that, but I'm having a contraction right now, so I need you to wait." She had an attitude and put her hand inside of me to check.

"Didn't I tell you to wait!" As she was pulling her hand out of my vagina, I dug my nails into her skin and scratched her arm. "Oh my God! I can't believe you did that. I'm just trying to do my job!"

"I told you to wait! Ain't nobody tryin' to stop you from doin' your job! I told you to wait!" She left the room immediately. My mother whispered in my ear, "You know you can't talk to people like that just because you are in pain."

"Whatever! I told her I was having a contraction and to wait. She's a dummy for stickin' her arm up there!"

After all of the trouble of trying to make me feel the contractions, they were ready to give me an epidural. "Okay, I need you to sit on the side edge of the bed, bend over as far as you can, and hold your knees. The epidural will burn just a little as it goes down your back, but whatever you do, you cannot move," the anesthesiologist told me.

"Okay." I knew that it couldn't hurt worse than the burst of contractions that I was having. I gladly bent over to get the epidural. It burned just like the doctor said it would; there was a tingly feeling, then beautiful numbness.

"Wow, now, that was a great invention," I told him. "Thank you so much."

Shortly after the epidural Allen ran into the room panting and trying to catch his breath. "Did the baby come yet?" We all looked at him and laughed.

"Nope! I'm still pregnant!" I told him.

The doctor came into the room. "Alright, everyone is here. It's baby time."

"Yeah, you missed all the drama, Allen! They had to induce labor on me two times!"

"Okay, bring your bottom all the way down to the end here. Now, don't push until I tell you to." She had a careful eye on the monitor.

"Okay, take a deep breath, bear down, and push." I tried to push, but the epidural had me so that I couldn't feel anything. I made the face as if I were pushing really hard. Dr. Lewis looked at me and rolled her eyes. "You are not pushing. Lay back, relax, and wait for me to give you the signal. Okay, take a deep breath, bear down, and give me a big push!" Aunt Yvonne was holding one leg and another nurse was holding the other. Allen was standing to the side watching. I made the face again. Allen looked at me, laughed, walked over to the birthing table, and whispered in my ear, "Just because you are making the face, doesn't mean that you are pushing."

I chuckled, "Well dang, I can't feel nothin'! I don't know if I'm pushin' or not, and I don't want to boo boo on the table!" We waited for the signal again. When it was time to push, he lifted my back up and our baby boy came right out. "Awww!" we sighed. "He's so cute!" They cut the umbilical cord and placed him on my stomach. "Ew, he's diiiiiiiirty!" We laughed.

I gave birth to a beautiful six pound nine ounce baby boy named Jordan Allen Carter. The birth of my son gave me a different and more profound feeling of true love. Instantly, I was happy that I had not had the abortion. *He's a tiny miracle. Thank you for him, God. I'm going to take good care of him, no matter how hard it gets.* I didn't cry on the outside, but I was streaming tears of joy inside.

Notes from My Journal

Something new and special has entered into my life. Something so wonderful and miraculous I could never explain the joyous feeling I have every time I hear him. Every time he looks into my eyes I see a world of wonder. I see someone I made, something I created. A miracle. It's so hard to explain. It's so remarkable how a human being can bring another human into the world. It's hard to believe that that sweet innocent person is the one who made me sick for nine months. The one who made me gain all that weight is so little and helpless. It's hard to believe that not long ago he was inside of me, so dependent on me. Everything I do will affect him. I pray every day that I will raise him right and be a good mother able to give him all he needs.

I couldn't have asked for a better child while I was a teenage mother. Jordan was so good. There were no nights when I was awake for hours with no end, no crying for no reason. I did home school while I was on maternity leave. I would go to the school on Fridays to take whatever tests I needed to and get my work for the following week. I went back to work at my part-time job four weeks after giving birth, and back to school at six weeks. Allen left college and came home to live. He told me that he missed Jordan and me and that he wanted to get a job to help take care of him. He came home but only worked on occasion. When Jordan needed diapers, if Mom or I didn't have enough money, Angela would bring them.

When I started back to school, my grades were okay, but I was very disappointed that Mrs. Williams had given me a C in Counterpoints. All of my tests came out fine, but I didn't have a good percentage in participation. *Well, she knew I was pregnant before I started this choir. I would've participated if I wasn't fat and pregnant. I have never gotten a C in Choir.* I withdrew from the class for the second semester. On the outside I tried to make it seem like it wasn't a big deal, but on the inside it was everything. Representatives from the University of Cincinnati had come to talk to us about getting full scholarships to go to their school for music. College had never been a thought for me, but there was no way that I could take my newborn to Cincinnati by myself.

The last semester of school was pretty uneventful. I didn't get to go to the games on Fridays or the weekend parties. Mom would only watch Jordan for me while I was working. She and I also fought a lot. I felt that I should have the freedom to come and go when I wanted and do whatever I wanted. She didn't agree. At first the resolution was for me to pay rent—fifty dollars a month. That's not a lot of money, but I wasn't making a lot either, so it seemed like more. We argued constantly. Angela invited me to move in with her and Allen into her sister's house. We could stay in the basement and set it up like our own apartment. I felt like I was an adult and enjoyed being able to have sex anytime. Angela and Delta were so nice, helpful, and supportive. Always willing and able to babysit, putting their plans aside just to watch Jordan. That is another reason life really wasn't that hard while I was a teenage mother. To me, Angela was my friend, so I listened to her instead of my family. My family was all about tough love. His family was more anything goes, so with them I went. Even though I was in high school, I had no curfew. I wasn't wild, hanging out partying, but the whole thing was that Angela gave me freedom I wasn't even asking for, opening my mind to new things.

Friends from school would visit and look at me crazy when I'd check downstairs before I let them come down to make sure my man had clothes on. They never said anything, but I could see it in their faces. But there was nothing to say because I was grown. When it was time for me to go to work, I would wait for him to watch Jordan, but he wouldn't show up. I would blow up his pager; he wouldn't call back. Either Mom, Angela, Delta, one of my friends, or a co-worker who worked another shift would watch him for me. Not working was not an option for me, because Allen couldn't buy him the things that he needed. It was all on me. When he would come home later that night we would argue. "You knew that you had to watch Jordan. Why didn't you return my page?"

"I was out with Junior and a few friends, and I knew I wouldn't be back before you needed to leave."

"Why didn't you call me back? My mom had something else to do, but instead she was stuck with Jordan!"

"It's okay, you got to work, didn't you? I'll be working soon, so you won't have to work, okay."

"You have to actually look for a job in order to get one. You know that, right?"

Journal Entry

March 2, 1996

So much new has happed to me I don't know where to begin. First of all I am finally a senior in high school. I had a beautiful baby boy on October 27th, 1995. His name is Jordan Allen Carter. Allen is back into my life for good I hope. I told him that if he messes up again I'm finished with him for good. I think he thinks I'm playin'. Although I'd hate to do it I'm serious! As a matter of fact we live together. We had to; Mom was on one of her trippin' moods and she kicked me & Jordan out on January 1st just because we had one of our fallouts ... My best friend is pregnant too. She's due next month. Her parents were trippin' too, but now everything is cool. She has her own place with her boyfriend. Anywayz back to me. So now I'm up in Allen's aunt's house living with him and his mamma. So far everything's cool. She's a real sweetie. I hope she doesn't start acting like those other mothers-in-law like you see on Ricki Lake and stuff. So far Allen still doesn't have a job, but I'm not going to say anything else about it because everything will work out in due time.

Angela started being too overbearing and demanding about Jordan. She had something to say about everything I did with my son, like I wasn't doing a good enough job. I knew I was young and not perfect, but I also knew that I wasn't a bad mother. I loved Jordan, and he was well taken care of because of me. We constantly moved from Mom's to Angela's.

As helpful and loving as Allen's family were, they also caused me a lot of unnecessary grief. I know now that it was because I let them have too much control. Too much say about Jordan, with no limitations of visits, etc. Not to mention too much control over me because I was always in and out of their houses, running from my issues and away from my mother. One of the times that I was living with Angela, I was running low on money. I bought Jordan some stage two baby food instead of stage three (which I had recently switched him to) so that I could get more food for my money. As I put the jars of baby food in the cabinet, Angela went off on me and started throwing the baby food away. "You can't feed that boy stage two baby food; he's going to starve to death."

I wasn't mad at the fact that she wanted me to give him the stage three food but because of her whole approach. I was already broke, and she was throwing away food and money that I didn't have. She said, "If you need some money for baby food than just ask!" I was already livid and pissed. I took my baby's food out of the trash and once again left with my child.

The morning of graduation I had to have my Aunt Patricia babysit, because everyone else would be at the actual ceremony. Mom watched him that evening, and I went to the final parties. It felt so good to get out because it had been such a long time.

About six months after graduation Allen took me to the spot where we had met. He told me, "I am so happy with you in my life.

I know I don't always do right, but I'm going to do better. I'm going to do right by you. Will you marry me?" I was so happy. We hadn't talked about marriage, but it was what I wanted. I just knew that if we got married, everything would work out just fine. We would make the perfect family with our son. For whatever reason I only told my friends; I didn't tell my mother or anyone else in my family. We never made any wedding plans. We were simply engaged. I never received any financial help from Allen. I never thought of it really, despite the advice I got from my granny. He did buy him a few toys and a few outfits for Christmas, but no money came to me. I didn't know why Granny stressed me about child support. In my eyes we were together, so it would be stupid to take him to court for child support. My Granny would tell me, "You better watch his mom; she's sneaky. She is trying to appease you by jumping the gun if Jordan needs something so you won't even think of taking him to court for child support. You'd better watch them; they have too much control over Jordan. He is your baby; don't forget that."

Another incident between Angela and me happened on Jordan's first Fourth of July. He was nine months old, and it was tradition to go to Grandmere's house for a BBQ. Angela asked if she could take him to her family's for their BBQ and said she would drop him off over Grandmere's. I saw no problem with that and agreed. I put his clothes on him, an outfit that my aunt bought him, so she could see him in it. He was adorable. I went downstairs and saw Angela ironing another outfit for Jordan. "Angela, what are you doing?"

"I wanted him to wear this outfit."

"No, Angela, he can't go out visiting like that. That's a play outfit. It has a missing button and no matching top."

"Oh, he'll be okay."

Eventually she gave in to my request and changed his clothes again. I was unaware that she had put the outfit she wanted in his diaper bag and taken it with her. I told her that I would see her at four p.m. I went to my Grandmere's and watched as the time passed: four turned to five; five turned to six, and so on, until it was past seven. I went back to the house, and she pulled up. I was sitting on the porch, and I started yelling at her. "Where have you been, Angela? I was trying to work with you, but you didn't hold up your end of the deal. You were supposed to meet me at four o'clock at my Grandmere's." I looked at my sleeping baby, and he had on the outfit that I had not wanted him to wear. I was pissed beyond pisstivity—if that were a real word, that's what I would have been. She laughed and tried to brush me off, as if my say-so as a mother meant absolutely nothing. "I'm not going to give you an opportunity to screw me over again." Allen showed up shortly after, and I told him what had happened as she pleaded her case to him. "Hey, I've got nothing to do with this. Ya'll work it out."

"See, Dream, you've got him thinking that he has nothing to do with his son's life!"

"This has nothing to do with him having something to do with him. He wasn't even with you guys," I yelled back.

My blood was boiling. Not only was it a pointless never-ending battle with someone who was so convenient; he wasn't even sticking up for me or trying to calm the situation down. I was once again stuck in a rut, a circle of drama, with no control.

My father and I had always talked periodically throughout my school years. I hated him most of the time and would not answer, or return, his phone calls. Other times, I loved him and wanted to rekindle our father/daughter relationship. My car broke down and needed a new engine. I was told by every shade tree mechanic I asked that the car was not worth investing all of that money in. I called Dad to see if he could help. He was really great with working with his hands and could fix anything. *Maybe he can fix my car.* My back was against the wall. I had to have reliable transportation to get to work and take Jordan to the baby sitters.

"Praise the Lord." *No, this nigga didn't answer the phone like he's all sanctified. Keep your cool, Dream, keep your cool.*

"Hey, Dad. It's Dream."

"Hey, Dream, how's it going?"

"Not so good, my car broke down, and I was wondering if you could take a look at it for me."

"Sure, no problem. What's it doing?"

"That's just it. It's not doing anything," I laughed. "I had a few people look at it. They told me I blew a gasket, and they say I need a new engine. Do you know how to replace an engine?"

"It's not worth fixing if it needs a new engine."

I was disappointed and trying to figure out what my next move would be; he interrupted my thoughts. "I do have an extra car that I'm not using. I'll come get you and bring you to the house so you can pick it up." There was a glimmer of hope on the horizon.

"Are you serious?" I squealed. I bragged to all my friends about how my dad was going to give me a car and solve all of my problems with just one phone call. The next day, Dad picked up me and Jordan and took us to his house. He had a red '84 Dodge Prizm sitting in his driveway. "I'm going to look at it first and give it a tune up. You can drive this car until I get it running real good for you. There's nothing major wrong with it; I just haven't driven it in a while."

"Okay. Thanks."

"This is your first time to my house. Come on in, and I'll give you and Jordan a tour."

I don't want to go in your house. All I want is the car. If I have to go in your house to get the car, then I just won't get the car. My mind started to race. *I don't think he would try anything with me now because I'm older, but I've got Jordan here with me. I'm way on the other side of town. How am I gonna get away if something goes down?* I entered into the doorway holding Jordan tightly to my chest. *If nothing else, I'll just run as fast as I can down the street yelling "Fire." Mom says to always yell "Fire" because people will come faster to help than if you just yell "Help" or "Rape," because they don't want to be involved.*

I followed him and only partially listened to him talk. I don't know what I expected or what I was looking for, but quietly I wanted to find some type of clue to prove to me that he was still a monster. The house was very small. A lot smaller than ours. It was two bedrooms. "This is just an extra room that I use for storage right now. If you and Jordan ever need a place to stay, you are more than welcome to have this room for free."

This fool is really serious! He must think I'm stupid to even fix his mouth and think I'ma move in here with him with my child. I remember what you did to me; and I know what you did to Tisha and Derrick.

There weren't any children's toys, and I glanced into the bathroom and saw his crushed velvet robe hanging on the wall. I started to remember the first time he had molested me and every inappropriate touch I had had from a man thereafter. I clutched Jordan closer and closed my eyes. *He can't touch you; it's okay. It's not going to happen anymore.* After the tour he asked if we were hungry. There were hot dogs on the stove. *How'd those hot dogs get there? He didn't put those on after I got here. Ugh, is he trying to feed me old hot dogs? No, he's trying to lure us in. Ah, comfort food.*

"No thanks I'm good."

"How about you, Jordan, do you like hot dogs?" Jordan was only eight months and not talking yet, but he held his hand out to get a hot dog. I silently watched as Dad put the hot dog on the plate, chopped it into small pieces, and squirted ketchup on it. I held Jordan's hand tight. He was excited about the food, but I was determined not to let go or lose focus. I had to figure out how I was going to get us out of the house unharmed. We left as soon as Jordan finished his food.

A week later Dad called: "Hey, Dream. I got the car up and running. Can you meet me Friday after work at my part-time job?"

"Where is it?"

"At the theatre in East Gate."

"Okay. What time?"

"I'm closing, so it will be kind of late. I'll just say eleven o'clock."

"Okay, see you Friday." I didn't think anything else about what had happened at the house, but Allen was on top of it. "I'm going with you. There ain't no way I'ma let you go meet him that late at night."

"That's fine, but I really don't think that anything is going to happen."

"I know nothing's gonna happen, because I'm not gonna let it."

That Friday we went to the cinema and waited in the car for the staff to finish closing. Dad walked out, and as he neared the car he looked shocked to see Allen in the car with me. I wasn't sure if it was because he had only seen him once before or if it was because he had another plan up his sleeve. We swapped cars, thanked him, and drove home.

A few weeks later, Dad called: "Hey, Dream. There is a job opening at the cinema. I can put in a good word for you if you are looking for a job." I wasn't looking for a job, but I thought I could use a change. I had been at my current job for two years. I went to the interview, and the manager told me, "Wow, I didn't know Walter had a daughter."

"Yeah, there's five of us." I could see that he looked awkward and changed the subject. I was hired on the spot. I quit my job at the clothing store to work at the cinema, making one dollar twenty-five cents less, on the other side of town.

One night, as we were closing, I was washing dishes, and Dad was sweeping the floor. I dropped a utensil. "Danggit!"

"What did you just say?"

"I said 'Danggit.'"

"Aw, that better have been all you said." I glared right through him and stared him down. *You have no right to tell me what I can and can't say. You lost that right when you molested me.* Shortly after, I quit the cinema.

Journal Entry

July 4, 1996

Dear Diary,

Well, Allen's mother did get like some of those mothers-in-law on Ricki Lake. It wasn't really all that bad, but she was forgetting that she wasn't Jordan's mother, I am. She acted like she didn't have to tell me where she was taking him (swimming) and she didn't have to bring him back when I said to. So Dream and Allen didn't see Jordan until 7:45 on the 4th of July. Me and Kim are about to get a place together until our men find the guts to marry us because this ½ way mess isn't gettin' it. I'm just not happy. I'm better than this and I deserve better. Allen finally got a job. He's been there for about 3 months. He works in the warehouse. Tisha's pregnant again (6 months). It's a boy (they say). I quit my job at Cash Bargain Center and now I'm at East Gate General Cinema. I really don't like it. Kim and I still plan on going to college. Kim and Allen had a huge fallout a few months ago and that affected our relationship. He blocked her number out and now he acts like I can't call her or go visit her. He can't come between us and he needs to realize that, just like she can't come between me and him. They had a fallout because he went to King's Island with his cousin and a whole bunch of freshmen and sophomores and she & her boyfriend were the chaperones. They saw him holdin' some hootchie mamma's hand. It's not their fault he's a dog! He even knew she was there.

P.S. Dad gave me a car and he works part time at the cinema.

P.P.S. I graduated June 5th 1996.

When Jordan had his first birthday party, Allen didn't show up until the party was ending. I kept paging him 9-1-1, but he never returned my pages, nor did he show up—and the party was at his home. He had gone out with some friends. When he finally showed up, I fussed at him, and he laughed but promised me that he would be on time the next time. I was so embarrassed. Here I had been bragging on our perfect relationship and family, and he didn't show up and, much worse, laughed it off. I had to show face by myself, trying to hide my discontent.

One evening, Jordan and I went to visit Allen before he went to work. We met him at his best friend Ricky's house. As soon as we got back home, the phone rang. It was his mother on the phone, and she was telling me to come to the hospital because Allen had been in a car accident and the doctors didn't think that he was going to make it. I was so overwhelmed and confused; I had just left him fifteen minutes before that. I got to the hospital, and they had him on life support and told us that he was brain dead and was in a coma. If he ever made it out of his coma, he would be a vegetable. We knew that was not how he would've wanted to live his life, so Angela said that she would wait until her mother and brothers came into town the next day from Atlanta and then she would take him off of life support. It was so hard for me to grasp this new reality.

In less than an hour Jordan's dad had been in a near-fatal accident and wasn't expected to live. I was soon to be fiancé-less, left to raise my one-year-old son on my own. Angela's only son was dying, and she had serious decisions to make. Delta's only brother, only sibling, was near death. Ricky's best friend from childhood was leaving this earth. One simple second, one stop light, changed all our lives dramatically.

The first few hours seemed to drag on as if they were days and then weeks. It seemed as if the world had stopped and stood still, but it hadn't. The world kept on turning, and we had to keep on living. I remember Ricky and his whole family there crying. He was in college, but he was also Jordan's godfather. With tears falling down his face, he promised that if there was ever anything that I needed for Jordan, he would handle it. No matter how big or how small it was.

I was the last one at the hospital with Angela and Delta. They told me to go home because there was nothing more that I could do that day. It was approximately one-thirty a.m. I went home in tears, crying because once again my life was falling apart.

The next morning Angela called me. "Dream, what are you going to do today?"

"I'm going to visit Allen in the hospital."

"He's already gone; we took him off of life support last night."

I fell to the floor in tears; it felt like someone had reached into my chest, pulled out my heart, and squeezed my lungs until I couldn't breathe. They took him off of life support right after I left the hospital. That wasn't the plan. I was so angry because they didn't stick to the plan. They told me to go home, which means they knew that they were going to take him off of life support. I felt so cheated. I wasn't his wife, but I was his fiancée. I was the mother of his only child, and that meant nothing to them. Now I was all alone in the world again, with my one-and-a-half-year-old son, who didn't understand what death meant.

I was at a loss for words and felt only emptiness. Angela had derailed my plans and thwarted me. It was Sunday morning. I had nowhere else to go, so Jordan and I got dressed in all black and went to church. I was in a dazed state. Church members came over and greeted us: "Good morning, how are you guys doing today?"

"Not too good. Jordan's dad died this morning."

"Oh no, sweetie, I'm so sorry to hear that. What happened?"

"He was in a car accident."

"Oh no, was he drunk driving?"

Just because he's young doesn't mean he was drunk driving, ya big dummy! I hate when church folks do that. "No, he was just in an accident."

I walked into my Sunday school class and told the teacher, Mrs. Smith. Mrs. Smith had always been very kind to me. She nurtured me musically, as she was a musician herself, as well as being someone I could talk to. "I know it's hard right now. It seems like it's the end of the world, but it's not. You need this time to grieve. There are actually seven stages of grieving, and you'll go through all of them. Right now you are in shock and denial, then there's pain and guilt, anger and bargaining. You'll even go through depression and loneliness. Those are the hardest parts; it will take you a while to get through them all. In about a year or so you'll go through the upwards-turn stage, reconstruction and working through, then finally acceptance and hope."

She makes it sound so easy. "I hear you and everything, but you
don't understand. I loved him so much. I put up with things I knew
I shouldn't have because I just loved him. I don't see myself getting
over it or getting to the upwards turn. I don't think I'll be okay in a
year. I'm here right now, stuck. I have to raise Jordan by myself. I can't
even fight with him about Jordan, because he's gone!"

"I know, sweetie, I know. Come on, let's pray about it. God has gotten you through worse." We prayed, but I still didn't feel better. I was
still sad, and I was mad. I was mad at God for taking him away after
we finally seemed to be on the right track.

I kept my head up the best I could. On top of Jordan's constant
crying and looking for his father, we had to plan the funeral. I had
very little experience with death. The only other person besides Allen
that I knew who had passed was my grandfather. I was a small child
then, and I didn't even go to his funeral. Angela made arrangements at
Stuart's Funeral Home, and she, Delta, Big Al, and myself went to meet
with them. There was an older lady who assisted us. She was nice, but
very monotone, with a stereotypical funeral person's demeanor. She
sat us down, and we talked to her about what things we would like regarding the funeral. "Okay, we can accommodate you and everything
that you are asking. First, I need you to pick out a casket. Follow me."
She then opened a door and led us into a room that was full of empty
caskets. My heart started pounding, and I couldn't walk through
the door. I burst into tears and turned around and walked out. "Oh
Dream! It's okay, it's okay. Here, take a tissue." Angela and Delta tried
to console me. "I didn't know there were going to be actual caskets in
a big ass room like that! She made it seem like we were shopping for
shoes! I was thinking we would look through a catalog or something!
I don't think I can do this." I waited for a moment and had a glass of
water. I got my nerves together and walked back through the door.
My heart was still pounding out of my chest, but somehow I kept my
composure. "Now, this is our top-of-the-line section right here. They
are more expensive, but you get a lot for your money. They are all

leak-proof, so no water or bugs will get in …" *So who's gonna check to see if water and bugs get in anyway? Who's gonna dig it up to make sure that the casket does what you are saying it will?* My eyes watched as she rubbed the side of the casket, showing all of the 'special' features and how soft it was. *Does she think he's going to pop up and say, "Hey I need some more cushion in here! Can you fluff my pillow please?"* She reminded me of the models on *The Price Is Right* rubbing on a top-of-the-line vacuum cleaner or the newest car. "Oh yeah, I think Allen would like this one," Angela said. Delta and Big Al both nodded their heads in agreement. *Are they crazy? He wouldn't like any casket. No one wants to be dead lying in a casket!*

"What do you think, Dream?"

"I don't. Whatever you decide is fine, but I'm curious to know the features of the cheaper caskets." They all looked at me with confused expressions. I stared back like a rebellious child.

The lady who worked there pulled me to the side before we left: "Have you gone down to the social security office to get SSI for your son?"

"What's SSI?"

"Well, the government will give you money each month to help you raise your son. Go down there. It will give you some help." I had no idea that you could do that; I didn't understand the full story about it, but I knew that I didn't want to feel like I was getting paid off of his death. More importantly, I wasn't used to getting money for Jordan when he was alive, so what was the difference now?

The night before the funeral, Jordan and I stayed at Angela's. All three of us climbed into her bed to sleep. The only one who got any sleep was Jordan. I would wake Angela up from my crying, and when I fell asleep she would wake me up. The next morning we got dressed for the funeral. I wore all white with gold accessories and sunglasses. I didn't want to be the typical grieving widow in all black. The limo came to the house to pick us up. *Wow, I never thought my first limo ride would be to Allen's funeral.*

I asked a friend to hold Jordan during the funeral. He had fallen asleep. I didn't want him to wake up and see his father lying in a casket and make a big scene. We greeted people as they came in to show their respects. Allen's favorite color was red; his cousins Junior and Bryan came in with red pinstriped suites on. My heart leaped out of my chest as I watched them close the casket. I cried uncontrollably. I wanted to run to the casket and shake him until he woke up. As the casket top lowered, it seemed as if the world was moving in slow motion. I envisioned myself in an open field screaming "Nooooooooooooooooooooo!" at the top of my lungs. But in reality, I just looked around to see how everyone else was taking it all in. Angela was crying but smiling as the pastor spoke. "Yes, this too shall pass! Amen! Amen!" Big Al was hunched over being consoled by other family members. I turned around, and the funeral home was packed. There was a line of people still outside that couldn't come in. There was a row of people standing in the back. Some faces I recognized, others I didn't. Allen's cousin Renee sang "His Eye Is on the Sparrow." I knew that I wouldn't have been able to make it through any song, so I didn't volunteer to sing, although I knew he would've liked it.

The funeral was as much of a success as a funeral could be. When Allen died, it seemed like the world had come to a screeching, crashing halt. Only too soon, I learned that life moves on; I still had to wake up, eat, and, most importantly, take care of Jordan. If I couldn't be strong for anyone else, I had to stand strong for him.

Dealing with Jordan was harder than dealing with Allen's death. Every time he heard a car with loud music come down the street, he would get excited and say, "Daddy! My daddy's here!" That would tear me up all over again. It was so hard because he was only one and didn't understand what death was or meant. I had to keep re-explaining, "Daddy is in Heaven with Jesus." It was like dealing with an Alzheimer's patient when you had to tell them about the death of a loved one and they would relive the heartache and pain over and over again.

I soon found out that Allen had a ten-thousand-dollar life insurance policy and Jordan was the sole beneficiary. To me, a single mother on minimum wage, that was a lot of money. But again, I didn't want to feel like I was getting paid off of his death. I felt like a zombie. All I did was cry. There would be no wedding and no wedding plans. I felt like I was seventeen and pregnant again. I couldn't see my life past the day he died.

I wrote Jordan, telling him of all my memories of his father, good and bad, while they were fresh in my head. I kept the letter in a safe place to give to him when he got older. I explained exactly what happened in the accident and in our relationship. Allen was far from perfect in our relationship, but I do know that he loved Jordan. He wasn't the best father, but I wasn't the best mother either. We were too young to be parents and were just flying by the seat of our pants. We were both imperfect and unstable, but we had both come a long way. Although I felt very alone, I did have a lot of support from Allen's family, and especially from Ricky and Ricky's family. Ricky was in college an hour away, but he would come into town and visit, and he would take Jordan to hang out and give me a much needed break.

All of Allen's family and friends said they would always be there for me and Jordan. The only one that was there constantly was Ricky and his family. Angela and Delta were there physically, but they were driving me crazy. Allen's friends were only there for a few months, leaving me in grief mode. Everyone else just kept moving, living as if Allen had never existed. I felt so lonely. I didn't understand how people who claimed they loved him so much could go about their happy lives as if nothing had changed. I felt pitiful. *Why don't they see things the same as me? I can't get out of grief mode, because if I do I'll forget about him.*

As more time went by, I started forgetting what his face looked like. I'd panic and stare at his pictures to re-soak him in my memory. I tried dating, but it just didn't feel right. I didn't have sex for over a year, but I thought I would never have sex again. I was simply heart-broken.

Diary Entry

July 24, 1997

Dear Diary,

This has been the longest 2 weeks of my life. Allen died last Sunday on July 13, 1997. His funeral was on Friday July 18. He was in a car accident and he didn't have his seatbelt on. He hit his head on a drainage sewer, causing him to be brain dead. His internal organs stopped working, so they took him off the respirator. My baby was only 20 years old! There were so many people at the funeral. 756 signed the book. The room seated 128, but the building fit 1,500. People were still standing outside trying to squeeze in. Fortunately he had just gotten saved a few months ago. But I can't help to praise God through all of this because Jordan and I could've been in the car with him. It just so happened that I had been wanting this car for about 6 months. I finally got it the day before the accident. If I didn't have that car Jordan and I would've been with Allen. Then a few days afterwards I had to take the car back. I also think Allen knew, because he said the spirit talked to him while he was in Atlanta and he rushed home and got saved and started living right. So God is good; I can't complain. Everything happens for a reason that may not be for us to know. But I'm about to start singing again.

Praise God

The company that held the life insurance policy would send me a statement in the mail. It informed me how much the policy was worth and my options for saving, cashing out the money, etc. I knew that I didn't know enough about insurance or the process, and again I really didn't want to feel like I got paid off of his death. I had already spoken to a representative, and she told me that I didn't have to make a decision as of yet and that I could take as much time as I needed. Most of the time, I wouldn't even open the statements. One day, I was visiting Angela and I saw a star emblem on an envelope that was under some other mail. It was the exact same emblem that was on the insurance information that I would get in the mail. My first thought was, *Wow, Allen had insurance on Angela too.* I pulled the envelope out from under all of the other mail and the label read my son's name, care of Dream, with Angela's address on it. I was floored. It hit me like a ton of bricks. I couldn't believe this woman who laughed in my face, kept my child close, would have the nerve to change my address to be hers! I confronted her about it when she came back in the room: "Angela, did you switch my address to yours?" She laughed to herself, trying to hide her surprise that her dirty little secret had been found out. "Yes, I didn't want you to waste the money on buying something like a car!" she answered. For whatever reason, I was so shocked at her bold reply, I stood up and got in her face: "If I need a car to get back and forth to work so that I can feed and clothe my child, then it's not a waste of money!" She tried to be as calm as she possibly could, because she could see that I was visibly irritated. She said, "I wanted to use the money to buy Jordan and Rasheeda some clothes and pay for Allen's headstone." I could've sworn that steam was coming out of my ears and out of the top of my head, like it does in the cartoons. *Am I really hearing those words come out of her mouth?* I yelled, "Rasheeda has a mother and a father. I am taking care of Jordan by myself, and he has never been in need of clothes. That insurance money is for Jordan, not clothes for Rasheeda and for damn sure not for a headstone for Allen!" I took Jordan and went back home.

For the next few months I was in a complete daze. I always felt like I was looking at myself from the outside. My body was just a shell. Jordan started having night terrors and would cry nonstop at night. It was so scary when it started because even though his eyes were open, it looked as though he had never awakened. I would talk really softly to him or try to wake him up, but nothing ever worked. Sometimes I'd just join in and cry with him.

I started back working, but there was still a void that I was looking to fill. My friends would keep in contact on a daily basis and always try to surround me for support. We got word of a fashion show that needed a few musical acts to complete their show. "Dream, do you think you are up to doing it?" they asked.

"Yeah, sure. It sounds like fun. O'Leta, me and you are gonna have to split up Jada's part since she's still off at school."

We started practicing again and performed a short medley and got a standing ovation. It felt like my spirit had jumped back into my body, instead of looking at me walk around. *Welcome back, Dream!*

Kim and I both decided to move out of our mothers' homes and share an apartment. She had a son named Demetrius, who was six months younger than Jordan. It was a perfect setup. We were best friends and got along great, and the boys were the same age and would keep each other company. We found a very nice three-bedroom, two-bath townhome that wasn't far from our mothers' houses. The townhouse was in a good neighborhood, and our rent was five hundred and ninety-five dollars a month. We would split that. We were so excited. We signed our lease and moved on Halloween. O'Leta, Allen's cousin Junior, and a few other friends helped us move our things in. We ordered pizza, drank Pepsi, and talked all night long, falling asleep on the floor. When we woke up, we realized how much fun we had had and vowed to make it a move-in tradition. The boys had so much fun running around their new place. We gave them the master bedroom so they would have more than enough room to play. After we got settled in, we would have parties every weekend. Demetrius would go to his father's house, and Jordan would visit Angela.

One day, Angela was visiting and brought up the insurance money again: "So, what are your plans for the insurance money?"

"I don't want to talk about it, Angela." She, of course, was persistent in trying to get the information out of me. I kept replying, "I don't want to talk about it."

This kept going until Kim jumped in and yelled at her, "Dammit, Angela, do you listen? She said she doesn't want to talk about it. She doesn't have to talk about it. It's none of your business what she's going to do with the money. You are gonna make me kick your ass out of the house if you don't stop harassing her!"

"I'm not even talking to you! Me and her are having a conversation, but I will leave it alone for now, but we will talk about it later!"

DaSangaz started singing a lot more, and we came across some guys who said they had their own entertainment company, named Basement Enterprise Productions. They had a camp of singers, rappers, and producers. They wanted to sign us and put us in the studio. We were eager and happy. We hadn't signed a contract, but we were on a temporary trial to see how we could work together.

They set us up with this producer named Carl. Carl was a nice guy and seemed to be very talented. He brought some of his recording equipment from his house and showed me how to create a track from scratch from a song that I had written. We recorded it, and although it wasn't exactly the way that it was in my head, I was very excited and was a sponge eager to learn more. We would always meet over the CEO's house for weekly meetings. No shows were ever set up, and we would mostly just clown and vibe off of each other's songs. It was something to do for the time being, but quietly I still wanted more.

My friend Elisha from high school had come back to Indianapolis from Texas. I let her stay with us in our apartment. Her parents had moved to Texas after we graduated, but she missed Indianapolis. Elisha had always been known to have a great singing voice. Our senior year, she was voted most likely to succeed. She started working with another guy we both went to school with named Sean. Sean used to sing, but he was a producer too. She would be in the studio daily and late at night. One day, I went to the studio with her. I had only been in the studio a few times before, but I learned a lot in just watching her in action. I studied her technique and quickly caught on to Sean's studio language. I was in awe. *Wow, she's better than I thought she was. Does she ever mess up?* After a few weeks of her staying with us, she came to me and said, "Dream, I know you are doing your singing thing with O'Leta and Kim, but Sean has something on the table, and I want to know if you want to be a part of it."

"Something like what?"

"Well he knows a guy who's over the group Public Announcement."

"R. Kelly's old group?"

"Yeah. His name is Phillip, and he wants to start a girl group, and I'm gonna be a member, but I wanted to know if you wanted to audition too."

"Really? Yeah!"

"Okay, now these people are professional, so we are gonna have to be on our A-Game. This ain't no Basement Enterprise Productions."

"It's cool. I got you!"

"Okay, the audition is Saturday at this club. Sean's gonna pick us up and take us."

"Okay, cool."

I heard everything that she said, and I was very excited. Not only was she very talented; Elisha had a way of always coming across people who were big time in the music business. My plan was to audition for the group and, if I made it, see where it took me. In my mind I wasn't dropping DaSangaz, but I saw a window of opportunity that I just couldn't let close.

I was in my second year of college. I never had a major; I was getting my general studies out of the way until I could figure out what I wanted to major in. I was still depressed over the loss of Allen. I couldn't fathom me ever dating or falling in love again. I still wore my engagement ring, and I actually started wearing the wedding band that came with it. I knew that I would never legally be Mrs. Carter or have the wedding for him to put the wedding band on my finger, but somehow it just made me feel better.

Our audition was set after Public Announcement's microphone check. Elisha and I watched as the group went through their performance. There were only a handful of girls waiting to audition too. Phillip had us all go to the microphone, introduce ourselves, and sing our audition piece. A heavyset girl named Shataria was first. I tried to hide my astonishment when I heard her sing. She sang effortlessly and didn't really need a microphone. *Whew! I already know they are gonna let her in.* Elisha was next. She had a very squeaky speaking voice, but when she sang it all changed. After she was done, we all applauded; it was also a given that she was going to make the group. Sean glanced over at me to tell me to go up next. I walked up to the stage; I wasn't nervous at all.

"Hi, I am Dream, I am nineteen years old, and I'm going to sing a verse from the song 'Tonight' by Xscape. Come a little bit closer and look into my eyes …" The other girls auditioned, and afterwards Phillip, Sean, and the group's manager went to the other side of the club to discuss whom they wanted to keep. They walked back to render their verdict. Phillip began to speak: "You ladies did a very good job, but we are making a four-girl group. Elisha, you have an amazing talent. You are the reason I came down from Chicago to form a group. You are in. Shataria, you have a beautiful and powerful voice. I'll be honest with you: there is just one dilemma as far as you fitting in the group. I'll just be as candid as I possibly can. Would you be willing to lose some weight to be in the group?"

Her eyes were on fire: "Excuse me? Lose some weight? Ain't a damn thang wrong with my weight! No I will not lose any weight to fit into your little group. I'm a damn good singer; I will make it without this group!" She grabbed her coat and purse and left the club. *Oh my God, I can't believe he said that to her!* I didn't know Shataria personally, but she and Elisha had used to sing in a girl group together, so I knew of her.

"Wow, okay, I guess that's a no to her wanting to be in the group," Phillip chuckled to himself. Phillip continued, "Our next member is Dream. Very nice job, welcome to the group." I was excited and hopeful. Things were looking up. Elisha and I were the only two girls who made the group that night. We held auditions at a studio for the next two members.

The next morning I broke the news to O'Leta and Kim. I was shocked to learn that they were mad at me about it: "Dream, I can't believe you would betray us like that. We are best friends! We already have a group doing things. You betta believe ya'll lil' group won't ever sound as good as us. That ol' squeaky voice girl done came in here and you done went crazy. Ya'll ain't gone make it! So get your head out of the clouds!"

Kim's mouth was running like an unstoppable train. O'Leta looked up and said, "Dream, why didn't you just tell us that you were going to audition for the group? I mean, I understand why you did it, I guess, but it would've just been nice for you to tell us before you went to the audition, ya know?"

"I mean, I didn't know that it would be such a big deal. I didn't even know if I would make the group, and even if I did that doesn't mean that I can't still sing with ya'll. Ya'll actin' like I gotta record deal or something. I just want to see where this goes. Plus I've been in more than one group at the same time before. It's going to be alright."

"Well, she's got a point, Kim. It's not like we do a lot of shows or even go to a real studio. I mean, this sounds like a really good opportunity. It's cool with me. I just wish you would've told me first."

"I know, I should've, but I really wasn't thinking it would be about all this. I am excited though!"

"Whatever! I can't believe that you are condoning this, O'Leta! I am mad as hell. Just know ya'll won't be doing no practicing in this house, and I don't want to hear none of your songs either!" O'Leta glanced over at me, trying not to laugh at the obvious overreaction. Kim was always known to be way over the top, but this was the worst I had ever seen firsthand.

I stopped going to my classes. I still didn't have a major, and there was absolutely nothing else in the world that I could see myself doing for the rest of my life besides music. I knew you should have something to fall back on, but I was not motivated enough to finish.

We held auditions for the next two members of the group at the studio that Elisha had recorded at before. A few girls came in. One was Sean's sister Serena. She was sixteen, very pretty, and had a beautiful voice. One of the other girls that came in was Raya. She had this really cool vibe about her. She sang "Silver and Gold" by Kirk Franklin. Phillip and Sean were impressed and added them to the group. Raya asked, "What's the name of the group gonna be?"

"MSST," Phillip answered. "I don't know what it means, but I like the way it sounds."

Things with the group took off quickly. We were in the studio four to five times a week. We were in the studio from seven p.m. until one a.m. all of the time. It was fun and exciting. We had a photo shoot, and Phillip hired choreographers, fashion designers, a bodyguard, and a makeup artist. The work was hard, but I absolutely loved it.

Our first performance was in Louisville, Kentucky. We held hands, and Elisha prayed before we went out. Elisha and Serena sang the lead verses. Raya and I made sure everything else gelled together. "Great job, ladies," Phillip told us after the show.

"You guys did really well for it to be your first performance. I'm gonna take you guys to Chicago for a show in a few weeks."

Wow! I'm glad I auditioned. DaSangaz never did any of this. Kim is going to be so mad when she finds out I'm going to Chicago!

We drove to Chicago and got ready for our show; our makeup was stunning. I loved having someone put my makeup on. I got into performance mode. I was always Dream, but Dream the performer would take on another persona. The performer was beautiful, confident, and a superstar.

We were set to be the opening act for Public Announcement at the House of Blues. We had one song to sing. We warmed up our vocal cords backstage, and once again Elisha prayed. We dominated the stage. I could see my dreams coming true. I was happy that my life was finally moving in the right direction.

After a few shows, Elisha found out that she was pregnant and went back to Texas. I was sad to see her go, but I was happy that things would still progress with the group. The following weekend Sean brought another girl that he had worked with who was currently in one of his other girl groups, named Ni'chelle. She and Raya had grown up together. She came to the studio during a recording session. We hadn't heard her sing, but they called her in the booth to record a verse. She started to sing, and we all were very impressed. She had a very strong voice, and Phillip was so taken by her that she became our new lead singer. We started to teach her the other songs and the choreography. We synced and worked very well together as a group.

When I was with my group and traveling, Angela told me that I needed to sign papers so she could have joint custody of Jordan. As naive as I was, I knew that something wasn't right. I asked her, "Why do you need joint custody?"

"So when you are away with your group, I can take Jordan to the doctor if he needs to go."

"Well, you have his Medicaid card. If he needs to go, just use his card. You wouldn't need joint custody for that." I saw the disappointment in her face; I just left that situation alone. Kim and I decided not to renew our lease. We still weren't getting along from me joining the group. I didn't want to live by myself with Jordan, nor did I think that I could afford it. Delta told me that she would be happy to let us stay with her. Things were fine at first. We got along better than we ever had, but my issue had never been with Delta; it was always with Angela. We were on the road so much I asked Delta if when we got our record deal and were on tour Jordan could stay with her instead of Angela. Her daughter Rasheeda was a few years older than Jordan, and she was already into the parenting routine. Angela probably would've ended up being around Delta or using Delta to do the majority of the caretaking anyway. She happily agreed, so everything was set; all I needed was my record deal. The more we traveled, the more antsy Delta grew. One day she was very aggressive toward me, drilling me with all types of questions: "When are you guys going on tour? What is your tour schedule going to be?"

"I don't know, and I can't give an estimated timeframe because I don't even have a record deal." That really agitated her. We also had some real bonding heart-to-heart moments. She told me things that I swore never to repeat; she told me that Allen had cheated on me with one of her friends shortly before he passed, and to watch her family because they always tried to take other people's children because they believed that no one could take better care of them than they could.

Things weren't necessarily great at Delta's, but they were tolerable. She would do or say little things to me that got under my skin about my parental skills and what she would like for me to do, but never anything worth fighting about like I had to with Angela.

One day, Jordan and I came home to Delta's house and, as I opened the door, I looked at something hanging on the wall. As I stared, I realized it was Allen's shirt and pants that he had been in the accident in. The clothes had been ripped and cut off of him by the paramedics, and there was still blood on the clothes. They were hung up as if there was a person on the wall. I immediately knew that Delta was in an unstable mental state. I calmly asked, "Delta, what's this all about?"

"Oh, I'm just trying to remember Allen," she replied in a very matter-of-fact tone, as if it was normal. I walked into my room, packed some things for me and Jordan, and left as I watched young Rasheeda playing on the floor. I felt sorry for her, but it was not my battle, and my main concern and priority was Jordan. I sucked up my pride and once again asked my mother if we could move back in.

I still spoke with the family after this major incident, but I started keeping my distance. Something just wasn't right. I can't imagine how they felt, because I had not lost my only son or only brother, but I did lose my fiancé, my first love, and my son's father. I had been really down before, and I wasn't totally over his death, but I couldn't imagine going to the extremes that Delta was going to.

No matter what Delta was doing, I still had to push forward and focus on the group. We were making great strides and were the opening act to the majority of Public Announcement's tour. We met Kelly Price backstage and opened for her during the Black Expo. Once again, I was on cloud nine. We would meet superstars and be in the same room with them. Jay-Z, Puff Daddy, and Ja Rule, to name a few, were mere inches from my grasp. I've never done drugs or gotten high or even drank, but this was my high; it was a great rush.

The baby of the group, Serena, had not been herself lately, being late to practice, and she didn't show up at the airport when we were set to fly to Palm Springs, California, for a music conference. We were worried about her and tried to call her to see what had happened. We had as much fun as we could without the baby of the group. Phillip gave us the full 'star experience.' A limousine picked us up at the airport; we had seating at a nice restaurant any time we were hungry. We had a very good show and headed back to Indianapolis. When we got back, we went to Serena's house. "I can't be in the group anymore. I just found out that I'm pregnant," she cried.

"Why didn't you tell us? We've been trying to call you."

"I just didn't know how to tell you." The other girls didn't understand, but I understood exactly what she meant. I had been there just a few years ago.

The group debated if we should find another member. Phillip told us that it would be our decision. We chose to keep the group as three members. Phillip was fine with that and flew us to Miami, Florida, for another music conference.

We were so excited to be in sunny Florida on the Ocean Boulevard strip. We were there for a few days and had time to shop and sightsee. When we first landed, the limousine picked us up at the airport and drove us to the Fontainebleau hotel. "Wow, we are really doing it big! This is a nice hotel!" we said to each other. We waited in the lobby for Phillip. Our bodyguard Bear informed us, "This is Phillip's hotel; you guys are going to stay in another hotel. We already have your reservations, and Public Announcement is already in their rooms not far from where you will be." We were disappointed that we wouldn't get to stay in that hotel but were still excited. "Well, what's taking so long? We've been down here waiting for over an hour," I asked.

"There was a little accident in Phillip's room, and the hotel staff is in there. The hotel staff is wrapping it up, though, so I'll go ahead and take you up." We got in the elevator and headed to his room. We walked in, and there were a few housekeeping employees as well as security. They were cleaning up broken glass from the bathroom mirror. *Something's just not right*, I thought to myself. Phillip greeted us but had a dazed, glassy look on his face. *Oh my God, he's high! I can't believe it! I didn't see this coming.*

After we left Phillip's hotel room, we checked into our hotel room and showered and changed our clothes. Usually when we traveled, Phillip provided us with transportation, and all meals were set up and paid for. We would travel as a group with Public Announcement and the other groups that were with us. We tried calling Phillip but never got an answer. We called the guys in Public Announcement to see if they had heard anything from him, but they hadn't. I had thirty dollars in my purse and figured I'd buy whatever food we needed if we couldn't find Phillip. We agreed to go out and walk the Ocean Boulevard strip.

We met other famous singers and various up-and-coming performers. We took pictures with everyone who was nobody and snapped close-up shots of JZ, Puffy, and Stone Cold Steve Austin. "It's getting late, I'm sure everyone else is hungry too," I said. We headed back to the hotel to try to reach Phillip again. When we opened our room door, we saw what seemed to be flying ants everywhere. "Oh my God! What is this?" We were giggling but really uneasy about what we saw. We looked closer and realized, "Ah! These are not flying ants! These are termites, and they are in our luggage and everything."

Words cannot truly describe the emotions that came over us. We laughed to keep from crying, but it was no laughing matter. We tried to shake our clothes out, but it seemed as if nothing would keep them off. We went to the lobby to complain, and the manager told us there was nothing he could do because they were in the whole hotel and that another room would not help. We picked up the phone to call Phillip, but there was no answer. We called Public Announcement, and they didn't know where Phillip was either, but their manager agreed to pick us up, even though we didn't know where we would stay.

When we met with the guys, we were still distraught and hungry. "Man we haven't eaten, Phillip done disappeared, ya'll have your manager, but we don't have anybody. This is my first time in Miami, and I'm supposed to be having fun, but instead this is the worst time of my life," I whined.

"Ya'll ain't ate yet?"

"No!" we all chimed.

"Okay, here's a little bit of money. Go get ya'll something to eat. That's messed up he's got ya'll out here with no food and transportation in a termite hotel." They tried to make light of the situation to make us feel better, but it didn't work. We went to a restaurant and had a big dinner. As we were eating, we looked up and saw Sean come through the door. "Sean!" we yelled and jumped up, ran and hugged, and looked up at him like a trio of lonely, lost orphans.

"Hey, what's wrong? Ya'll alright?"

"No, we are not alright. Phillip done went and turned into a crackhead and left us stranded here in Miami; our hotel has termites; we don't know where we are going to sleep tonight! Sean, why did you hook us up with him if he was a crazy crackhead?" We were talking over each other and going into a mad frenzy. "I'm sorry, he had what we were looking for at the time. I had no idea he was on drugs. It's okay, though, I'm here. All the hotels are booked, but you can stay in my room. I've got a double bed."

We piled into Sean's rental car and drove to his hotel. We showered and got ready for bed. We three girls lay flip side of each other in one bed, and he lay in the other bed. "How crazy is this? I've got three beautiful ladies in my hotel room, but I'm alone in my bed. Ya'll better be glad we are like family." We giggled and fell asleep. The next morning, Sean drove us to the airport and made sure we got off okay.

After we got back, things changed drastically. Phillip was in and out of the picture. We didn't have any more shows booked for us. We tried to go to the studio but were told we couldn't because Phillip still had an outstanding balance. We were still hungry for the business and would book our own shows at colleges, and we still went to our vocal lessons. Things started to die down, as we were very limited on funds and had no money or management team to back us.

Diary Entry

August 31, 1998

Dear Diary,

It's been a little over a year since I've written. This time I'm in much better spirits. A lot has happened in this year. I'm not totally happy yet, but I had to stop trying so hard because I was only living in fake temporary happiness. Now I stopped looking for happiness or for someone to make me happy and I'm A LOT happier! Well this year has been different for me. I don't know what happened to me. I guess I was more depressed about Allen than I thought; or maybe just lonely or probably both … Dad wrote Mom a letter last week saying that he FORGIVES her and he's been living with hatred in his heart for her all of these years. With bible verses everywhere. Mom wrote him back saying I don't know why you have hatred for me, I don't have hatred for you. But he really pissed me off doing that.

One day, Angela called me to see if Jordan could come over for a few hours. At first I didn't think anything of it, but as she went on she was saying that she had made a cake and that they were going to have a birthday party for Allen. I guess you could say that I did the Scooby sound when he's confused about what Shaggy is saying, "Ru Ru?" I refused to even entertain the thought of my child being caught up with them singing "Happy Birthday" to someone who was not there.

I told my family and best friends about it, voicing all of the questions that were going through my mind but that I dared not ask because I was afraid of the answer. *Who's going to blow out the candles on the cake? Who opens the presents? If no one opens the presents, what do you do with them? Why are you spending money on presents for someone who is not there? Why can't we just have a memorial celebration with no cake! Are they purposely trying to drive me crazy? What kind of mother would I be to let my two-year-old son, who still doesn't understand the concept of death, go to a party where they are singing "Happy Birthday" to someone who is not there that he still asks about day to day? If she had the nerve to ask me if he could come over for a birthday party, then what are they doing with him when I'm not around that they don't ask or tell me about?*

My mind was blown! After all that I had been through with this family, this was one of the ultimate Looney Tunes acts I had ever witnessed. I wouldn't even be able to conjure these scenarios in my head, and I consider myself to be a very creative person. With all of the events that had taken place with them and now this, I knew for a fact that no matter how things went between my mother and me, Jordan and I would not be moving back in with any of them ever again. If it meant that I couldn't travel with my group, that would just be a sacrifice I would have to make, because I was not about to let them drive my child crazy and have him think that birthday parties for dead people were okay and normal.

I was tired, tired of his family treating me as if I were my child's sister instead of his mother. I was tired of our instability of moving from house to house, having clothes and toys between four or five houses around the city. I needed a change. I didn't know what kind of change or how I would go about it, but I needed a change all the same.

In the summer of 1999, I had moved back in with my mother from Delta's house. There was an announcement on the radio that Lauryn Hill was coming to Indianapolis for a concert. The Roots were the opening act. I was so excited and knew I had to be there.

A few weeks before I was going to buy my ticket, our well busted and flooded our front yard. We knew it wasn't worth the money to get it fixed, and everyone else on the street had switched to the city line a few years prior. Mom didn't have enough money to switch to the city line a few years earlier. She didn't have money for the conversion then. I gave her the majority of my paychecks until we had enough to switch the water. Since I had given her all of my money, I didn't have enough money to buy any tickets. So I tried winning them on the radio. My co-workers and I frantically called when they played a Lauryn Hill song but were still unable to get through. *I have no choice but to get these tickets. I'm going to have to do something drastic.* Early one morning, I drove to WLTC 105.7 radio station. I told the security guard, "Hi, my name is Dream, and I'm here to see Guy Black."

"Is he expecting you?"

"No, but it's important that I see him, just for a quick moment."

"Well he's on the air right now. Let me see if he can come out."

"Okay. Thanks."

A few minutes later Guy Black stuck his head out of the sound room. "Can I help you?"

"Hey! Let me first tell you that I'm not a crazy stalker chick, but I've got to get tickets to the Lauryn Hill concert. I had every intention of buying them, but my mamma's well busted and I had to give all of my paycheck so she could get it fixed. Can you puh-lease give me some tickets?"

"Where ya'll live to still be using a well?"

"Our whole neighborhood was on it and switched to the city line a few years ago; we just never did," I laughed.

"I can't just give you the tickets. You have to be the tenth caller and sing one of her songs on the radio."

"I know, but I have to get those tickets. I will sing for you right now! Do you want me to do cartwheels too?" He laughed.

"Okay, I'll tell you what. I'ma give you these sneak peak tickets to the movies and you call in and sing in the morning."

"I appreciate that and all, but I'd rather just have the Lauryn Hill tickets."

"Damn girl, you don't give up do you?"

"Nope! Never!" I joked.

"Okay, don't tell nobody, I mean nobody! Give me your number. I'll call you in the morning; be up and ready to sing. I will introduce you as the tenth caller and you betta sound good, ya hear me?"

"Oh, I got you! Thank you so much! So, do I still get the movie tickets?"

"Yeah, go ahead. Go enjoy yourself. I'll call you around six a.m. so be ready."

"I will!"

That night Raya and I went to the movies. We had a great time, but I was ready for morning to come so I could sing for my tickets. I set my alarm for five a.m. I didn't want Guy Black to call me and my voice not be ready to be heard. I brushed my teeth and hummed to myself to warm up my voice. Around five forty-five the phone rang. "Hello," I answered, trying not to sound too excited.

"Are you awake?"

"Yep, I'm awake and ready."

"Calm down, little grasshopper, it's not time yet. I'll call you back in about thirty minutes."

"Okay."

I called a few of my closest friends and co-workers to make sure they were listening to the radio. When the phone rang again, I answered and went into the garage.

"Are you ready?"

"Yes."

"Okay, just follow along." He placed me on hold, and when he came back on, I knew I was on the radio. "Good morning. WTLC. Who is this?"

"This is Dream. Oh my God, am I the right caller?"

"Yes, you are caller number ten. Are you a true Lauryn Hill fan?"

"I am her biggest fan. I play her CD all day; it's all I listen to."

"Okay, well here's the test. I'm gonna play one of her songs, and when it stops you keep singing until I tell you to stop. If you mess up any words, you don't win."

"Okay, I can handle that." I anticipated the music starting. The piano started to play, and Lauryn started to sing: "It could all be so simple, but you'd rather make it hard. Loving you is like a battle, but we both end up with scars ..." The music stopped, and I started to sing: "No matter how I think we grow you always seem to let me know ..."

"Okay, so you know one Lauryn Hill song. That doesn't make you a fan. Let's try another one."

The music started again. In the back of my mind I was happy, because all of the other callers got to sing only one song. I was winning tickets and singing over the radio. Lauryn's voice came on again, "Stromin' my pain with his finger ..." I joined in.

"Killing me softly with his song, killing me softly with his song ..." Guy Black came back again. "So, you know a classic song. Let's try something else." I heard the horns and the background vocals to "That Thing." *He must not know this is my song. I do this every weekend at karaoke.* I sang the song effortlessly and didn't fumble on the rap. "So, you just might be her biggest fan. Congratulations, you won the tickets." I was elated. I hung up, and the phone rang off the hook with all of my family and friends congratulating me.

The day before Thanksgiving in 1999 I went to visit my high school friend Leyla in Kentucky. The plan was for me to spend the night then drive back on Thanksgiving Day and meet my family over my Grandmere's house for dinner. I left Kentucky early in the afternoon. I hadn't been gone that long and, as I was driving back, I started having car problems with my '87 Ford Mustang. I pulled over at a rest stop to try to figure out what was wrong. The car would run; I just had problems steering. Men who were stopping through would pop the hood to try to help but weren't willing to take up too much time, seeing as they couldn't easily spot the problem and had other places to go.

I used my calling card to call my mother on the pay phone and told her what was going on. There weren't any mechanic shops or even dealerships open, because it was Thanksgiving. I hung out at the rest stop, buying everything in the vending machine, laughing and joking with the staff there. An older guy who worked there also looked at my car. It was almost nightfall, and he told me that he would drive me home after his shift ended. I, having my issues with men because of my past, was already skeptical of any man. I did my best- and worst-case scenarios in my head, sized him up, took into account his age, and figured that I could take him if I needed to. We got into his truck, and he filled up the gas tank. He told me to drive so that he could rest and drive back. From that moment, I knew that I would be okay; if he tried something, I would run us off of the road and make a mad dash for help.

I prayed in my head the whole way home that the demons that tormented me before did not revisit me. God was with me the whole way home. When we entered Indianapolis, his brakes started to screech and grind. I had to mash the brakes to the floor for the truck to stop. Not only had I hitchhiked from Kentucky and driven a strange man across state lines, but now his brakes were going out. *What a day!* I felt so bad, because I didn't want him to be stranded in Indianapolis or get in an accident on his way home. He had been nice to me, but I was in no position to help him back, and there was no way that my family or I would let him spend the night at our house. As I turned onto Spring Street there was a sigh of relief and anxious thoughts. *Should I pull into our driveway or into a trusted neighbor's so he won't know where I live and come back and get me?* I took a risk and pulled into our driveway. "Thank you so much for bringing me home; I really appreciate it. Let me give you some gas money."

"No, it's okay, I don't need any money."

"Well, at least let me give you a plate of Thanksgiving dinner."

"No really, I'm fine. I don't need anything. You have a good night."

"Okay, you too, drive safely. Thanks again!" He drove off and out of sight. My only dilemma now was how I was going to get my car.

When I got in, I told my mother the story. She was glad to see me, and I gulped down my Thanksgiving leftovers. Mom was the leader of Kevia's Girl Scout troop, and they had a singing engagement downtown the next day, but she said that we could get up early and get my car. She woke me up at about five thirty a.m. and we headed out. We got back to the rest stop, and none of the people who had kept me company the night before were there. I got in my car and assumed my mother would follow me to a service station to get it fixed. She told me that she hadn't planned on staying and drove off. I was so mad at her for deserting me in the middle of nowhere again! I was literally right back where I started. *I could've stayed overnight in Kentucky if I would've known that was what she was going to do.*

I sat in my car and turned the key and slowly drove off. I was driving down the highway about thirty-five miles per hour. I figured that I would get off at the first exit and pray there would be some place that could fix my car. I felt like I was moving like a turtle. I was happy to see a Chevron gas station with a service station attached.

I pulled into the service part, and a tall red-neck white man with a long ponytail came out to see how he could help me. I explained the car troubles that I was having; he popped the hood and immediately saw that a belt had come loose. The piece that was supposedly holding it up had apparently fallen off without me knowing, and that was why I couldn't steer. He took a nut and bolt out of the top of a box with a lot of nuts and bolts and put it in where the piece had fallen off, and in less than ten minutes my car was fixed. I was so happy I could've laid one sloppy wet kiss on this greasy, long-haired white man. He told me that my charge was only twenty dollars. I was so elated, which made everything even better. I drove off in true Mustang style, fast and carefree. As I drove off, my heart was happy, and uncontrollable tears streamed down my face. A thought came to me in the back of my mind. It was God. He said, "You're going to be okay. You don't need anyone to have your back but me."

It was so clear! I had heard stories of God speaking to people in the Bible, and I had always believed them. I just figured that it hadn't happened to me, but this time it had. There was no question in my mind.

I called my mother from my prepaid cell once I hit the Indiana line to tell her I was on my way. She told me that she was just pulling up to my sister's performance. All of a sudden I wasn't mad at her anymore. I guess I realized that it was a test, and I felt in my heart that I had passed it.

Before I made it home, I started making plans. Very big plans. *I am moving. Jordan and I are going to move. To where? Either Chicago, California, New York, or Atlanta. I weighed my options with all of them. Chicago is too close to home, and I'm always there anyway with MSST. California is too far away and has earthquakes. New York is too far away, and the rats are too big. Atlanta is the perfect place. Not too far and not too close, an eight-hour drive if I need to get back to Indianapolis. I'm going to step out on faith and trust God because he told me that I would be alright.*

I had never been to Atlanta before, and I didn't know anyone there, but I was going to be the star that I was born to be. We could still be a group and could travel for gigs and studio time.

Journal Entry

I Miss Allen, February 14, 2000

I miss Allen. Not like I did before, but I still miss him. I think now I'm finally coming to grips with myself and the truth is, he's not coming back. I still hurt and I still cry sometimes, but it's okay. I had a dream about him just last week and it made me realize how far I've really come dealing with the hardest heartbreak of my life. I dreamed I was in a store and I looked out the window and I saw him, right there in the parking lot, and he was looking at me. He was sitting in his gold

Cadillac with the music bumpin', lookin' as fine as ever, and just looking at me. I dropped whatever I was buying and ran outside and opened his passenger door to get a better look. The closer I got the more he changed. He turned from my Allen to a total and complete stranger. I touched his face and he was an old man in a different Cadillac, but the same color. And the man was looking at me like I was crazy. But I didn't get upset; I kind of expected it. I remember when I first lost him I thought I would live out the rest of my days living like he had just died. I had lost all the desires that I ever had. I didn't want to laugh even if something was funny. I couldn't look my son in the face. I didn't want to carry the load all by myself. I used any and everything that I could to "replace" Allen: friends, guys, and family members. This was a worst-case scenario to me. No one in the world loved a man the way that I loved Allen. No woman in the world had his child that looked just like him and then lost him forever. This was no ordinary heart-break; this was the worst heartbreak ever because we couldn't even fight about anything. About him not coming around, taking care of his responsibilities, returning my pages. If anything, to make it easier for me he could've just been a deadbeat dad, but he would've still been alive. I didn't know how to tell my one-and-a-half-year-old that his daddy was dead and explain that he was never coming back. Now I look back and see how bad off I was emotionally. How I couldn't see past that day. My sleepless nights and tiresome days. And I can only say, "Thank You, Jesus." For pulling me out, for showing me another way, a better way, Your way. And yes, even though I was mad at God for taking him away, despite all that He still gave me joy, even when I didn't want it. So much joy I couldn't help but take it. Love! The love I thought I never had, I'd never get, I'd never give. More love than any one person could use, and most of all peace in my soul and courage to keep on. And now I look back two-and-a-half whole years later, and I realize it wasn't that bad after all. I can still do things. But I have learned I have to love myself totally and completely before I love another as much as I loved Allen, and before another loves me totally and completely. And it's true, "This too shall pass," and "Joy comes in the morning."

Thank You, Jesus

Reign

Ms. Perfectionist

I WAS DOING OKAY not being with Junior, but I was hurting without my children. Every chance he had to rip them from me, he took. I sat on the porch and thought back. *I was hospitalized a month ago. I know I needed help, but I wasn't that bad.* I was in the mental health portion of the hospital. Each day consisted of a jail inmate, an elderly woman, and a boy who was faking crazy.

The jail inmate was handcuffed to the bed. He was in the hospital because he had gone 'mad' in the local jail. He spent his nights jackin' off with his free hand. Every night I had to hear the sounds of him moaning and groaning.

The elderly woman walked the halls and screamed out for her dead brother. She wailed, "My brother, where is my brother?" At any given moment, she might begin her shuffle through the hallway. Hearing her slippers sent me into a frenzy. I thought I was completely insane because I was surrounded by unstable people.

I did make one friend in the hospital—a guy named Lamont who was supposed to turn himself into prison to serve a five-year sentence. He was afraid of the idea of prison, so he faked a suicide attempt. They rushed him to the hospital, and he was hiding out. He never knew that the girl he loved talking to had actually attempted to take her life. Being around these people showed me that I was not crazy. I was being driven crazy. Someone or something was trying to kill me.

While at the hospital, I tried to call the kids. Junior answered and hung up. He knew it was me because everyone knew I was there. I called and Sophia answered: "What do you want, Reign? Your children don't want to speak with you. Babygirl was riding her bike and got hit by a car."

"What happened? Can I talk to her?"

I was never allowed to talk to her or any of the kids. Babygirl was never in an accident; she was with her granddad. I called once a day for a while, but they never allowed me to talk to the kids. After I left the hospital, Junior and I planned times when I could visit with them. There were times we were supposed to meet and exchange the children and he wouldn't show. On holidays, if I called to have the children, he wouldn't answer the phone. Phone numbers were changed, and when I called Sophia for help, she wouldn't answer. To further hurt me, they contacted my family members and allowed them to see the kids, while telling them how unfit I was to raise them.

Once I spoke with Sophia, and she asked how I was still alive. She said, "I thought you killed yourself. You lost your husband and your children. You should be dead by now."

"That's a good question." I didn't have an answer.

Junior and I were no longer together, and that was one thing. If he thought he could take my children from me, he had better think again. I was their mother. They deserved to have me in their life.

One afternoon, I went to the daycare and picked them up.

"Reign, what are you doing here?" the sitter asked me.

"I am here to take my children home."

"Mom!" they yelled in unison. I hugged and kissed them. It had been three months since Junior had allowed me to see them. Between him and Sophia, they made sure that I would not only suffer through the divorce but also lose my mind not seeing my children. My concern was not me; it was them.

We went to Mom's, and I listened to and talked with the kids. "Mom we had so much fun at Disney World. The only thing missing was you," Big Smooth said. He told me all about the rides, the games, and all of the action. Princess described all of the buffet foods they had.

"Mom, we had waffles for dinner and nachos for breakfast."

She told me all about the plane ride. It was the first time they had been on an airplane. I was so sad. I wished I could have been there for their first plane ride.

Big Smooth told me a funny story about him calling the police. There was a Mickey Mouse phone at the hotel. He asked his sisters if they thought it was real, and the girls said no. Big Smooth, being who he is, called 9-1-1.

"Momma, a mean, large black woman came to the door and knocked. Grandma and Daddy were in another room. Princess got the door, and the lady asked if someone had called 9-1-1. She was so country, Momma."

The kids laughed as they told me the tale. They said they got in big trouble, but it was still funny.

"They tried to make me forget about you, but I can't. You are my mom. I love you. I could never forget about you or my granny." Babygirl had tears in her eyes. She wrapped her arms around me and held me tight. I breathed in her skin and hair. We talked for hours about Disney. I was happy for them, but I felt betrayed by Junior and Sophia.

Even if they hated me, why would they take my kids away from me? I didn't deserve that. I am their mom, and I was there. Every minute with my daughter, I was there. I had stayed with Junior for so long because I loved my children so much. I would have loved to have shared every moment with them in Florida. I was a fool to think they would wait for me to leave the hospital and go with my children. I should have known they had never cared anything about me. Nor did they care about my children's feelings.

Listening to the kids tell their stories, I could tell they wished I had been there, but one thing that touched me was when my cancer survivor told me she didn't get her wish, because her wish always included me.

It was time for me to pour all of my love into my children. God had spared my life, and they needed me. I had a getaway plan in my head. I had to make sure Junior and his family wouldn't get my children again.

I decided that night that the cycle of abuse, depression, and pain would end and I would leave it in Indianapolis. That night we left town for Evansville.

"Did someone call for a cab?"

I got into the cab and told the driver, "Take me to Evansville, Indiana."

"Did you say Evansville? You do know that's four hours away?"

I didn't care how far away it was. I had saved enough money to care for my children and myself for a few months. The kids slept most of the way. When they did wake up, I told them, "We are going to a safe place, and no one will ever take you away from me." Princess smiled and drifted off to sleep. The driver stopped so Babygirl could use the restroom. I freshened up and looked into the mirror. *Reign, are you sure you know what you are doing? How can you live without Junior? How will you make it alone? I must; I have no choice.*

We pulled up to the women's shelter, and I dragged the kids and our bags up the stairs. The driver made sure I was at the right place. Even though I tried to give him the full fare of two hundred dollars, he said, "Just give me one hundred bucks. Promise me you will never go back to a man who will abuse you and take your children."

"I won't," I promised.

A stern lady came to the door and asked, "What's your name? Fill this out."

I began to fill out a plethora of paperwork, copied my ID, and went over the rules. It was two a.m. when we finally got into our room.

We adapted to shelter life well. All of the counselors were kind. A child therapist talked to the children. She was very in tune with them, and they loved her as well. She listened, and she gave them a chance to be children. We talked as a family and begin to work past the abuse they had seen and I had endured. I explained to them the depression I dealt with and my triggers. I also apologized for everything I had put them through.

I immediately began to explore our new surroundings. I took

them on a walk downtown on our second day there. On the weekends, we would ride buses on all sides of town and learn the area. The people of Evansville seemed nice enough. I liked being around them because of their country twang.

The area was known as Kentuckiana, because it's along the border of Indiana and Kentucky. It's right along the Ohio River. What we enjoyed the most was walking along the river. It was so peaceful and serene. For a family who dealt with chaos 24/7, sitting near the river was like heaven. Many days and nights, we would walk, and Princess would sing country songs. We would talk about our future together to get through the pain of our past.

I began bonding with the kids again and making up for lost time. We took many trips to the local ice cream shop, Lick's. The workers came to know us well. One day we went to a conference in a nice hotel. We snuck in and didn't pay for the food. We had a fancy meal with three courses and drank iced tea. Just imagine a nice conference with businesspeople all dressed up with attaché cases, and my children and I dressed up too. We coined the phrase "Act fancy not smantzy." I said that to them whenever we went somewhere and acted fancy or pretended to be rich. I taught them how to use their knives and forks properly. We would fold our cloth napkins over our laps. Although times were rough, I never let them know it.

I put them in school, and they did well. No matter what situation they were in at any point in their lives, they always did well academically. In an unstable environment, you have to hold on to something. They have always loved school, loved to read, and enjoyed learning.

I began to look for a job and eventually found one at a Max & Erma's inside of the Argosy Casino, right next to the shelter. I also found a church that we enjoyed called Memorial Baptist. There was a nice couple who would pick us up in the church bus. The congregation fell in love with the children.

Junior would often call my cell phone. When I picked up, I could hear him breathing. After a while, I disconnected it and got a new one. When Mom came down to visit us, the kids would stay at a hotel with her. Shelter rules stated I could not stay out all night or I would lose my room. I made some friends at the shelter but found most women were addicted to crack cocaine, running from the law, or just plain triflin'. I felt different from them, and I was. I had a plan: get my children to safety, get a job, find a place, get back into school, and get on with my life. Most of the women who worked at the shelter knew that. One lady saw how hard I worked and how well behaved my children were. She came to my room one morning and gave me an envelope with three hundred dollars in it. I asked, "Why did you choose me over the other women and their children?"

"I admire you."

A woman who has a degree, has her life together, and was never abused admires me—wow!

"I see how hard you work and how you ride the bus. I watch you learn the city. I hear you and your kids pray in the morning and at night. Take this money and buy your babies something for Christmas or save it. Do whatever you wish. It is yours."

I held that money in that envelope until my next journey, which led me to Hotlanta, the black Mecca.

"Reign, someone is looking for you. Kenneth 'Babyface' Edmonds is looking for you. He remembers hearing about you, and he wants to start a girl group."

I was on the phone with my brother Dave. Dave had connections to the Edmonds family. I called my dad.

"I still want to sing, but Atlanta? I am just getting settled in Evansville. Things are going good. Should I rock the boat? Okay, let's do it!"

I made a decision. I didn't feel great about it, but it was too late: my mother was on her way. We piled into the back of her Honda Civic. We had so much stuff we had to leave some of it in Evansville. We set out for Atlanta.

Uncle Jim was cool about us coming. He welcomed the kids and me. He had a daughter and was a single dad. He had a beautiful home with more than enough room for us.

As soon as we got there, Uncle Jim and I caught up on old times. He had me laughing as soon as we arrived. The cousins played and argued. He so was helpful in getting the kids into school, and once again they did well from the start. We begin working on music, but not as much as I wanted to. He had a lot of projects in the works. We did the vocals on a State Farm commercial. It was a paid gig, and I was able to get some things for the kids.

I took advantage of the programs Atlanta had to offer. I was in job training, and I signed the kids up for PeachCare health insurance and for food and cash assistance with Family & Children's Services. The kid's daycare was paid for, and I found a job at an Applebee's restaurant.

As I settled in Atlanta, I realized I was not doing much musically. I felt like I had been tricked. I never got in touch with Babyface. I never did anything outside of Uncle Jim's studio, but I needed to be in Atlanta at that time. Just being in that beautiful place lifted my spirits. Uncle Jim always had me laughing, and there was always something to do. We took the kids skating, went to a black-owned mall, and saw black people running things. Once we went to a bank, and there was a black president working at the local Wachovia. That was all new for us. Uncle Jim had cool friends who had BBQs and parties. The nightlife was vibrant, and I went out with Uncle Jim's friends often. I was never depressed when I was down there, but after a while I knew I had to go back home and finish the business I had left. I had to go home and at least give Junior the chance to co-parent his children.

In February 2003, we went back to Indianapolis, and I was among my family and friends. I was back at Mom's and was planning a Valentine's party that night with the children. As we cruised through Circle Center Mall, we picked out napkins, streamers, and party hats.

We picked up a cookie cake and headed home. I put on my fake smile and tried to have a good time for the kids' sake; still in the back of my mind, I wished I had a special Valentine. I told myself, *My kids are my Valentines this year. I am so sick of all of the commercials, the goofy couples, and the cupid hearts.*

"Blah, this is bull," I sighed. *I may as well head to the bar.* I put the kids to bed and headed out for the night.

As I made my way out of the bar, I stumbled toward a bright yellow cab. I stepped inside and saw a familiar face. We began the five-mile ride home. I was quiet most of the way and didn't want to make any small talk. I thought I was home free, but as we pulled in front of the house, he looked back into the seat.

"Don't I know you from somewhere?"

"Oh yes. Is it Mikel?" I answered.

"How's life? How are your husband and the kids doing?"

I laughed and informed him, "There is no husband, and life is great."

We exchanged numbers, and that night I sent him a text message. The text read, "I am impressed that you never tried to holla' at me, although I have known you for a while."

He texted back, "I don't holla' at married women, but now we both single and available, let's do this. How 'bout dinner tomorrow?"

I sent a final text: "Yeah, that would be cool."

I got ready for my date two hours early.

"Where are you going, Momma?" Princess asked.

"Momma has a date, babies." Babygirl didn't seem too happy. Big Smooth just looked down, but Princess told me, "Momma, you smell good," and helped me get ready. It was the first time I had been out in a year. I had met guys in bars, and of course there was Rico, but there were no dates.

"Mom, what ya think about my hair? Trish did a good job, right?"

My mom pulled at the curls in the back.

"Yeah, baby, you look nice, but be careful."

I had on a tight pink shirt that framed my figured. My Express jeans had been ironed twice. *Why am I so nervous? I have known this dude for years.* I knew Mikel as my cab driver and the nice guy with the cute daughter. Back in 1998, he came and picked me up in the mornings, and his little girl was in the front with him. I always thought he was cute; those eyes and strong arms caught my attention, but never for more than a minute. I was married then and had no intention to be with any other man. I recalled the night before. I was somewhere in between tipsy and drunk, but I remembered those eyes. *I wonder why we connected now when we never did before.*

Okay, ten minutes, Reign. I grabbed my pink superstar belt and peeked out of the window. He was walking up the steps. I wasn't ready for Mom or the children to meet him yet. I cut him off before he could ring the doorbell.

"Hey, Reign, so where do you want to go?"

I had no idea. I had not done anything meaningful in so long. All I really wanted to do was talk and have someone listen.

"How about Rock Bottom? They have some good food," he said.

We headed to the car, and he opened the door for me.

"Are you warm enough?" he asked. It was a cold February night, two days after Valentine's Day, and I was finally on my date. In the back of my mind, I wondered if this would be a date from hell.

We pulled up in front of the Rock Bottom restaurant. I had been there before with some people from work. I knew the food was pretty good. He ordered a steak. I got the same thing I always ate, chicken quesadillas. We ordered Cokes to drink. "How have you been, and what have you been up to?" he asked. He seemed to be listening to every word I said. When I answered a question, he would ask follow-up questions. He wanted to know all of the details of my life.

Most people say you should never discuss past relationships on a first date, but we both talked about our relationship failures. We went on about our children. When he asked questions about my children, my defenses went up. I kept my thoughts to myself. *Hmm, he could be a child molester—don't no man care about no kids.*

Then came my turn with the questions. I thought Mikel was just a cab driver. Between our salads and the main course I found out he was much more than that. He had many talents. "I'm the oldest of three. I have two sisters. My mom and dad have been married for thirty years. I went to private schools and played sports. I am good with my hands and used to take things apart and put them back together." *Wow, he answered all of my questions.* He seemed to be both street smart and book smart. We both called that 'boughetto,' a word combining bourgeois and ghetto.

I didn't pay much attention to my food. I was paying more attention to his voice.

"So, what kind of things do you like to do, Reign? I mean what is your passion?"

I couldn't stop looking into his beautiful hazel eyes. *Wow, this man wants to know about me. This is new.*

"Did you hear me, Reign? I asked you what you like to do? What would you do for free?"

I thought for a minute, even though I didn't need to. *Should I share my dreams with this man?*

"I want to perform. I want to sing, act, and write music. I want to make people feel good with my talent. I want them to get lost in my voice. I love to sing."

"Maybe one day I can make you sing." He took my hand.

My mind battled with my heart. *This dude thinks he is slick. I don't trust him or any other man. He is not getting my cookies. Then again, maybe he will; it has been a while. This guy has a lot of game. I can see through the bull, though. This date is going well, too well.* Back to the questions.

"So, Mikel, where is your girlfriend? Does she know you are out with me tonight?"

I waited for him to come up with something. He immediately

countered, "I don't have a girlfriend. My daughters' mom left me a few years ago. I have a two-year-old daughter and an eight-year-old daughter; that is all we share."

"So, you have a two-year-old? That's pretty recent. What happened with you and her mother?" I was curious and wanted to know why he was not with a woman he had a small child with. "How did the relationship end, and why did it end?"

I was a firm believer in staying together for the sake of the child. *It didn't work for me, but why didn't it work for him?*

"She wasn't the one for me. She never fully satisfied me. When I was with her, I always needed someone else. She never fully gave me what I needed."

I looked at him sideways: "Well, why did you have children with her? Obviously you loved her enough to create life."

He thought for a moment. "I didn't say I never loved her. I said she never gave me everything I needed in a woman. She just wasn't enough"

This guy is so full of it. Still prying for more, I asked, "So, what did she need to do? I mean, what did you need that she wasn't giving?"

I cocked my head and waited on his answer.

"I need a total experience. I need a total package. She wasn't that. Let's change the subject."

We finished our meal, and he paid the server. He left a seven-dollar tip. As much as I didn't want to, I liked this man.

"You know, I used to wait tables part time, and I loved people like you. I worked hard, and I was fast. I always made nice money—I mean for a part-time job."

He laughed. "I feel you. I have been driving cabs for nine years, and I know how it is to work hard. I treat others like I would want to be treated. If they give me crappy service, I still tip, just not as much as I normally would."

We had a lot in common. We were both divorced, both had children, and both worked in the service industry.

As we headed out to the car, we realized that it was gone. It was not in the place where we had parked. We walked around dumbfounded.

"I could have sworn the car was right there." He pointed. I agreed. As we came closer to the spot, we noticed a No Parking sign.

"Oh no!" I was scared. The date was about to go downhill. Or was it?

"I guess they towed it." He was calm and already thinking.

"Well, what are you gonna do?" I waited for the blowup.

"Do you have gloves and a hat with you? We are going to have to walk to the City- County building and pay the fine before we find out where the car is."

I checked my pockets. I had a hat but no gloves. I put it on, and he took my hand. Instead of cursing, complaining, and going off, we walked and talked. I forgot how cold it was and that the car had been towed. *Oooh, I am lovin' this man.*

We went into the office, and Mikel gave his name. He paid the ticket like it was a normal habit. The officer gave him the information on where the car was located. While we waited on paperwork, he joked with the officer and with me. I saw how calm he was. *I have never been calm in my life. I don't even think I am calm when I'm asleep.*

We took a cab to get the car and talked to the driver along the way. The driver knew him and asked about his family. He seemed to like talking to people. *Yet another thing we have in common.* Per his request, I waited in the cab until he got the car and warmed it up. Once again, he tipped beyond the normal fifteen percent. I hopped in the car, and we started our conversation where we had left off.

"So, you want to know if I have a girlfriend. How about I show you. You want to ride somewhere with me?"

I wasn't worried about anything bad happening. He didn't seem crazy or deranged, but then again, I had made judgment mistakes in the past. Something told me to go. I thought it was my mind, but it definitely was my body.

"Cool, let's go."

"Here we are. Come on in."

He took my hand and led me into the living room. There was a clothes basket in the front room. There were clothes strewn about the place. All of the lights were on, and the radio was on.

"Okay, your girlfriend keeps a dirty place."

He opened the refrigerator, and there was a half-full orange juice container, some lunchmeat, and a few apples.

"You win. No woman would have that little bit of food in the house. You don't have chocolate candy or anything. I'm sorry. I was wrong."

We talked for hours, well into the night. I looked at my phone, and it was two o'clock in the morning. I yawned and stretched to give him the clue I was ready to go.

"Tired? You can lie down for a while, and I will take you home." He took my hand and showed me to his room. It was pretty simple: a bed, a lamp, and more clothes on the floor. *At least the sheets and blankets are clean.* I lay on top of the bed and relaxed. He went back into his other room and turned on some music. Now I was supposed to be relaxing a bit. The next thing I knew, I was sitting straight up in the bed frightened by the sound of DMX yelling, "Ya'll gone make me lose my mind up in here, up in here!"

"Mikel, what the …" I couldn't get my sentence out. He came back into the room.

"What, you don't like DMX?"

"I like the wild man just fine, but not early in the morning while trying to sleep."

"Let me find something you may like. Be right back."

"You can have anything I own, work my fingers all the way to the bone," Jaheim was stirring in the front of the apartment, and I thought I was asleep. But if I was asleep, I was having a vivid dream. I was being held around the waist and kissed all over my neck. I was reciprocating the kisses softly. Too scared to open my eyes and wake from my dream, I slowly pushed one lid open and saw Mikel kissing me and heard him whispering in my ear.

"I had a good time tonight with you. Has anyone ever told you how beautiful you are? I always thought you were an attractive woman, but I didn't know you had been hurt so much. If you were my woman, I would make love to you every night and take good care of you. All night I have wanted to taste your lips."

Reign, don't fall for this. Of course this man is saying this. He wants what is in your pants. He wants sex, just like they all do. Mmm hmm, I am beautiful. I have been fed that line before. They always say that at the beginning. After they marry you and knock you up, they bounce on you. My mind was giving me all of the logical information, but my lust was strong. Had he been any other man, I am sure he would have taken me right then. Instead, he kissed me for hours. He rubbed my back and every inch of my body. I was shaking and scared. *This feels so good.*

I hope he can't tell that it has been a while since anyone has touched me or even kissed me. Reign, please stop shaking and get your head right.

He kept whispering in my ear: "I know you need this, so let me make you feel better. I am so sorry that you have been through so much. Come on, baby."

I did what he asked me to do and fell asleep.

"Oh my gosh. My mom is gonna kill me. I have been gone all night and my kids will wonder where I am. I have to be at work this morning. You have to take me home now!"

It was six a.m. and Mom was usually up by then. I would wake the kids up at seven and had to be at work by nine.

"Be cool, baby. I will get you home in no time. I will grab you some coffee and donuts on the way. Can I at least do that for you?"

This dude is a trip. *I spend the night in your bed on our first date and you want to offer me breakfast—coffee and donuts at that?* I was so embarrassed and wanted to get out of there. I just smiled at him.

"Sure, some donuts would be cool."

He warmed up the car, and I waited inside his apartment. The night before replayed in my mind. *Well, I kept my clothes on, and we didn't have sex. I still spent the night with a man on the first date. What was I thinking? I'm breaking all of my rules already. Whatever. He is just some dude I already knew, plus I'll never see him again. Shoot, I had some fun and felt like I have not felt in a long time.* Mikel startled me as he came back through the front door.

"I live here. Why did you jump?"

I laughed and put on my coat. "I know you live here. You just scared me."

He opened the car door and made sure I put my seatbelt on, and we headed for the donut shop. I felt my phone vibrate in my pocket.

"So, how was your hot date?" My best friend, Betty, was on the phone.

"It was fine. I will call you back and tell you all about it. The date is still in progress."

She laughed and told me to call her back as soon as I could.

I hung up with her and called Mom.

"Yes, Reign, where are you?"

"I stayed at Mikel's, since his car was towed and it was late when we got it back."

"So, you spent the night? You need to be careful."

I wanted to argue, but she was right.

"Mikel is cool, Momma; we just talked most of the night."

That was technically true.

"I hate this place. I mean, the donuts are good, but they are so rude when I come in."

I was telling Mikel about how they treated me at the local donut shop.

"Really? I have never had a problem, and I have been coming here all of my life. My parents live right down the street, and I have lived here most of my life."

He opened the door to the shop, and I walked in. As soon as the attendants saw him, they smiled and waved.

"Welcome to Long's. How are you doing, Mikel?"

He ordered for both of us and we left.

"I bet they won't treat you mean again. Now they know you are with me."

This man is insane. I am not with him. I went out with him once. He is crazy. "Yeahhh okaaaayy," I said.

We arrived in front of my house and said our goodbyes. I didn't want the date to end, but it was time to get back to reality.

"Thanks for the date, Mikel. I had a good time."

"Do you remember my full name?" This was a test; we had played twenty questions the night before.

"Thank you, Mikel Andre, for the date. Enjoy the rest of your day."

I walked up the steps slowly. I was on cloud nine, but not for long. I was pulling out my keys when I ended up on my butt. I had fallen on the ice that was on the steps. I heard Mikel yell and open the car door to help me. I hurried and got back up.

"No, I am fine. I don't need help. Just go, please."

I unlocked the door and slammed it. I peeked out of the window, and he was still out of his car looking toward the door. I watched until he drove down the street. *Way to go, Reign. Date number one was a total failure.* I erased his name out of my phone, sure there would be no second date.

The next day after work, Mikel called to make sure I was okay.

"You took a hard tumble yesterday. You seemed so embarrassed so I didn't call you right away."

I put the phone down.

"Yeah, I was embarrassed. I am such a klutz. I am always falling and dropping stuff. I figured you were telling all of your boys that I was the jump-off chick who fell at the end of the date."

"Actually I had a good time and wanted to see you again. I could tell you needed to be held, and that is why what happened went down. It is what it is; don't trip. So, you wanna see a movie tonight?"

That was the beginning of many dates and times spent together. I enjoyed his company. I learned a lot about him and his family. I introduced him to my family. Mom had some reservations, but in time she saw that he made me happy.

We dated for a while and had our ups and downs. I had never met a guy so laid back. He always allowed me to pick where we would eat or what we would do. One day, he called me unexpectedly with something in mind.

"Hey Reign, where you at, baby?"

"I'm at church."

"At church? Well, how long are you gonna be there? Why don't I come and pick you up for dinner?"

"Okay, I should be home in an hour."

"Cool, I will be at your house in two hours."

I left church and got ready for our date. I was becoming very comfortable around him. He allowed me to be myself. I dressed the way I wanted to. I had always been a jeans type of girl. I would wear a nice shirt and my favorite pair of jeans. Something as simple as what we call a 'wife beater' and some fitted jeans would excite Mikel. He always complimented my hair and my scent, but if he didn't like something, he would tell me that too.

He arrived at my house exactly two hours later. He was always precise. If he said he would do something or be somewhere that is what he did.

"Where are we going?

"It's a surprise." Twenty minutes later, we were at his apartment.

"You wanna cook with me?"

"Yeah."

"Cool, we are making steak and veggies. I'm using the George Foreman grill to cook the steak."

That's odd. The grill is fine, but I didn't think it was good for steak. I made my steaks the old-fashioned way: frying pan, onions, mushrooms, peppers, and a little seasoning. He told me to start the veggies. I threw them in a pot and begin boiling them on medium.

"Reign, what are you doing? You have to slow-cook those vegetables. They will burn and stick to the bottom of the pan. They have cheese in them."

I backed up and looked at this man.

"Negro, it's frozen veggies, not rocket science. What are you blabbing about? Do you know me? I have been cooking since I was sixteen. I have been a mother since the age of seventeen. Nana and my dad taught me to cook real shit. You are talking about some damn frozen veggies. Get out of here."

"Reign, I don't care who taught you what. I do know that these are not just frozen veggies. They have cheese in them, and if you cook them too high the cheese will burn. I have burnt them before. Can you just turn them down?"

"Nope, I can't. Don't you think that if I smelled some cheese burning I would turn it off? More importantly, do you think I would stand here and watch the veggies burning? Plus who uses a George Foreman to make steaks? What are you, twelve? That grill is for burgers maybe, hot dogs. Steaks are cooked in a skillet. Do you have one of those? I am calling my dad. This is some mess."

I went way over the top.

"Daddy, this dude is a dummy. Please tell me how to cook vegetables."

I put the phone on speaker so Mikel could hear.

"Daddy, tell this dude I am in school for cooking right now. I wear a chef's hat. I know how to make foods from different countries, and you are telling me about some frozen veggies. I tell you what, take me home!"

He finished the steaks, wrapped the food up, and got his keys. When we got out to the car, he reached under his seat. I saw the nine-millimeter in his hand. Flashbacks of my past ran into my head.

"What the hell. So, you're gonna shoot me over some steak."

He ignored me and put the gun in his trunk. "Reign, I don't know what you are used to, but this ain't that. I put the gun in the trunk because you said you are scared of guns. Is that still the case?"

I put my head down and nodded. We rode home in silence.

I got to my house and jumped out of the car. He yelled out of the window.

"Bye, sweetheart. If I did anything to hurt you, I am sorry. I thought making dinner together would be fun."

I slammed the door and promised myself I would never see him again. *The only thing I know is that I am hungry.*

The next day, I thought about what I had done. I could admit I was way over the top. All the man was trying to do was cook and spend some time with me. I faced the situation and called him.

"Hey, Reign, what's up?"

"I'm sorry."

"Okay, no problem. Are you okay? You seemed really upset. I wanted to call you, but I thought I better let you calm down."

"I was trippin' and it wasn't cool. I just felt like you were attacking me and I had to defend myself. I hate when people tell me what to do. So, what did you do last night?

"Shit, I was full of two steaks and a whole pot of vegetables. What about you?"

"You wrong for that boy, so we going out tonight or what?"

"Be there in thirty minutes."

I used so many tactics to push Mikel away from me. If I saw anything that upset me, it was over. If he made one mistake, I would tell him we were through. The man never stood a chance with me. History had shown me that men change and that I had no need for them. I wasn't interested in any relationship. What I did do was use him to take my past pain away. That was not his job, and that was not something any man could do.

"I have tickets to the Isley Brothers; wanna come?" I flashed the tickets in front of his face.

"Sure, sounds fun. Tell me when and where."

The next week, we were shopping for clothes for the show. I decided on all brown. I like browns; they blend with my skin in a caramel-color mesh. They also bring out the light-brown color in my eyes. I picked out brown for Mikel too. We were all ready for the show the following weekend.

On the day of the concert, I had school and Mikel was working. We were to meet at his house that evening. By this time, he had given me a key to his place. I went to his apartment and showered. I prepared my clothes and watched television. I called him to see what we were doing for dinner.

He sounded alarmed when he answered the phone.

"Someone broke into my parents' house. I will be there in a few, but I have to leave again."

I began to pray for him and his family. After he came home, he went back to his parents to check on things. I waited patiently at the apartment. Back in the day, that wouldn't have worked, as I am an impatient person. Being around Mikel for six months had changed me a bit. I was no longer concerned with the concert but with the safety of his family. I just wanted him to be okay and not to worry. I wanted to be with him. I didn't add to the mayhem. I just waited like he told me to.

After I had prayed for what seemed like hours, he walked back in the door.

"I'm sorry, we don't have time for a nice dinner. The show starts in an hour, and I have no time to iron my clothes."

I showed him I had already done that.

"Jump in the shower if you still want to go. We can eat at Arby's downtown."

"You sure you're not gonna be mad if we don't go to a sit-down restaurant for dinner?"

I locked eyes with him. "Mikel, I don't care where we eat. We don't even have to go to the show. I just want to be with you. I love you, Mikel."

There, I said it.

"I love you too, Reign." He kissed me.

He loves me too. Wow, Reign, be careful, chile.

The Isleys were amazing on stage. They did all of my favorite old-school joints. They did some of the new stuff too, but the old stuff was off the hook. We talked music and sipped on beers. I sang along with the brothers, and he didn't seem to mind. We discussed the music our parents listened to. We swayed back and forth to the music. I could feel his breath on my neck, and he wrapped his arms around me. It was a magical night, and it wasn't over yet.

We grabbed a quick bite to eat at Waffle House. No matter how much time we spent together, we always had great conversations. There were never moments of awkward silence. There was always plenty of laughing and touching.

Back at his apartment, he taught me how to be still and stay in the moment. I turned on some music; he turned it off. I turned off the lights, and he turned them on. He massaged every inch of my five-foot-four-inch frame. Each time I tried to speak, he wouldn't allow me to. I attempted to return the love with my hands, and he pushed them away.

"Don't do anything, Reign; just let me touch you."

I exhaled and closed my eyes. *This is it!* "M-M-Mikel, will you make love to me?"

I whispered so soft I didn't know if he could hear me.

"Are you sure, Reign? I mean, are you ready for this?"

I thought again and raised my head up. "Yes, Mikel, please. I have wanted to since the first night."

"Are you sure you are ready?"

Is this man a fool? I am telling him I want to give him some, and he is asking me again. Maybe I should run now. He reached into a nightstand drawer and came out with a condom. I looked at it and watched him put it on. He very carefully showed me every movement he made. We had both discussed not having any more children and how dangerous it is to have sex with no protection. This was a must and took nothing away from the mood that was set.

I was shaking and couldn't will my body to stop. The moment he entered my body, I began to speak.

"I knew it. I knew it. I knew it." I was still and let him get a rhythm.

"You knew what, baby? You knew what?"

"I knew the physical connection would be the same as the mental."

I said those last words. For the next few hours, I was on a roller-coaster ride. I was in the front seat. First, we drifted smooth and slow. Then we sped up and it was an exciting rush. We hit the first hill. Then came the part when the ride slows down almost to a stop and you know the big hill is coming up. Your toes curl with excitement. I was in the back seat, then forward, and backward. There were mutual exchanges of every fantasy I had imagined. Then there was a great release and silence. I lay in his arms for hours. For the next three days, we made love over and over. We hardly ate anything. We left the house once and got a pizza. Every time one of us would get hungry, we would devour each other. Between the sexual episodes, we would talk about any and everything.

The conversation was just as orgasmic as the sex. The sex was so good; not just the intercourse. It was the total experience that I was hooked on. The touches, the caresses, the looks, and the sounds made him very good at pleasing me. But I knew it was all wrong. I knew I should be sexing my husband. But I didn't have a husband. Getting married again was not an option for me. I was gonna have to keep this up; it was too good.

Things were going great with Mikel and me. We would talk on the phone for hours. We talked about real stuff: politics, the world, school, and our children. We discussed our future and our past. We made love mentally and physically, and either way it was mind blowing.

In my past relationships, I had felt ugly, unloved, and unworthy of a man. He made me feel beautiful, adored, almost worshipped. He would stare at me for hours while I was naked. He would stand me up in all my glory and smile. He was so sweet and gentle with me, and he always made sure I was comfortable and happy. I was scared of the way I felt around him. I began to wonder what he wanted from me.

It took a while for me to allow him around the children. I was scared that he might be a hidden sex offender or child molester. I checked out his criminal history and spoke with his exes. While they were happy to tell me about him as a boyfriend, I wanted to know about him as a father.

One day, he asked us out to breakfast and paid more attention to them than me. He seemed to know my fears and treated my children with care. He remembered them from our past meetings and was shocked at how they had grown. *Why is he so nice to my children? Will he hurt them? Is he some kind of nutcase?* I still wondered what he wanted from me and when the real Mikel would show up. *When will the abuse begin? When will it be over? When will he throw me away like Junior did?*

Soon after, I began to change; my past had shown me that giving your heart to a man meant getting hurt. D never really loved me, Dad didn't love Mom enough to make us a family, and Junior left me when I needed him the most. I began to ignore phone calls and go out on dates with other friends. I was talking to Rico here and there. I began to talk to the man who hurt me the most, Junior. He was seeing the kids every now and then, and sometimes when we exchanged them, we would go out. We would act like we were dating again. Junior wasn't really providing for the children. He always had an excuse for why he didn't have any money. He managed to buy a new truck but never bought his children anything during that time. However, I still dealt with him. If I became mad at Mikel, I would call Junior. I acted a complete fool, and any other man would have been gone.

I started telling Mikel about my past—all of my issues, the abuse, my childhood, and things between Junior and me. He listened and never judged me. I told deep, dark secrets that no one ever had a clue about; still he loved me.

I began to realize Mikel loved my children. *This man is kind, and loving.* He was the real deal. He would take the kids to breakfast, skating, and the movies. Princess was taken by him right away. The other two had some reservations. They were nervous that the flowers he sent meant we would be married soon. I was the first one to mention that I would never get married again and that I hated the thought of marriage.

We moved in together. Things were going okay. I was so happy in my life. I had a wonderful man, and my children were happy and doing well in school. I was loving life. Although things were going well, we were struggling financially. Our living room had no furniture. I would sit on the floor, sing, and hear my echo. I lay on the hardwood floor with a notebook and CD player, writing songs.

One day, as I was singing, he snuck up behind me and began to kiss and touch me. We made love for an hour as I sang. It was one of the sweetest moments of my existence. I had never met a man who made me want to sing. I wrote so many songs during this time. I wrote about my feelings. I cried, laughed, and wrote like a crazy woman.

The love Mikel showed reminded me of my first love, music. I thought about how I had said I would never sing again. *What the hell was I thinking? This feels so damn good, and I am good at it.* I have many talents, but I love to hear feelings come out of my body. I know many people say all black people can sing or that singers come a dime a dozen. But I adore it, and I do it well.

As good as I sing in front of an audience, I soar at home alone. I go into another world when I worship. There is a huge difference between singing and worshipping. When I think about my life and what God has brought me through, I don't even know my own voice. I pray and sing. I cry out to God with my voice. I can feel His spirit, and He speaks back to me. I don't have a pretty voice, and I make lots of mistakes when I sing. My voice is rough, and even when I sing a sweet song it aches. I know it doesn't make much sense, but when I am alone and I think about my children and what they have suffered, when I think of the many things they have seen that no child should, when I remember the abuse they have seen and the torment they have seen me go through—after all of the past, I am still blessed. I can't help but thank God in song. Even in the midst of all the wrong I was doing, I was still being kept by God, and I owed Him praise. I don't sing; I praise. It is the sweetest form of thanks I can give God.

As Mikel and I blended our lives, he was great with the children. He treated them like his own. He was taking on the role of father since Junior was not providing any care for them. When Mikel came into the picture, it was like Junior's job was over. I was done forcing him to love his children. I didn't beg him for money or to see his kids. He didn't offer any help other than stealing their tax money each year.

Once, Junior came by and saw that we were struggling to get the children what they needed. He made fun of our small home. He joked about the living room with no couch. He laughed at the kids' beds being in the living room. He then asked me for gas money to take our children to school. That was the last time he was in their lives.

Money was still tight, but we were family and had never been more stable. We had so much love. We would play games around the house. We watched movies on the weekend. Mikel and Princess would fall asleep watching football on Sundays. He taught the children things he knew. He taught them how to build a PC from scratch and to make certain meals. Him being in our lives made things easier on me. I could relax or take a nap. Once, I woke up and he had taken them to breakfast at Golden Corral and left me a note:

Reign,

You were sleeping so peacefully. I couldn't bring myself to wake you. The kids and I went to breakfast. If you wake up within the next two hours call me and I will bring you something home.

I love you so much

Mikel

Years ago, I would have lost my mind if he had left with my children. I was comfortable with the man I was in love with. I was secure with my children being around him. Mikel did these things on a consistent basis. He picked up where their 'sperm donor' left off. He had them active in sports. He enrolled Babygirl in basketball. He was at every event the children had. If he was not there, he was working two jobs: driving a cab and working for Hewlett Packard.

Big Smooth was having issues because his father had left. Instead of Mikel tearing him down, he said, "Man, I am here. I may not be your dad, but as long as you live in my house, you are my son. I see you as mine. I am going to be hard on you. I am gonna make you a man. As long as you are with me, you will be a responsible young man. I will make sure of that."

"Okay, it's just hard for me. I miss my real dad. Since you came around he doesn't want to see me."

Things were not perfect. I had to learn to adjust to letting a man discipline my children. For so long it had been Mom, the kids, and me. If I wanted things to work, I had to let go. After all, this was what I had prayed for and had always wanted. I was used to telling the children to do something and saying it repeatedly. Mikel had a loud voice and didn't sugarcoat anything. I would hear him calling them loudly, and I would lose it.

"Why are you yelling at them?" I would say, with my hands on my hips.

"I told them to wash these dishes, and look at the food on them."

Although I knew he was right, I wanted him to let me tell them that. For so long they had been in transition. Their dad and I provided an unstable environment. They watched me being abused by their dad, and then they watched us abuse each other. I was always trying to protect them. I wanted them to just be kids. Mikel provided stability, balance, and discipline. He gave them chores, responsibility, and an idea of taking pride in themselves. Many times, those chores were not done right, if at all. If they were not done, there was trouble for them. He usually would make them do them again, and I would become upset.

I would come to their rescue. "No, you don't have to do what he said. I'll do it. Just go play and be a kid."

He would get upset and try to explain. "Reign, I am just making sure they have some common sense. I want to teach them how to care for themselves. They have to learn to take care of each other and be responsible. They also have to take pride in themselves and in their home. I am not trying to hurt them by making them clean up, iron, and take care of each other."

I didn't need the lecture. I understood what he was trying to teach them. I began to let up and realize he was their dad and had stepped into that role. He was at the football games. He was at the band concerts. He was teaching skills about life, sports, and all the things that make a well-rounded person.

We moved into a bigger place. We began getting into church and learning about Jesus and His role in our life. I had been out of church since Junior and I had divorced. I didn't want to put my trust in any group of people. I felt that since I prayed and worshipped at home, I didn't need to go to a church house.

Uncle Cleo invited me to a new church he attended. I visited, and the Holy Spirit grabbed me on my first visit. I attended Sunday service, Bible study, and Holy Spirit baptism classes. I started with becoming closer to God and ended up meeting a group of people who were broken just like me.

The church was called Healing Streams. It was a perfect name because in my new members' class I met people who had been addicted to drugs and alcohol. I prayed with people who battled with depression, guilt, and low self-esteem. I made new friends who were looking for what I was looking for. We had all been hurt and wounded. We all needed Jesus and each other. Our pastor was a loving man of God who not only gave us the message but also massaged our souls.

To him we were family, and he loved us. His wife took me under her wing and was always available to talk or email. My healing began at Healing Streams, but it wasn't done yet.

Shortly after joining the church, I met a couple who were involved in a deliverance ministry. I had never heard of this ministry and wasn't sure what they did. They talked to me one day and told me about the program. I laughed because it sounded crazy to me. They said something about casting out demons and healing past hurts. I could picture these ghosts and goblins coming out of someone while incense burned. Uncle Cleo talked with me about some of my past issues.

"Reign, do you want to be delivered so you can enjoy the life God has for you?"

"Sure, but you make it sound easy, like after this my life will be perfect."

"Your life will never be perfect, but you have the power to defeat these things. They are spirits, the spirits of depression and fear. You need to use the power God has placed in you."

"Okay, I'll try it, but it ain't gonna work."

A month later, I was in another church and a team of people were praying for me. The couple from Healing Streams were there. I filled out a form and talked to them about my past and the issues I dealt with. For the next seven hours, they prayed for me. I called out the people who had haunted me. I called out the names: D and Junior. I called out the things that had happened to me: the molestation, the accident, and the physical abuse.

"No, I don't want to forgive Junior. He treated me like a dog and left his children. I want him to have pain. Why does he get a new truck? Why does he have a good life? He should suffer daily like I do."

"Sweetie, you have to let this go. God can't get him if you still got him. Do you love him? Do you still want to be with him? If not, let him go and forgive him tonight."

"What about D? He took my virginity; he raped me. Why should I forgive him? He never said sorry. He should be raped and see how it feels. He has moved on and is married with kids. He shouldn't be allowed around kids. Naw, I will not forgive him. I wish death on him."

I cried and attempted to run out of the church. I shook my head no and threw up. One of the ministers grabbed me and laid me back on the floor of the church. She cleaned me up and began to pray over me. I cried and screamed no. Finally, after more prayer and more tears, I said it.

"Lord, I forgive D. Please take him out of my heart. Please take him away from me. I want to be free. I want to be free. Release him right now, in the name of Jesus."

"You must forgive Junior too."

"I forgive Junior. Please take him out of my heart. Please take him away from me. I want to be set free. I want to be free. Release him right now, in the name of Jesus."

That night, I put the anger and pain behind me, and at one a.m. I left them there in that church. I came out renewed and ready to bring my family into my newfound freedom.

The children and I had been attending Healing Streams, and Mikel started going with us. He would come, sit quietly, and like a sponge take in all of what he needed. It was great to see him being transformed by the Lord. I had gotten stronger by attending, and now we were all becoming better.

Our church was like a family. We had lots of support from our pastor and first lady. Uncle Cleo, Aunt Betty, and many friends attended and were equally supportive. For me it was a relearning of things I had been taught before. For Mikel it was a personal relationship with Jesus that he had never known.

During church, we would all chat and visit. I called it fellowship. Mikel would read and meditate. For the most part, he was quiet during service. He would sit up in his seat attentive to what the pastor was saying. The pastor and Mikel shared a special relationship. He felt comfortable talking with the pastor about things. Few men share the same values that Mikel holds dear. We were becoming active in the church. The children were in children's activities. I was singing in the Super Sunday Choir and attending church every time the doors were opened. Things were progressing quite nicely. But God was still not pleased.

One afternoon, we were alone, and Mikel took me into the living room. He asked me to sit.

"This is my grandmother's ring. It is the only thing I have left from my biological father's side of the family. Reign, you are the total package I spoke of when we first met. You are what no other woman has ever been. You are beautiful, funny, smart, and energetic, and you always have an opinion. You see in color where I see in black and white. You see in bright radiant colors. You gave me the hope to dream again. You showed me how to live life again with no boundaries. You are spontaneous. I love you, Reign"

He got down on his knee next to our davenport couch and asked, "Reign, will you marry me?"

I laughed. "You know the answer to that, boy. Of course I will marry you."

I couldn't believe a man who had said he would never marry again and a woman who had said the same were engaged to be married.

There we were in Vegas, in front of a man named Jesus—not Jesus Christ, a man named Jesus. We were laughing and smiling. This was nothing either of us had imagined we would be doing. We both had bad experiences with marriage, both with children from previous bad situations. Who would have thought we would be in Vegas getting married? *What will my mom think? What will his family think? They already don't seem to like me. I am not his ex, and I am not the mother of his children.*

With all that in mind, we did it. We had a ball all weekend. It was great finally finding someone who understood me. I was ready for everything I deserved, the perfect life that I saw on the *Cosby Show.*

In February 2007, we decided to have an actual ceremony to renew our wedding vows. Mikel and I didn't make big plans for our ceremony. We decided that since we had run off and got married, we should now include our children. We decided to have a small intimate ceremony for close family and friends. This wasn't something we did for us.

In our eyes, we had made our vows and were husband and wife back in Las Vegas. The invites to the wedding included only those who supported us in our union. There were those who thought we had too many children to get married. *What kind of sense does that make?* Mikel was amazing. He didn't hurt or betray me, and he showed my children and me unconditional love.

We loved each other and, more importantly, we were great friends. A friend is someone you will always have in your life. You would be with him or her even if you were not in a relationship or married. That love will trickle down to all the children.

On February 16, 2007, the same day we had met four years earlier, we were set to have a small ceremony. Both sides of our families were in town, but most importantly all of our children were there.

That morning, I text messaged Mikel like we had done when we first met. We shared the same messages we had so many mornings before. Mom and I got up and began to prepare for the big day. The kids busied themselves with getting breakfast and shining shoes. It was very bad outside that day. There were was at least four inches of snow. It was not pretty and warm like my first wedding day. It was not your typical wedding day, but Mikel and I were not your typical couple. We got to the church and had to walk over mounds of snow and ice. I dragged bags and boxes of stuff through the snow. My mother-in-law was in the kitchen preparing the items for the reception.

I sat in the basement of the church and waited. After an hour, our pastor still wasn't there. Mikel was passing cell phones down and calling me. He was worried and concerned. We came to find out that

I had told the pastor a certain time to be there and then changed it. I had never notified him of the change. *My bad.* Uncle Cleo called him, and he quickly arrived.

It was absolutely simple and perfect. There were no lavish dresses, no bridesmaids or groomsmen. I wore a cream ball dress, and Mikel matched me with a suit in the same hue. My hair was perfect in crimps, and Mikel was clean-shaven and handsome. Mikel's Aunt Michelle brought flowers and decorated the church beautifully.

When I looked into his eyes, his love for me took over my soul. I walked down the aisle and smiled at everyone. He looked at me and grinned so big. He was about to cry and was overwhelmed with love for our children and me. That was news to me, because Mikel seldom cries, even when that seems to be a natural reaction.

Our wedding was not a show or a circus, but a union that would include everyone we invited. Everyone sat down, and only the two of us were up front. I addressed the crowd and thanked them for being there. I explained to them why they were there and why we had decided to have the ceremony. I made jokes and had some fun with the family. I read from a pre-written note:

> Our idea for this ceremony is to publicly unite the two families. Please witness and share the love that Mikel and I have had for the last four years. We are two families uniting under one God.

Our pastor sang a song, and we exchanged vows. This time, I felt our marriage was blessed. I felt this was the right way to do things. It felt sacred.

After the vows, I sang to Mikel and expressed my love in the best way I knew how. "I could feel it coming from a mile away as I opened up the door. I saw everything that I've been waiting for …" I began the song. When the song ended, we decreed again that we were husband and wife and would be forever. We had a modest kiss, so as not to gross the kids out too much.

We hung around upstairs and hugged everyone. Mikel stared at me as I walked down the stairs. He held my hand while we entered the reception. Mikel told me it was the happiest he had ever been.

We had a small reception in the basement of the church, with cake I ordered from a bakery. The real idea was to bring our children together and allow them to see that our love was real. I also needed to let Mikel's children know that although they didn't live with us, they were included in our family, all three of them. We are not complete without them. They are special to me and share the same spot as the children who live under our roof. Our home is also their home, no matter how far apart we are.

After the ceremony, all of the family went to dinner. We had a ball. It was a lot of fun having all of our children together at once, because that didn't happen often. It was great to see the children interacting like biological brothers and sisters.

That night we got a nice hotel. We made love into the wee hours of the morning and talked like it was our first date. It was a beautiful day that I will never forget. I am so glad that we decided to do that, and I am glad our families were united

Now our marriage was blessed, the connection was like electricity. Even when we held hands, we could both feel it. There was hot passion even when we were fully clothed. We could be on different sides of the country and still feel the spiritual connection. The Reign from years back would have never trusted a man to go on business trips for work. Mikel would call me in the middle of the night to talk while he was away. I would go on most of his trips, and if I couldn't he would spend the night on IM chatting with me.

As soon as we began settling in, things took a turn. Mikel was offered a job in Ohio, so we packed up and moved. He had always been a man to put others before himself, so he wanted to make sure I was okay with us moving. I had a good feeling about what would happen in Ohio. I wasn't sure what it was; I just knew it would be best for him, which would be best for us. This decision was something we prayed about.

Upon moving to Ohio, he was able to excel in his field and gain the respect of everyone he met. While Mikel was moving up the corporate ladder at his company, I was in bed with pains. I made an appointment with the doctor and was told I was pregnant. This was great news! I told my family and friends. I was so excited that we were making a new life. Finally, I was having a baby that was planned, with my husband. Life was wonderful.

Since we were in a new state and didn't know our way around, Mikel thought we should explore.

"Let's get out and check out the city, babe."

"Aight, cool."

"Why don't you drive this time?"

"You been drinking or smoking? You know you don't want me driving the car."

"Yes I do. I'm getting out, and unless you wanna stay here all day you betta come on."

We were in the middle of the street, near the airport, and I was scared. I reluctantly got into the driver's seat. *Here we go again; back to 30th and Tacoma, near the bakery. I know I'm gonna hit someone or they're gonna hit me.* I put the car in drive and let up off the brake. This time I slowly put my foot on the gas and drove. I drove down the street and around the corner. There was a car close to me. I was a little nervous, but I didn't freak out.

"Okay, stop, baby. Reign, I love you. I am not the other people in your life. I want you to be independent. I want you to be able to do anything you want. You don't need to be scared. I am right here. Even if we are not together, I want you to be able to take care of yourself. If I die or you are not with me, I want you to be better than you were when we met."

Between wet eyes, I drove around our neighborhood until I felt comfortable. No one died. There was no accident. *I am driving. So much for me being chauffeured in limos.*

"Well, that was fun, but don't get it twisted. I ain't driving all the time. I am cool with driving around here, but that's it."

"That's what you think."

"Shoot, you gon' be mad when I start driving. I'll be in Indianapolis, Atlanta, and Kentucky. You ain't gone never see me."

"I can't wait! I'm not here to hold you back. I am here to push you. When you get to Atlanta, call me."

"Granny!"

The kids were so happy to see Mom in the driveway as we pulled up.

"I came because I heard I have a grandbaby in there."

She placed her hands on my stomach. I told her I thought it was a boy and we would name him Miguel Addison. I thought that was a nice name for a little Mikel.

We had a nice visit. We showed Mom the sights in Columbus. We hung out at the Scioto River, the local movie theatre, and our favorite restaurant, Mongolian BBQ. Mikel was able to rest while we hung out with Mom. Big Smooth had been in plays and had a play that week. Mom and I were in the front row. Babygirl read with her granny all week, and we attended Princess's drum ensemble.

On Saturday, I decided to give Mom a letter I had written. The last time I had given her a letter had been fourteen years ago, and it had revealed secrets of sexual abuse. But the name on the envelope read D. She opened the letter, and it read like this:

Dear D,

I am writing to let you know that I forgive you. Before I left Indy, I went to church and I was delivered. For years, I have held you in my heart. I have had you in my life for nineteen years. You have been in my spirit tormenting me. Every relationship I have been in, you were there. In my mind, I am still nine years old and you are taking my innocence away.

I have hated you for so long. I have loved you for so long. I wondered why you had not been killed, murdered, or put in jail. I wanted to know how you could reproduce. How could a woman love and marry you? I went to church and I found out that the reason God has not reigned His wrath on you is because I am saving you. I have hated you so much, and the bitterness has killed me. But while I was holding you in my heart, it made it impossible for God to place His vengeance on you.

Since I was nine, I have not trusted a single soul. I have never had faith in God or anyone else in my life. I wait for people to hurt me because I have made up my mind that they will. I have never been able to keep a job, a relationship, or a friend. I have moved so many times I can't begin to think of what my past addresses were. I am afraid of the dark, the boogeyman, and any man who approaches me.

When a man gives me attention, I think he wants to sleep with me, even when he doesn't. I have had intercourse with four men, but I have performed sex acts with over ten men. I have been abused, mistreated, and used. For years, I thought that is what men were supposed to do.

You have made a negative impact on my life and so many others'. I cannot begin to think of the others you have or may have hurt. We both know there is at least one, since you molested us together on Halloween. I pray for your wife and children every night. I check on the sex offender list to see if you have been found out.

I never let my children out of the house without me. When they went to daycare, if a man worked there, I removed them promptly. I don't allow my children to go to sleepovers, no matter who it is. My children are questioned often about someone trying to molest them. I am very overprotective and will continue to be that way forever, I am sure. When I met my husband I didn't allow him near my kids for a while, and when I did I watched him carefully. I worry about my children whenever they are away, even when they are with family. I check the sex offender list in my city once a week.

I have been in counseling five times in my life. I have been on medication for anxiety, bipolar disorder, depression, and post-traumatic stress. I have panic attacks and do not drive much. I have never had a driver's license, and I am now twenty-eight years old. I am currently in counseling and taking anxiety meds, but I am spiritually well. I can now say I forgive you and I release you to God so He can show you He is God.

I do hope that you get help before it's too late. You are a sick man. I pray that you stay away from children, like you should have stayed *away from me. They say that people who are victims of offenders will abuse others. Well, that is a bunch of BULL! I have never and will never hurt my children or any child. I can only protect my children and any child I come in contact with. I hope no one ever hurts your children.*

Thank you for making me a strong person. What you did to me actually gave me a shock reflex. Whenever I am in pain, I can't feel it. My body goes into shock just like it did in those days. I have had three children, all natural, and I delivered my son in a car. I pulled him out and held him until I got to the hospital. I was hit by a car and tried to walk away. I had no idea my arm was broken. I was abused by my first husband, a three-hundred-pound man, on a regular basis and never felt a thing. Sometimes I beat him up for no reason at all. I have been in over twenty fights and have never lost one. Most times, I don't feel a thing.

But I feel emotional pain. I get my feelings hurt often. People say things to me and don't know the impact words have on me. I have been rejected by so many people. I have always wanted intimacy from relationships. Not just partner relationships, but ALL relationships. I have always needed attention since I never got any when I needed it the most. No one noticed that an eighteen-year-old man was raping me on a regular.

You have hurt my mother, my father, my children, and every man I have ever met. But no more; I will no longer use you as an excuse. Please do not write me back. I don't need an explanation. I am not in Indy, so please don't try to contact my mom or me. If you want to become a problem and bring some drama, my husband I am with now packs heat and he will kill you on the spot. I am trying to allow God to deal with you, but if you come at me trust you will meet the Devil sooner rather than later. I AM NO LONGER A NINE-YEAR-OLD GIRL

I release you. I forgive you. Thank you,

Reign

I gave the letter to my mom and sealed the envelope. When she returned to Indy, she gave the letter to D's mom, and the rest is history.

I am not sure if Aunt Peaches read the letter. I don't even know if D ever got it. What I do know is that I wrote it and I have released him.

Two months later, I was back at the OBGYN office. There was a problem: no heartbeat, no movement, nothing. I was sent to OSU hospital, where they performed various tests. Mikel and I were given the horrible news that the baby was gone. The nurse stood near me.

"I am so sorry, Reign. What you are seeing is a sac, an empty sac. I don't think the baby was ever fully formed."

Empty sac. She just called our baby an empty sac. I buried my head into Mikel's chest. That day my soul died, and I wanted to die with it. I was so angry. *Why? Why is this happening? I love this man. Is this my punishment for having kids so young? What did I do? Why is this happening?* I was angry at God. I blamed Mikel. He never really cried; he seemed sad for me but not about losing the baby. When I went in for surgery to pass the sac, he cried as I lay on the table. I could tell from his eyes he wanted to take the pain for me.

From November until January, I was in a state of depression. I had fleeting suicidal thoughts. I had a plan to shoot myself in the head and just end it. I would hold the gun in my hand and shake. One night, I shot through the bathroom wall. It scared Mikel so much. He hid the gun and held me all night. I lost my job. I shopped for Christmas and bought more than we could afford or needed. Mikel and I began to argue about nothing and everything.

At four in the morning, we awoke to a call that changed our lives forever. Mikel's dad had been murdered violently in Indy. He was a kind man. He ran a food pantry for the community. He would run people to the doctor's in his cab for free. He took my children to school and me to work in the late '90s. He was a cab driver, but it was a ministry not a job. He used his cab to help people not just to make a living, and he died in his cab helping people, working the neighborhood.

Mikel took it hard; his father was the only person he talked to who he felt understood him. He called him for everything. He called to talk, to listen, to vent, to ask for advice, help, and money. I was there for him, but in the back of my mind I felt guilty. I felt that I was to blame for the move from Indy and taking Mikel away from his family.

Chip, Mikel's dad, always said, "You didn't live in Ohio; you just lived on the east side of Indy." But on the eighty-five-mile-per-hour ride to Nap we all knew we should have been there.

Mikel talked on and off on the way to Indianapolis.

"If I had been driving cabs, would I have taken that run? Would my dad have called me to go into that 'hood? Would my dad have been out that late if I had called him that night?"

Once again we had questions of *why?* Now we had a dead baby and a dead father.

The next year was stressful. Mikel was still dealing heavily with the loss of his dad. We moved into a new home. It should have been a happy time. The kids were doing excellently in school—good grades, activities, and honors. They were flourishing. I was at a new job and enjoying it. Our money was good, but the hole in Mikel's heart was growing by the day. He was a time bomb waiting to explode. I was in denial and thinking everything was great.

Things around the house were normal. We were living the normal suburban life: sports, school, work, dinner, Wal-Mart, and shopping malls. The blended family thing was working fine. We had all the children with us, hanging out and having a good time. Then Mikel began to go inside himself. He would be in a room full of people and have this blank stare like he wasn't there. When he laughed it was forced. We could be in the same bed talking, but his eyes showed he was miles away. He was up and down. Around the family and friends he was fine, but at home with the children and me he was unpredictable. He lashed out about anything. Sometimes I went into the girls' room and slept with them. We were often afraid of his mood swings.

I called his mom and sisters in hopes they would call and see about him, but they would call him and tell him what I said. Mikel was two different people, a calm man at work and around his family. At home he presented a different person: an angry, out-of-control man.

"Mikel, I am not happy; I want to leave. I want a divorce."

He shook, cried, and begged me not to go. "Reign, please just stay while I am grieving. I don't want to be alone."

I went to Indiana twice, but I always came back As much as I loved him, and for all he went through with me, why couldn't I stay with him while he went through the toughest time in his life? It was time to stop thinking about myself. It was time to be a wife. I recited my vows in my mind, and I held my husband all night, for as long as he needed me to. For the first time, he cried in my arms. The healing process began for us.

For years, black people have said that counseling is for the weak, the rich, and the white. What we don't get is that we take assistance for everything else. We will take welfare and food stamps in a heart-beat. We will be at the WIC office as soon as we find out we are preg-nant. When it comes to our mental health, we medicate with drugs and alcohol.

For many years, I was laughed at by my own family for being depressed. I was made fun of for going to counseling and stress cen-ters. I was ridiculed by a very close cousin for attempting suicide and for taking antidepressants to balance my moods. This same cousin was hooked on weed for years. This same family is full of alcoholics and dope fiends. Yeah, I said dope fiends. These people made me feel bad for seeking help. If it's not church, they don't want to hear it. But church hasn't helped them yet. You can't only pray; you must also do! You must act. I don't allow people to tell me I am crazy any-more. I don't hide behind old traditions from a poisoned people. We believe in family therapy, and we are not ashamed. Our family stopped that cycle. We began to put the broken fragments of our lives back together. We started with me—the molestation, the depression, the loss of the child. We then transitioned Mikel—his dad's murder, and him being the man he wanted to be for the entire family. Then we brought the children into the fold. We began self-esteem classes, blended family therapy, and parenting.

I am aware of how blessed I am to have divorced my first husband. At first, I felt ashamed and guilty, but when I think about it, had I not, I would have never found the man God had for me. I wouldn't know how it feels to wake up every morning and be totally loved. My children wouldn't know what a healthy relationship looks like. Princess wouldn't know what it's like to be told by your father that you are adored. Babygirl wouldn't have anyone to shoot free throws with. Big Smooth wouldn't know the call to be a real man.

Princess had her last cancer screen on May 11, 2006, at the age of twelve. She has now been cancer free for seven years. She is healthy and happy. Everything she does, she does with a zeal and zest for life. She helps other children and loves being around babies.

She also plays drums in her school's marching band. Princess is a straight A student with three college scholarships. She is a joy to be around and has touched the lives of so many with her testimony. She has stomped on cancer and now lives for the Lord. On September 28, 2008, she was baptized; she continues to work for the Kingdom of God and remember her calling to please the Lord in all she does. She challenges me to be a better mother, a better person, and a better child of God. Princess is more than a conqueror.

Big Smooth plays trumpet and sings. He doesn't even know what a good voice he has. He doesn't want to sing professionally, but if he did, he could. I don't have that much influence over him with that. Right now, he wants to be a stunt man. So I am dealing with that revelation. He is very tolerant and teaches others to be that way. He makes friends with children from all over the globe. He has friends calling the house from Somalia, Japan, China, and Pakistan. His best friend's name is Hussein. He is learning Japanese, and we are tossing around the idea of him being a language expert. I hope that beats the stunt man.

Babygirl is a basketball player and an avid reader. She is so tough and feisty. If you mess with her, you may want to run. She gets straight A's and could be anything she wants to be. She has many talents, from drawing to sports, and is very creative. I admire her because she stands alone. She doesn't follow the crowd and does things based on what is right. She doesn't need attention to do anything. She helps others and makes friends with those who are mistreated.

Supporting my children keeps me busy. They are active in our church, and they want to do things God's way. I couldn't ask for more. I wish I had been like them when I was their age.

My husband has shown me the love of Christ. I realized I never knew real love. Not only did I learn about human unconditional love; I learned about God's love for me. If a man could love and care for me this much, how much more can the man who made me love me? Much more!

Things are not perfect, but we are perfectly imperfect together. We provide the balance for each other, parts becoming one whole. We are so much stronger than we were. We are the strongest, most powerful, most loving family on the planet. We have been through hell, and we are still here and still strong. I am still Mrs. Perfectionist. I always have the kids looking nice. If they are not perfect, I become upset. If one of them gets a B, I am upset. I am working on allowing myself to make mistakes.

As far as my music career, I have prayed about this, and God has told me with a loud voice that the music business is not for me. Not only is there no more money in being an artist; God has said He will not bless anything I do unless it's to glorify Him.

What He has told me is to *look to my children*. Whenever someone approaches me about singing, even in a choir or a group, I hear the same words, *Look to your children.*

I have a small studio in my home where they record songs, and I still sing in the shower. I worship in my home. I sing "Happy Birthday" in a jazzy tune and sometimes post videos on YouTube for fun, to keep me active. My big dreams are not about music anymore. My big dreams are bigger and include three college graduates. They include a lifetime of happiness with a husband who loves me more than I could ever imagine. Music will always be inside of me. It has helped me through depression, death, marriage, pain, cancer, divorce, remarriage, happiness, joy, and thirty-two years of life.

Personally, I know why I have had the life I've had. I know why I am so deep and why I view things the way I do. I know why I struggle so much with things. I have many talents: writing, singing, culinary arts, interpreting and raising children, but my purpose in life is to help others like me, other women, and girls, who need to reveal themselves and heal. Let me stop lying to myself again; God revealed His purpose to me years ago. I have been called to the ministry; I am just scared. I don't feel like I am ready. Are you guys ready for a neck-rolling tell-it-like-it-is minister? I am afraid, and feel like I have to be in a pulpit or have a church. I feel like I have to wear a white collar and a dress down to my feet. I talked with Uncle Cleo about this, and he informed me that my ministry is this book. I don't have to be ordained to be a minister. I do have to save souls, and it begins with my soul. There is so much I have to do, so many people I am going to help.

I am learning that my testimony is my ministry; my ministry is not my testimony. Thanks to Uncle Cleo, I have a new outlook on life, and on this book. My ministry will be different from what society thinks ministry should be. When I make a decision, I have to think about what God says. I am already ministering to you as you read these pages. I am a witness, and you just read my testimony.

God talks to me often, and sometimes I still don't listen. I still have demons that haunt me daily. I have to work at this thing. Be patient with me; God is not through with me yet ... He is working on me. He talks to me, and sometimes I still don't listen. You guessed it, guys. I am Rhasha Janel Halliburton Williams Hoosier, Miss Victim no more, Mrs. Depressed no more, Ms. Perfectionist, and this was my story.

Reign's Epilogue

AS I WRITE THIS BOOK, my dad and I are closer. I no longer blame him and my mom for the bad that has happened to me. I am actually glad they divorced; had they not, I would have never met Momma Lisa, who has been a Godsend to me. She and I have a special relationship. I only called her my stepmom for this book's sake. I didn't want to confuse my biological mother with my stepmom. Momma Lisa has always treated me and my siblings with love. She treats us no different from her biological children. My only wish is that I could be a stepmom to my stepchildren.

I stay in contact with my dad. If we don't talk for a while, I call him, text him, and email him like crazy. After dealing with the loss of Mikel's dad, it makes me appreciate my dad more. My dad is an excellent granddad. He is very into his grandchildren and is always there for them and to support me in raising them. I try not to dwell on the past. I try to start from today. I am attempting to bring my siblings together. My dad is the conduit; he is what connects us.

Let me address the women who wish to be married. Many women focus on the wedding instead of the working on the marriage. What people don't get about a wedding is that the event can be as beautiful as you want it to be. You can have family members paying for expensive dresses, choose pretty flowers, and have it in June. Women are often caught up in how their wedding will be. The wedding doesn't matter at all. What can you do in the marriage? What kind of life do you want? What plans will you make for that? How much work are you prepared to do? Being married is work! If you are in it just for the wedding or to say you are married, hang it up.

In the story, I call myself Reign. The name Rhasha interpreted in Swahili, letter for letter, means romantic reign. That name fits me so well. I have always wanted love, protection, and romance. I don't mean in the man/woman sense but in a love sense. I always wanted intimacy from all relationships. I wanted intimacy with my mom and dad. I wanted it in male/female relationships. I also wanted it with the Lord. I love deeply and very hard.

As far as the name Reign goes, I reign over any situation I am in. I reign over my children. I reign as a wife, although maybe not in the way most would think. I do not reign like a tyrant; I reign as a strong woman. I reign over darkness and evil that tries to control my life and my family. I reign over the curses that haunt my family. I reign in any place I reside.

I am a leader in most circles, and I will dominate most groups I am involved with (other than my opinionated co-authors). It has always been this way. When I walk into a room, I can change the energy in that room. If I am angry, the room fills with anger. If I am happy, all is good in my space. I do not shrink, nor have I ever shrunk, even while I was being abused. I reign in love. I am just that: Romantic Reign.

This is what I wish someone had told me when I was being molested, physically abused, and victimized, when I was hurting myself. Know that you are not alone: there are people who can help you. I don't care if you think you are by yourself; you are not. There is always a pastor, teacher, aunt, cousin, friend—someone who loves you. Talk to that person and tell them what is happening to you. If you have a feeling something is not right, it's probably not. Secrets are never good if you are being hurt. Find someone and tell him or her what is bothering you. There is someone; I promise. You may not see them at first; just look a little closer. There is one friend who will never leave you; he's always there, even when you turn your back on him. This leads me to my next point.

Prayer changes things. I know it sounds clichéd. You hear the church people saying it, and you think, *Please, what is prayer gonna do for me?* Let me be a witness. Prayer worked for me when I was too dumb to pray for myself. You did read the story right? My Uncle Cleo prayed for me and walked around my house with a box of dough-nuts. My mother, Aunt Betty, and a whole church prayed for me. Sometimes I could feel it. I learned very recently how to pray and taught my children. Now that's a trait to pass down to the next gen-eration. I have always been loud and boisterous, but I would never pray, and if I did, it was quietly or silently. I was worried about using big words and speaking in tongues. I learned that I am praying to my heavenly father, not to a crowded room.

If someone is abusing you physically, leave. Please leave! Leave if you are abusing someone else. I was abused and then became an abuser. It will never get better; it will only get worse. The person will not change; you can't change them. If they tell you to stay, that they will get help, tell them you will support them from afar. To those of you who have children, it's not safe for them to see you being abused. It is not best to stay with someone who is hurting you and use the children as your reason. I don't care if you have to go to a shelter or move three states away. If you have to leave everything you have and go for broke, do it! You could be saving your own life.

Lastly, I would say, love yourself. Most of my issues and problems began because I hated myself. I hated what I saw in the mirror. I was ashamed and felt guilty about the molestation. When things happened to me, I felt it was my fault. I never felt worthy of love. I tried to take my life because I didn't think my life held any value. Because of that, I make sure to tell my babies how much I adore them. I tell them how beautiful, smart, and talented they are. When they have a bad hair day or a pimple, I don't let them think for one moment that it makes them ugly. I don't blame them for the things that have happened to them. I tell them who is responsible so they never feel ashamed or guilty. I remind them of how important they are to me and to God, but here is the awesome part: so are you! Thank you for taking this journey of revealing and healing with me. When will you begin to reveal and heal? When will you be ready to write your story?

Rhasha

Reality

Growing Up Twice

LIFE CHANGED DRASTICALLY FOR ME. My third pregnancy took me completely by surprise. I was once again pregnant and alone, although I didn't have to be. Tony made it clear that he would be there for me and the baby. I didn't want to be pregnant by someone I didn't love or care to be with, so I pushed him away. I let him know about all my doctor's appointments and filled him in on how things were progressing, but I kept him at arm's length. I didn't want him as my boyfriend, and I didn't want him thinking that's what I wanted. Besides, Jeremy was a factor in it, too. We had never stopped messing around.

Before I got pregnant, Jeremy would pay me for sex sometimes. I obliged, partly because I still loved him, and partly because I knew I could. Jeremy knew about the pregnancy, but I assured him that my baby wasn't his. He was a little nervous because he had a girlfriend. She knew about me and felt threatened by me, even though they had bought a house together. She was the one who told me about their marriage plans. *He's getting married? Why didn't he tell me?*

Charise started treating me differently after she knew I was going to keep the baby. It started with avoidance; then she lost her job. When her birthday came around, I bought her a present. She had a job interview the Monday after her birthday, but she blew it off. She went out of town and stayed gone for about a month or so, leaving me behind to foot all of the bills in the apartment. I was down on myself because it really hurt me. I felt like the person I trusted the most had turned her back on me when I needed her. The more Charise pulled away from me, the closer I got to Betty.

Betty was already two months pregnant, so we formed an even tighter bond. We knew our children would be friends for life. We were always out together, shopping, going to the movies, or just hanging out.

There were times we would be out shopping and one of us would decide we wanted watermelon, so we would go to the store, buy the slices, and eat the watermelon right in the car. When one of us had a craving, we would call the other one to voice the craving, and a few minutes later, we were headed to the restaurant to satisfy the urge. I thought she was strong because she actually worked three jobs to support herself. Her baby's father had left for the Army, so he wasn't around. She bought him a ring and was ready to become a family when he returned.

She was about seven months pregnant, I was five, when her baby's father came back from the Army. He told her that he didn't want her; she was too fat, and he didn't love her. It crushed her, and it crushed me to witness it. Being the friend that I am, I was ready to give him a serious beatdown, belly and all. I felt her pain and her angst. I was so angry that he would say that to someone who was about to deliver his baby. I know she cared about him. I tried to be there for her through that time. I wanted to make her feel better, so I took her to the movies that day.

I continued to grow, but I must admit, I was beautiful when I was pregnant. So beautiful that an older guy at work named Bruce tried to get with me. I hesitated at first, but he reeled me in with his charisma and charm. I had never felt sexier, because guys were still trying to talk to me. I looked like a nicely built, plus-size woman. Many people didn't realize I was pregnant until the very end of my pregnancy.

I found out that I was having a girl, and I couldn't have been happier. Ever since I had been a little girl, I had wanted to have my son first and my daughter second. A girl needed a big brother to protect her. Being the oldest, I never had anyone to protect me. I was always the protector.

During my pregnancy, I was relatively calm. I tried to not let things get to me, but sometimes they did. When it got closer for me to deliver, I would sometimes cry for no reason at all. I worked and saved up as much money as I could. I asked my co-workers to give me a baby shower, but I planned my own baby shower at my mother's house.

Even though I helped plan Betty's baby shower, she didn't help one bit with mine. I didn't have the money, but I bought her baby some basic things like blankets and sleepers. She, in turn, gave me used stuff her baby couldn't fit. I really didn't understand why that happened. The baby shower I threw for myself wasn't grand at all. I really didn't get a lot of things, and I had to decorate my mom's apartment myself.

My co-workers gave me a baby shower at work on October 22, 1999. I received so many gifts. *This is ridiculous. How could my co-workers do more for me than my own people?* The people at work were so generous to me, and I cried on the way home. The shower was right on time, because I went into labor on October 24, 1999.

Betty decided to help me in my distress by taking me to the mall. I was emotional all the time, and I think she knew it was about time for me to deliver.

"Girl, slow down. You are walking the shit outta me!"

"You'll be in labor soon, probably tomorrow. C'mon, keep walking."

"I'm tired. Take me to Momma's house."

I went to my mother's house to pick up Prince. As we stood in the kitchen, the familiar pains started.

"What's wrong with you?" she asked.

"Betty walked me to death today," I said, frowning.

"Girl, get your ass on home and rest."

I grabbed Prince's things and left.

I went home and not even two hours later, I picked up the phone and paged Tony. He called back a few minutes later.

"Yeah."

"Hey, it's time. I need to go to the hospital. I'm in labor."

"Okay, I'll be there in a few," Tony said.

My next call was to my mother.

"Ma, I'm having contractions. Tony is taking me to the hospital. Can you come get Prince?"

"Alright. I'll be there in a minute."

Tony took forever to get there, and my pain was mounting. When he finally did get to my house, he waited until we were in the car and said, "We've got to stop and get some gas or else we ain't gonna make it to the hospital."

"Tony! Are you kidding me? You think this baby cares about some damn gas? Hurry up!" I wanted to cuss him out because I knew this was his form of payback for keeping him at arm's length, but I hurt too much to say anything.

We made it to the hospital, and they took me back to the maternity ward. This labor was different than when I had had Prince, because I was having extremely hard contractions but I wasn't dilating. The nurses made me walk around. I walked the halls with Tony by my side until I couldn't take it anymore.

The doctors were going to send me home because my contractions weren't producing any results; my cervix just wasn't opening. If they had looked closer, they would have realized that the scar tissue on my cervix from the cryosurgery I had had at sixteen was preventing the dilation. Before they sent me home, they hooked me up to the monitor and stepped out. A few minutes later, a team of nurses and doctors flooded my room. "Sir, I'm sorry, but I'm going to have to ask you to step out."

I didn't know why they were making Tony leave, and it freaked me out.

I soon learned that my unborn baby's heartbeat had decelerated during a contraction. Her head was in position, so the doctor essentially ripped the scar tissue from my cervix, which was more painful than the contractions. She wiggled her fingers on top of my baby's head. The heartbeat started again. I was admitted.

After the baby and I were stabilized, the doctors took me into a birthing room and let Tony back in. I squeezed Tony's hand so hard when they gave me the epidural that he punched me in the arm. The nurse saw this and raised an eyebrow, but she didn't say anything and neither did I. It shocked me, but I figured that was a part of my payback.

At six a.m., I called my mother and filled her in on the progress.

At eight ten a.m. on October 25, I gave birth to a healthy seven-pound baby girl. Tony stood in the corner as she was being born. The look on his face was priceless. I thought he was going to pass out.

I named her Cherub. She was the most beautiful baby I ever saw. As soon as she exited the womb, the doctor laid her on my chest. She didn't cry. She looked at me and yawned, her deep dimples sinking into her jaw. She had a puzzled look on her face, and I smiled.

"Oh, she has dimples!" I said, beaming. "She's perfect. Hi, my precious. Hi, Cherub. It's so nice to finally meet you."

Charise came in about five minutes after she was born, but Tony left.

"Dammit! I missed it," she said. She walked over to the incubator and looked at Cherub.

"Thank goodness she took after you in looks!"

Later that day, a doctor came into my room. I had just finished breast feeding for the second time. The doctor asked, "I see here that you want to have a tubal ligation. Are you sure?"

"Yes."

"What if you decide to have another child? What if something happens?"

"I don't want anymore."

"What if you lose one?"

"Even if I lose one."

"What if you get married?"

"I won't."

"Okay, we'll get it done this afternoon." He gave me a sideward glance and walked out the room. I still wonder what he was thinking. *I am twenty-three and I am never going to get married. That would be the only thing to change my mind. Who wants to marry someone with an already made family? It's me and them against the world.* That's the way that it had always been, so I had no reason to think differently.

I went home the next day. I couldn't have wished for a better baby. She was exceptionally good; she didn't cry at all. I would wake up in a panic sometimes because she didn't cry. She would be awake and would just lie there and look around. She wasn't spoiled as my first. *If she had been my first, high school would have been easier for me.*

Tony paid my rent for one month, but I still sought assistance from our local Trustee's Office. I was out of work for six weeks. I had managed to save a little money, but it wasn't enough.

Charise moved out, and I went back to work. My mother watched Cherub for me. On my first day back, Cherub contracted a fever. I rushed her to the hospital, and she was admitted. I missed another week of work, and another week of pay. They never found out what was wrong with her. They gave her a string of antibiotics, and she had no more health issues.

I didn't want to move, but I had no choice. I couldn't afford the rent since Charise had moved out. I moved into a low-income apartment shortly after Cherub's hospital stay. My cousin, Jake, and Sasha's boyfriend helped me move.

All the while, Bruce and I talked almost every day via the telephone. He was really cool. There were days when he would take me to work. He had a nice apartment and a nice car. Bruce was an older guy and very manipulative. He ran an adult website, and he only worked at my job for "human interaction."

When things got a little serious, he really tore me down and hurt my feelings. He was supposed to take me to get a manicure and pedicure, along with a dinner, for my birthday. The day of, he called me and said, "I talked to someone about that, and they said that kind of present was for a girlfriend, not just a friend." He came by my house and dropped off a birthday card. I was livid because this was a letdown. I lined up a babysitter and everything. I was so disappointed *I thought friends did things like that for each other, and this was just an excuse not to.*

We continued to talk on the phone, but our conversations were literally belittling to me. We talked about marriage, not to each other, but marriage in general. He told me, "You know, you probably won't get married, ever. I mean, you are what, twenty-three, twenty-four? If it doesn't happen by the age of thirty, then it probably won't happen at all. I mean you are a good girl and everything, but marriage? It just may not happen for you."

"I don't know what would make you say that. I know that I am a good person, mothafucka. Fuck you!" I said, and I hung up the phone. That was the end of him.

When Cherub was eight months old, Tony asked me to file for child support against him, but I knew that what he really wanted was a DNA test. I didn't blame him and went willingly. Two months later the DNA confirmed what I already knew: she was his child. He was happy, and we attempted to have a relationship. I really tried to love him for my daughter, but I just couldn't. At first things between us were okay. We were boyfriend and girlfriend, and he doted on his daughter, but he was also lazy, and that bothered me. He was broke, so to speak. He was a DJ but wasn't getting much work. We still, after all of that time, didn't have much in common.

He was a good guy, but he didn't have my heart. I told him I loved him, and I did, but it wasn't a romantic love. I loved him for giving me my baby girl. Prince loved him, but I wanted more, and he couldn't give it to me. He was a big kid.

I understood that dialysis took a lot out of him physically, but he could do everything else he wanted to do. He would hang out with his friends and play video games when he wanted to.

"Why do you always go play games? You live here."

"I don't live here. My name ain't on no bills."

"You have a key to my apartment. You are here every day and every night."

"Once again, my name ain't on any of the bills. I live with my parents."

One day, we got into a heated argument. I can't remember what the argument was about. I just remember saying, "Oh yeah? You can eat a fat pussy and suck a fat dick!"

The next thing I knew, he rushed me on the couch. He head butted me, and I jumped up and ran into the kitchen. He opened the freezer, smacked me in the face with a bag of frozen chicken breasts, and ripped the oven door off its hinges. I was stunned, and I had a bruise on my cheek. I fought him until the police came. I don't know who called the police. He packed up the food he had just bought and took it with him, leaving me with a little food. My children sat there and watched the whole thing. I already knew what they were feeling because I had felt the same thing when I watched my father beat my mom.

We seemed to get into more and more arguments. The more we argued, the harder we fought physically. One time, I threw a bar of soap down the steps at him. I didn't intend to hit him, but it bonked him hard, right in the back of his head. I had already started walking away when I heard him coming up the steps. I rushed into the bathroom and closed the door. He tore the door off and came in after me. Prince called my brothers. The two of them, along with friends, ran two blocks down the street to my house.

They ran up the stairs into my bedroom, where Tony was. They beat him up in my bed. When it was all over, Tony's mouth was bloody, and he left. Betty's brother, Samuel, had also heard about the fight and ran to my house. He told me, "He's lucky. If I was here that nigga woulda been dead. Matter of fact he better hope I don't find him."

The last straw was on a Saturday afternoon in June. I had just picked Tony up from the dialysis center. I was getting ready to go to the wedding of one of Betty's friends. I knew he was tired, but I also needed him to get ready for his part-time job at a local record store. We were already behind, and I was his ride.

I got out of the shower with a towel wrapped around me.

"Get yo' lazy ass up! C'mon, you're gonna make me late!"

"Okay," he said.

He still didn't move. Betty had arrived, and I was still undressed.

"C'mon, Tony, get up! I understand you tired, but we have got to go."

"I said, Okay."

I stomped around, agitated because he wouldn't budge. I can't remember exactly what happened next, or what was said, but he jumped up at me and pushed me into the closest. I fell backward and hit my head. The towel came off me as I jumped up, and I punched him repeatedly. He took the hits and didn't fight back. I walked away with a shiner on my head. I was unaware that Prince had called the police to the house again, until I heard the sirens coming down the street.

The police arrived, took one look at my head, and arrested him. It hurt my feelings, but I knew that I had had enough. My kids witnessed the abusive behavior, and I didn't want to go through it anymore. I still went to the wedding, which was beautiful. My heart ached because I longed for my own wedding day. I held back tears. I started to sink back down into my depressed state of mind. I felt lonelier than I ever had before.

I went to court for the fight between Tony and me. I told the judge that I didn't want him to go to jail, because he was a good father to his daughter. I knew that he loved her, and being separated from her wouldn't be good for her. If we could get along for her sake, I was okay. I suggested that he attend anger management classes, which he agreed to. Cherub still had her dad.

In December 2000, I got a job working at a mail hub. I really enjoyed the job because it paid very well, and I made a lot of money. One check was enough to last me for almost two months. I saved my money so that I could finally get a car. I was supposed to be hired on within 90 days; instead, I was laid off, and depressed again. I filed for bankruptcy, and it was discharged. I had nothing: no job, no car.

One night, Betty and I went to a small club on the west side of town. I ran into an old neighbor I had always had a crush on. He noticed me first.

"Hey, remember me?"

I turned around and looked up. I was surprised to see that it was Calvin.

"Hey, how are you?" I said as I gave him a hug. He was about six three and chocolate. My weakness.

"Fine. You are looking good."

"So are you."

"Lemme buy you a drink."

He bought my vodka and cranberry, and we went to a table. We talked the night away as we rested between dance breaks. He took my shoes off and massaged my feet in the club, even though I thought it was funny and way over the top. I gave him my number anyway.

Calvin was a nice person. I got to know the adult side of him versus the kid side that I had always known. I learned that he was moving to Gary, Indiana. Of course I was a little disappointed when I heard that news because I would rather he stay in Indianapolis so we could possibly get to know each other and maybe have a relationship.

I later found out he was divorced and had two kids. I already knew his sisters, who were the twins I lived next door to in the projects, so when he did make the move, we kept in touch. We stayed in contact via a popular networking site called BlackPlanet.

I was invited to a friend of mine named Brian's wedding, which opened up the perfect opportunity for me to go to Gary and visit Calvin.

I stayed with Calvin, his sister Karen, and her family. I was welcomed with open arms. I drove down on a Friday and left on Sunday. The wedding was that Saturday. Since I was in the area, I also visited my dad, who lived in Calumet City, Illinois. The visit with Dad was short, and I took Calvin to meet him.

Calvin and I had wonderful, body-tingling sex that weekend. I thought he was really feeling me, but, once again, I was in over my head.

He came to Indianapolis and stayed a weekend with me. I enjoyed his company. Shortly after the visit, he started getting religious on me; I mean like real deep.

"I feel like something in my soul ain't right, Reality."

"What do you mean?"

"I'm going to hell 'cause I'm laying up with you, and we are not married."

"Um, why do you say that?"

"Were you baptized in the name of Jesus or in the name of the Father, the Son, and the Holy Spirit?"

"I was baptized in the name of Jesus."

"You are not truly baptized. "

"What?"

"I can't do this. It's wrong. It's fornication. God don't like this."

I cared about him, but at the same time, I figured he had grown tired of me. Either that, or he was seeing someone else. At that point, I knew we were a pretty done deal.

I still kept things going on with Jeremy. He would tell his fiancée that he was going to work, and he would spend the night at my house. I attribute my stupidity to loneliness. Here he was, engaged to be married, yet he was spending nights with me. His fiancée would call me and, at times, come by my house. I didn't trip; she had the ring, the house, and the kid. I was a side item, but secretly I still loved him. I got increasingly agitated. I always had the feeling that while I was good enough to lay up with, I wasn't good enough to marry. That revelation stung me, especially since Bruce had told me that marriage was not in my future. *I guess it won't happen to me. Bruce was right. This man can still come over here and sleep with me while another woman has the ring. What am I doing?*

Jeremy came over around midnight one night as I sat at my computer writing poetry. He sat near me and watched me. It was obvious that he had smoked some weed. He looked especially handsome that night. We were silent. I looked over at him and said, "Jeremy, why are you here? Did you come to get some ass?"

He was stunned at what I had said, but he smiled. "I came to see you."

"Jeremy, go home to your girl." He looked down at his feet and then back up at me. He got up and walked out, but that wasn't the last time I would hear from him.

Coincidentally, his wedding date was March 25, my son's birthday. The day before his wedding, he called me constantly. I knew he wanted to come over, but I didn't answer the phone. I knew that if I did, Jeremy would be in my bed, and his 'wife' would have been left at the altar. I didn't want to ruin it, because he made that bed for himself. He told me that he was unsure. It wasn't my problem anymore. He made his choice, and it wasn't me.

I stayed on BlackPlanet when I was supposed to be working. I didn't think too seriously about it at first, but then I started chatting with guys who had some of the same interests as I did. One guy named Brad asked me to meet him at a local Subway. Brad was handsome but very quiet; I was not at all disappointed at what I saw.

Brad was the kind of person you would think was sad because he was so quiet. He was a poet, like myself, and we had some interesting conversations. We hung out a few times, and I found out that he was a fun person. He was extremely deep, and he made my mind work. He put thoughts into words, and I loved that. I got the sense that he was feeling me, but he started pulling away. I knew he had been laid off. His trade was cement work, and there were some job issues. I didn't think he needed the added pressures of a girlfriend. I did ask him if our relationship was going anywhere. He wasn't ready yet, so I backed off a little bit and gave him some space. I continued to chat on BlackPlanet, and I met Roger.

Roger was another story. He was all about the flash, and I saw a window of opportunity. I knew that with all that flash, cash had to be around somewhere. I tried to get in, but of course he was one step ahead of me.

He was hilarious, and whenever we talked on the phone, I would be in fits of laughter. He worked for an area pharmaceutical company, and he hustled on the side.

Roger turned me on to *Def Poetry Jam* because he knew I liked poetry. I would go to his house weekly to watch it, because I didn't have cable. Before I could get close to my opportunity to "get in where I fit in," he scored. He got me drunk as hell one night, and we had sex before I wanted to. Actually, I didn't want him or the sex. I just wanted some of his shine.

We still talked, and, I admit, I harassed the hell out of him. He got over when I had just started. I was pissed I hadn't stuck to my plan. Needless to say, it was a done deal. I chalked it up and kept moving.

That's when I met Corey. We chatted on BlackPlanet for a while, and eventually we talked on the phone. He was also hilarious, and he had a very attractive personality. We agreed to meet at a downtown movie theatre to see the movie *Training Day*.

He told me what he would be wearing, and he said he would have curly hair. I dressed in a black denim outfit that had a hint of red in it, and some really tall deep red boots, and drove downtown. I walked up the steps, saw this huge afro, and knew immediately it was him. I walked up behind him, put my hand in is hair, and said "Curly hair, huh?" He turned around, and the look on his face was priceless. He said, "My God, you're beautiful." I said, "Thanks. Did you get the tickets?"

He flashed them at me, and we walked to the concession stand, where I got my usual, popcorn and Coke. We walked into the theatre and talked before the movie came on. He seemed really cool.

As I fell in love with Denzel Washington being a bad boy, Corey reached over and held my hand. I wondered why he did that, but I didn't ask him about it. After it was over, Corey said, "I'm not ready for our date to be over." He ran to the ATM, withdrew some money, turned to me, and said, "Where do you want to go? Let's go have a drink."

We walked down to Jillian's, a restaurant that's also a bar, game room, bowling alley, and club. We went to the game room, and there I had my first shot of tequila. We stayed for a while, taking shots.

"I think I'm drunk. I'm ready to go," I said.

"Okay. Can you drop me off at home?"

I didn't know that he didn't have transportation, but we had had a great date, so I agreed to take him home.

We arrived at his house. He lived on the west side of town, close to an area called Haughville. I had to pee really badly.

"Corey, I really have to pee. Can I use your restroom?"

"Sure."

He ran in before me, as if trying to straighten up before I came in. I used the restroom and said, "Thanks."

"Thank you for trusting me to let you use my restroom."

I laughed and said, "Good night."

My phone was ringing when I walked through the door.

"Hello?"

"Hey, beautiful. I was just checking on you, you know, making sure you made it home alright."

"Yes I did. Thanks. I had a good time."

"Me, too. Well, goodnight."

"Goodnight."

Corey and I really clicked. He was really off brand, and his humor was different. We went around the town, to clubs and different restaurants. One day, we were walking down the street toward Jillian's, and I had my coat open.

"Reality, it really is cold out here. You should zip up."

"Naw, I'm not that cold."

"Really, I think you should."

He proceeded to walk in front of me and grabbed my coat like he was going to zip it. I backed away, but he pulled me closer and kissed me. The kiss shocked me. I had just thought we were good friends, and I really didn't expect for it to go further than that. I felt like he really was digging me, and that felt good.

Corey made decent money as a producer for a small video production company. Even with all of his good points, there was something about him that wasn't right. We had debates about religion, and he said he didn't believe in the Bible because it was man made. I had never heard this from anyone before, and that intrigued me, being a Southern Gal, knowing nothing but the Bible. Plus, I was in church every Sunday. The talks really opened my eyes to different views about things I never thought about. He was really interesting, from his music choices, to his clothing, to his views, and I liked it. That was the problem. I liked it a little too much and felt myself falling in that same trap of falling for someone too fast, before I get to really know them.

Corey was really freaky, but I liked that about him. Even with all of his freaky ways, we only had sex four times. Fear made me pull away from him.

I started standing him up for dates and not calling. He got tired of that.

"Hey, Reality. My brother and his girl are coming into town, and I want you to meet them."

"Okay. I'll call you when I get home."

"Okay, they are pulling up now, so we will wait on you."

"Okay."

I never called, and I never made it over there. I called about a week later.

"Oh, you know my number now?"

"Yeah. What's up?"

"I guess you think that I'm just supposed to be glad you're calling me?"

"Man, something came up. I'm sorry."

"Sorry? You embarrassed the hell outta me, and all you can say is 'I'm sorry'?"

"You're really mad, huh?"

"I tell you what, don't call me anymore. Okay?"

"Corey, it's not that deep, I mean ..."

DIAL TONE.

Did that really happen? I gave him a call a few days later, and he told me again to never call him again. I was devastated because of how things had happened. I wasn't in love with him, but Corey had potential, and it was me who messed things up. He was a good guy, handsome, funny, and got along with the family, but he wasn't my boyfriend. He always lived his dream and didn't let the world's opinions stop him. I was afraid of getting too close and being hurt, and I ended up being hurt anyway. I cried for days. I called Charise and cried to her because I had no one else to talk to.

A few weeks later, I got a call at work from Charise. Her boyfriend had a nephew named Jayme who was in work release.

She told me, "Girl, he is tall, dark, and handsome, just how you like them!"

"No criminals, please. I don't want to be a part of that."

"Come hang out for lunch. Chris is gonna cook."

As soon as I walked through the door, they bombarded me with compliments for all of Jayme's virtues.

"He's a good dude," said Chris. "You would like him."

I still said no. I went over the next day, for lunch, and again it was the same thing. They called me the next day, until I eventually caved in and told them to give him my number.

For about three days, I noticed a lot of payphone calls on my caller ID. I wondered who they were from. One particular day, I walked through my door just as the phone was ringing. It was a payphone call. I answered it.

"Hello?"

"Can I speak to … uh … Real?" said a very sexy deep voice.

"Real doesn't live here."

"Oh."

"Reality does."

"Yeah, that's who I want."

"This is she."

He laughed.

"What's so funny?"

"I'm sorry I got your name wrong."

"Who's this?"

"Jayme."

"Jayme? Oh, your Chris's nephew."

He told me that he was in work release and that he had two five-year-old kids, a boy and a girl. He also told me they had different mothers.

"Oh no. A hot boy," I said.

He laughed.

"Naw, not like that. I'm cool …"

I told him that I had two kids as well, a boy and a girl, and that they were ten and two. He told me he was twenty-four. I asked him what he was looking for.

"Nothing, nothing but friendship," he said.

"Cool with me. I don't have a man. Too much damn work."

He chuckled. "Naw, I'm not like that. For real. All you gotta do is keep it real with me, and everything will be cool."

"That's funny. I'm the same way," I replied.

"Well, since we are alike, can I call you sometime?"

"Yeah, you seem aight."

"Well, I gotta go. I'll be calling you, Miss Lady."

"I'm sure you will."

We both laughed.

"Okay then … talk to you soon."

We talked every day from that day forward. He'd call me at work and at home. We talked so often that I got a cell phone. His conversation enthralled me; his voice captivated me. He was smart, reserved, and funny. We talked on the phone for two weeks before I ever saw him.

Our first face-to-face meeting made me nervous. I took off from work and met him and Chris in the parking lot of a White Castle. I walked over to the car and didn't even look at him. I was so nervous. I spoke to Chris but didn't speak to Jayme. He leaned over and said, "Hello." He took my breath away.

He was the darkest, sexiest man I had ever seen. He was clean cut and had on Gucci glasses. He had on a baby blue sweater and dark blue jeans. His lips were nice, and his smile was electrifying. I managed to say hello back. He got out of the car, I saw his frame, and I knew instantly that I would be sexing him one day. His shoulders were broad, and he had long arms and legs. He was stocky and simply perfect.

We got in my car and went to the mall, where he filled out some applications for a job. I then took him back to the work release center where he was staying.

"Thanks for picking me up. It was good to see you in person."

"Likewise," I said.

"I'll call you later."

"Okay."

I sat in the car and watched him walk across the street; actually, I sat there for more than 15 minutes just staring. He had a fix on me, and I barely knew him. *This time, I'ma let it go where it goes.*

We were inseparable. I would leave work to pick him up. We went out to lunch with Chris and Charise, but he never tried to kiss me or touch me inappropriately. I thought it was very noble of him. One day, I had a cold and called in sick to work. He called the house, and asked me to come and pick him up. He wasn't too far from my house, so I did. I took him to look for a job, the reason he was out in the first place. Jayme took me to get some cough drops and medicine; then he took me to TGI Friday's for lunch.

We sat in a booth by the window. Our hands were on the table; he reached out and stroked my hand. I noticed his hand was sweaty and he was shaking.

"Babe, what's wrong?"

"You make me nervous."

"Why?"

"Because I never met anyone quite like you."

"What do you mean?"

"You're different. You like me even though I don't have nothing. You go to church and you take good care of your kids. You go to work every day, you got your own, you're ambitious, and to top it off, you are beautiful."

This nigga is buttering me up. I like him too.

He was truly different, and nothing like I had expected when we first met. He didn't try to bed me, he didn't slick talk me, and he was sweet. Even though I was sick, lunch was wonderful. We laughed and talked like we'd known each other our whole lives. When I took him back to the work release center, I parked the car, and we talked for a second. We locked eyes and enjoyed the moment. He reached over and embraced me; as he pulled away, I kissed him, cold and all. He didn't seem to mind, because he kissed me back.

His kiss sent shocks through my body. I trembled, and held my breath. His lips were so soft, and he smelled so good. He made me feel good, so good I couldn't even describe it. I had never had that feeling, and it scared me, but I didn't give in to the fear. *Reality, this is going too fast. But I like it. I like him.*

A few weeks later, I bought a new living room set. It would be delivered on March 4, between noon and four p.m. We made plans for him to come over, and I would cook lunch while we waited for the furniture to be delivered. *This would be our first time together at the house. Uh-oh.*

That morning, I went to work and left about eleven to met him at a Marsh, where he was filling out a job application. I forged a few signatures on his job tracking sheet so that we could get to my apartment. When we pulled up in front of my apartment, he told me that his cousin had lived in the exact same apartment. I thought that was neat.

He helped me move my old furniture out of the apartment. I vacuumed the floor and started the chicken wings and waffles, the lunch he asked me for. He put in the movie *Baby Boy*. As soon as we started the movie, the delivery guys were knocking on the door. As I cooked, they brought the furniture in and arranged it. We ate lunch and finished the movie sitting comfortably on the new furniture.

After the movie, he looked at me, smiled, and said, "Thank you for lunch."

"You're welcome." He kissed me on my shoulder. I looked him in the eyes, and he kissed me on the lips. Eventually, the necking led to my bedroom.

We didn't have much time, so it was fast. We got up and showered, and I drove him back to the work release center. He called me later that evening.

"Hey, Reality."

"Hey, babe."

"I, um, I want to talk about what happened today."

"Mmm hmm."

"I just didn't feel right just having sex with you, and you are not my girl."

"Mmm hmm."

"Will you be my lady?"

"You know I will."

It was official. We became an item.

My family thought I was crazy because he was a convicted criminal and still in work release. Everyone thought that it was infatuation or a phase, but we became really serious, really fast. At times, I thought I had lost my mind.

Your Music ...

May 2001

Mystical music surrounds me, moves me, engulfs me... it is your love
The notes I hear no one else can
Your passion ... music ... squeezes me and holds my breath
The warmth of you on my neck caresses me and your music creates a
*   sensation*
only you know.

How my passion, my fire, my soul all belong to you
Life is unfulfilled if it's not you I see
Your music is mesmerizing, hypnotizing
We are a bond
Too strong to be broken
Too weak to control

He first asked me to marry him in June. We had been official for about three months. I thought he was playing.

"Reality, I'm telling you, you will be by wife one day."

"Okay. Whatever you say."

I laughed at the notion. *Wife? Naw.* He was laying it on really thick. He was in my head, so yet again to protect my feelings, I tried to hold him at arm's length, but he was so damn irresistible. He wouldn't go away.

In July, he was late getting back to the work release center a few times and violated. They sent him back to prison for four months that August. He would be out in November. I cried because I didn't know what I would do. I couldn't figure out if I should stay with him or walk away. We had been dating for only four months, but I loved him, so I decided to stay.

While he was locked up, I visited virtually every week. I accepted phone calls and wrote many letters to him. He wrote me, and asked me again if I would marry him. He called me after I received that particular letter.

"Are you serious?"

"Reality, I am serious."

"Sure, okay," I replied.

We talked about where he was going to live once he came home, and he was adamant that he wouldn't come live with me. He and his cousin, Barry, had discussed living in the house his grandparents owned until he got on his feet. About two weeks after that conversation, Barry moved in with his girlfriend, and Chris moved into the house. He didn't want to live there, and he didn't want to move in with his mother. I told him, "You don't have to go through all that. Just come stay with me," with no hesitation. My mother always questioned me about where he was going to stay. I hadn't counted on him really moving in with me, but it happened.

November 6, 2002, was his release date. I went to the grocery store because I had told him I would cook him something nice for dinner. I had on sexy lingerie under my clothing. I went to the prison to pick up my man.

I waited about thirty minutes for him to come out. When he did, I smiled. I walked up to him, and he hugged me and said, "Let's get outta here."

I drove home, and the first thing he wanted to do was take a long hot shower. I had other plans. I undressed in front of him, and he caught a glimpse of my fishnet nightie.

He said "Aw yeah?" and stood up to grab me. We made love for hours. It was so passionate and hot that I could swear flames were coming out of my pores. Afterward, we showered, got dressed, and went visiting friends and family His friends came by and took him out to a strip club. When he came back, he was ready to do it again. I was in heaven.

He had to be on probation for two years, which I thought was okay. We set the date for the wedding, and still no one, including me, believed it would happen. I still didn't take him seriously, because I had been hurt and let down so many times before. I was waiting for the bomb to fall and reveal itself, but it never did.

On Valentine's Day in 2003, we got our rings. They didn't cost much, but he officially proposed to me on one knee inside the mall at the jewelry store. I was embarrassed, but he looked so handsome and sincere, and that's when I realized that he was really serious.

We started planning the wedding and took our engagement pictures. In March, we moved out of the low-income apartments and bought a house. March also marked our one-year anniversary.

I asked Charise, Betty, and his sister Janice to be in my wedding party. Charise was fine with it, until I told her I would like for her to have her hair done, and not in a big ghetto fabulous ponytail. Not that I had anything against the ponytail; I wanted my wedding to be elegant and chic. I wanted her to try a different look. She was angered and pulled out. Janice was gung ho from the start. She was hysterically funny, and I enjoyed having her around. However, she could not stand Betty.

We went to the bridal shop to pick out the dresses. My colors were white and periwinkle blue. The dresses would be standard dresses, but Betty's dress was different because she was the maid of honor. Her dress had a bare shoulder.

"I don't like it," she said.

"What do you mean? I like that dress," I replied.

"I mean, I don't think it's cute at all."

"Dammit,," Janice interjected, "If Reality wants me to wear this ugly ass fuckin' blue dress, then dammit I will. This ain't about what you like; it's about Reality, so shut the fuck up and get this shit ordered. Regardless, I'ma look good." Betty was stunned; I laughed. Janice was so straightforward, and she said it without raising her voice. I didn't know Janice that well, but I could tell we would be close.

A week before the wedding, Betty was supposed to give me a bridal shower. She was my best friend and maid of honor, so I figured this would be nice. I requested a male stripper.

"I don't want that going on," she said.

"If it's about money, I'll pay for it."

"I don't want that in my house."

"We can have it at the club house, then."

There was no stripper, and no food. A friend of mine made some taco dip, and then she went to Church's to get a box of chicken. The whole thing lasted maybe two hours. A trickle of gifts adorned her coffee table. I was thoroughly disappointed. *The people at work gave me a better bridal shower than this, and they barely know me. I should have planned it myself.* No one had fun, and I was embarrassed.

We were married on June 21, 2003. We had a very nice wedding considering our shoestring budget. I was in a daze as I admired my husband in his all-white tuxedo. Our children were pictures of perfection. His son was his little mini-me, and my son was Dapper Don in his tux. Our girls looked like little black princesses. My friend Reign sang at my wedding as the wedding party marched down. It was funny because she had to come up with songs off the top of her head because the march was so long.

As I walked down the aisle to Jahiem's "Forever," different emotions hit me at once. I wanted to cry, I wanted to run, I wanted to wait, I wanted to make sure this was for real. When I stood in front of him, he leaned in for a kiss, and the congregation laughed. My cousin Jake later said, "Man, he must really love her. He couldn't even wait for the preacher to start the ceremony!"

I had left the poem that I had written for him at home, so I pushed my nerves aside and recited as much as I could off the top of my head. We exchanged vows, and I was a married woman, and this fine black stallion of a man, this street nigga, ex-con, man of valor and substance, this man that no one could understand why I married, became my husband.

Our reception was nice as well. There was laughter, and there were children running around. Our families mingled. When it came time for the toast, Betty said, "If you hurt my girl, I'ma have to cut you." Jayme's sister, April, said, "Naw, now that's my brother you talkin' about. I don't think so!" Once again, Betty was stunned. I shook my head, did my toast, and danced off with my new husband.

Married life started out good. We didn't have much, but what we did have was good. Most of all we had love. There were nights when we would be up watching movies and making love, and then we'd decide we were hungry. Three a.m. trips to Steak N Shake were not unusual for us. We would lie in bed and talk all night. I would fall asleep with his arm over me, protecting me. I felt safe.

Reality soon started to set in; love can't pay the bills. He was a street nigga, one who knew how to hustle hard and get what he wanted. I was a female who had been there, done that, and I was hardworking with a legit job. We didn't see eye to eye on that. He would stay out late at night hanging out with his friends, which was a problem for me. His late and my late were two different things. I felt midnight was late; he felt it was early.

His children's mothers started acting a damn fool for no reason that I could see. Now, it's very possible that he could have been doing irritating things to them as well, but I didn't see them. My family was always in my ear telling me that he was all wrong for me, but that made me want my marriage to work even more.

Betty bet that our marriage wouldn't last longer than five years. I found this out from Reign. Even still, we would hang out and go shopping all the time. She would try to get Jayme's attention, but he would never pay any attention to her. This confused her. She would often say, "He don't like me." I would counter and say, "It ain't that he don't like you; he just thinks you're a cornball."

She would also say things like "Jayme doesn't have a personality" or "Does Jayme ever laugh? He has no sense of humor." He really did have a sense of humor, just not toward her. She could not get this one to notice her. I saw that it did something to her, because we stopped hanging out as frequently. I didn't trip; we were on separate paths in our lives.

I had this fantasy in my head about how my life would be. My son would be at the top of his class. My husband would leave the street life alone and become this successful barber, chef, DJ, mechanic—any profession was fine with me as long as it was a legal job and kept him out of trouble. We would raise our children together, and all would be well. We would have rough patches, of course, but we could work through them. That was not my reality; in fact, it was the exact opposite. It's funny how life has a way of waking you up.

Jayme has been arrested six times since we've been married. There's always been an issue, whether it's child support, drugs, or guns. He was incarcerated for a year and a half and served house arrest time to finish that sentence. Every time something doesn't go right, the first thing I'm asked is, "What does Jayme do?"

I keep holding on to that dream that he will get it together and leave all the bullshit alone, and that I can have the happy life that I've always dreamed of. My husband has a good heart. He has a brain that is sharp as a tack. He is honest, and he is deep. He has a good head on his shoulders, but he lets his past stop him.

Sometimes, I think I'm his crutch and that he doesn't love me as much as he says he does. Maybe it's my intuition or just my own insecurities; I don't know. I do know that after him being away for that year and half, my love for him has changed.

I still love him, but it's not like it used to be, especially since he is still going through a legal issue. I look at him sometimes and think about asking for a divorce. Sometimes, I tell myself that I can't do it. I just wanted to be loved, but this is not what I bargained for. It's too much for me to handle right now. I have no clue what to do, but I'm working on it.

Although I love him very much, one of the reasons I married him was to spite the people who told me that marriage would never happen to me and to prove a point. That point being that someone would love me enough to marry me and that being a single woman with two kids would not be my life. However, things didn't work out as I thought they would.

When you marry someone, marry them because you love them, and because you want to spend your life with them. Make sure they are the one for you and you are the one for them. Make sure your expectations of each other are clearly stated. Both of you should always be working on your next goals, individually and together. Know that the person who is your boyfriend or girlfriend will still be that same person when they are your husband or wife.

My mistake was that although I love my husband dearly, with all my heart, and I would travel the world to get to him, my expectations of our life changed, and I didn't talk about it. I didn't voice my feelings; I assumed and expected that he would just know. I thought that once we left the dating/fiancée stage of the relationship, I would be his life. I expected him to change. The kids and I would be the ones he would want to be around all the time. The street life would no longer be a factor. I expected him home every night no later than midnight, and when I didn't get that, we fought. Actually, we fought constantly about the street life. I was supposed to "save" him from that life and be his beacon light to leave the street life alone. I wasn't, and as a result of this caked-up fantasy, I was disappointed and hurt. Furthermore, I didn't tell him what I expected. Although we talked about everything else, we never talked about the expectation factor.

My second mistake was marrying him because "they" said, "He doesn't love you, he won't actually marry you, he'll just use you, cheat, abuse you, belittle you, and treat you like shit." "They" said it was all "jail talk." He was a thug, a nothing, and a nobody to them, but he meant the world to me. Besides, "they" didn't know him like I did.

"They" didn't know that he has a brain; he is witty and smart. "They" didn't know that his heart is as soft as cotton, despite his exterior. "They" didn't know about the conversations we had, or his positive nature, even though he had been dealt a raw deal. "They" didn't know that he really loved me for who I was and not for what he could get from me. "They" didn't understand it, and "they" just knew that he would hurt me, and get in trouble, and never work, and always be a burden on me. "They" were partially correct.

My husband cheated on me after almost three years of being married. I found out because after an afternoon of making love, he left the house in his car that had "beats," and he had it turned up really loud. He went to get some blunts and was coming back home. He had some weed and a gun in the car. The music caused the police to pay attention to him. They pulled him over, claimed they smelled the weed, and arrested him. His cousin, Joe, just happened to drive by and call me. I drove over to where they were arresting him and took his property, which included the cell phone. I used it to call Janice. I took his cigarettes, money, and hat home.

When I got home, I was upset because I had told him to not ride around like that. *So here we go again with another charge.* I noticed that he had a message in his inbox, so I checked it. It said, "What time? 'cause I get off at ten." I checked the log. The message that made me flip out was "Can I get some daddy dick tonite?" And his response? "Yes."

I lost my mind, and I couldn't get to him. I couldn't talk to him. I was livid to the point I screamed and hollered, " 'They' were right; he would cheat on me."

His brother came over, and I lashed out at him, accusing him of knowing what was going on. I called all his friends and cussed them out, accusing them of knowing what had happened. I called the female.

"Um, is this Yo-Yo?"

"Who is this?"

"Do you know Jayme?"

"Who is this?"

"This is his wife."

"He don't have a wife."

"Yes, he does."

"Don't be callin' me with this ..." she yelled.

"Hold on. I'm not trying to go off on you. I just want to know what happened. I can't be mad at you because I don't know what he told you. So keep it real with me."

She told me that they had been seeing each other for a while, but I knew she was lying. She said our Explorer was blue; it was black. She said his car was brown; it was maroon, and so was the interior. On days she said he was with her, he had been with me the whole day. In particular, she said on that past Sunday, she had cooked him dinner and he had been with her all day. That same Sunday, I cooked a Sunday dinner, and he stayed at home, not leaving once.

I stayed calm and let her talk. I knew she lied about some stuff. *I can't filter out the exact truth, other than the things I already know.* I was ready to leave him then, but I didn't. Something told me to talk with him first.

He was held for seven days in jail, and I couldn't talk to him. I accepted a collect call from him at work. I had to explain the situation to my boss before he called.

"I know about Yo-Yo."

"What do you mean?" he asked.

"Just keep it real with me, Jayme."

"Babe, it was a one-time thing, I swear. That girl is always texting me and harassing me."

"But what about you giving her money and being at the club with her?"

"I don't go to the club with her, and I damn sure don't give her no money. C'mon, why would I give that bitch anything?"

"Well, my first thought was to leave you. I won't kick you while you are down and going through your case. I can't guarantee that I'm gonna stay the duration, though."

He was released, and we worked on mending our relationship. Trust has always been an issue for me. Once it's broken, it can never be fully restored. He stayed on with the same lifestyle, which fueled my distrust even more.

Since the beginning of our marriage, I had thought about going back to school. Jayme encouraged me the whole time to do so. I got up the nerve, applied, and was accepted. I started in January 2007. When I started school, he picked up the slack as far as housework and cooking. I had dinner waiting for me on my late school nights; there were times when I even had a bath drawn. He stepped things up and supported me to the fullest.

In February of that year, the Friday before the Super Bowl, he was sentenced to four years in prison. In Indiana, each day is worth two days. So he would be locked up for two years. I was devastated. I left the courtroom in a daze. I don't know how I got home.

On Super Bowl Sunday, Todd was gunned down in his SUV. The news devastated my son. Although Todd had never really done anything for Prince, he was still his father. Todd survived the attack, but he was in critical condition.

When Jayme's property was sent to the house, I was queasy. Prince told me that a note was on the door from UPS, and I automatically knew what it was. I arranged for him and Cherub to be gone from the house.

I called UPS and told them to hold the package at the station. I walked in, and my legs almost buckled. I showed an ID and waited for the package to be brought to me. Tears fell when my eyes focused on the box. I took it to the car and cried. I drove off the lot.

I cried so hard that I had to stop at Janice's house because my vision was so bad.

"What's wrong, Reality?" Janice asked.

"It just h-h-hit me that h-h-he's gonna be gone for all that time," I wailed. I sat at her table and bawled. She rubbed my back and kept repeating, "It's gonna be alright."

I dried those tears and made the trek home. I got out and looked in the back seat at the box. I stared at it for five minutes before I decided I would go ahead and take it in the house.

Once in the house, I lit some candles and poured some Absolut vodka. I put on some soft music, never taking my eyes off the box.

I sat in front of it, took a pair of scissors, and opened it. As soon as the scissors touched the box, the tears flowed. I took out each piece of clothing. I wrapped myself in his coat and lay on the floor. I reached into the box and touched a small manila envelope. I opened it and turned it upside down—his ring. At that point, I lost it, completely. I lay on the floor, wrapped in his coat, and cried so hard I thought I was insane. The pain flowing thorough my veins was unbearable because, once again, I was alone.

It took all the strength I could muster just to wake up in the morning. I cried constantly for that first month. I worked, went to school, and took care of the kids the best I could, but I was thoroughly heart-broken. I thought that I wouldn't recover from that blow. I couldn't talk to him or visit him for that first month. All we could do was write to each other. He was moved to a prison that was thirty minutes away from Indianapolis.

I visited him every week. Wrote letters. Accepted phone calls. But I was lost. A married woman whose husband was alive, and I was alone. I slept with his T-shirt on my pillow. I lined the other pillows under me. The only way I could sleep was to cry. I started smoking weed again.

I lost weight. I barbequed on our anniversary, which was our tradition. I got so drunk that I was sick when I went to see him the next day. Every holiday ripped my heart out. His family was so good at including me in functions, but sometimes they were hard to bear. My grief was written on my face, and everyone knew it.

Todd succumbed to his injuries in January 2008. He was only thirty-four years old, but he had at least twenty children by a plethora of women. Prince found out that a boy he was cool with was actually his half-brother. I tried to hold him down as best I could. It showed that his father's death truly bothered him.

I had an infidelity of my own during this time. I hate to discuss it, simply because it was probably the stupidest thing I have ever done. Jacob, my infidel, capitalized on the fact that I was lonely, and I let my emotions overtake my brain. I had been sexless for a year, and I just longed to be touched. I wanted my husband home. I tried to use Jacob as a filler. I should have just held out. In essence, it wasn't worth the pain it caused my husband when I told him. Yes, I told him; the guilt was too much to bear. I felt obliged to tell him, and it opened up doors to more problems. I know many think I shouldn't have said anything, but I felt that being honest was best. It wasn't malicious; I had a void in my life.

He, on the other hand, worked his ass off to get time cuts, and suc-ceeded. He got a certification in food safety. He went to another work release center. He wasn't at home, but he was close enough. He had a decent job, and we got to see each other every day. He had a modification hearing, and the judge released him to house arrest. I was ecstatic.

However, the work release center wouldn't release him. I spoke to numerous people at Community Corrections. They, in turn, called the work release center. I guess the employees at the work release center were angry or something, because they prevented him from going to work. They also had the sheriff come take him to jail before he could be released. I came to find out he had a child support warrant from a court date missed due to incarceration, even though I called the court to tell them where he was. They did nothing about it. That warrant held him in jail for a week. He lost his job. And here we go again.

I was so stressed out after he came home. All of our bills were behind; the mortgage, the car payment, the lights. I thought I would have to leave the house because I didn't have a full-time job. I was angry because it seemed that no one appreciated the things I had done. I was on the brink of a mental meltdown. Jayme told me that he owed me nothing for staying in his corner. Prince was being a typical teenager, and things just weren't right.

One night, the day after Mom's birthday, Jayme and I got into an argument. The kids were asleep, and he left. I decided I was leaving. I filled a pint bottle of Absolut from a fifth of Absolut and walked out the front door, leaving everything, keys, phone, purse, and the door wide open. I started walking, sipping, crying, and talking to myself. Before I knew it, I had walked seven blocks east and four blocks north of my house and ended up in a shopping plaza. The only thing that kept me from going on was the fact that I had to pee. I had no idea where I was headed. I stopped at a payphone and called collect to the house.

"Reality, where are you?"

"In … Devington."

"What did you do? Why did you leave the door open? You know what? Don't answer that, I'm on my way."

He came to pick me up. The pint was about gone, and I was totally drunk. He pulled up to the house, and I jumped out. I cried, ran into the house, and packed.

"I'm sick of this! I'm sick of you, these damn kids, this damn house, just everything!"

I was seriously going through something mentally. I believe I checked out for a few days, my brain totally incapable of making sound decisions about our situation. Today I'm still here, with him and the kids.

I wouldn't have had the strength to do this, to reveal all my ills if it were not for my husband. I know there are people out there who wonder why I am still with him. Not only do I love him, but I feel like he is the only man in my life who has truly and unconditionally loved me. No matter what I may say, no matter what I may do, I will still be there, because no man, not even the man that helped make me, has ever done things that he has. No one. He has encouraged me to do things that I want to do, not what anyone else says I should. He has had my back through it all. I haven't been the perfect wife, but even when I'm a bitch, he still loves me. I thank him so much for what he's done for my vision of myself. Yet, still, I'd be lying to myself if I didn't say that I question my decision about staying. I almost lost everything and went through some pretty deep things mentally and emotionally that I am not totally healed from. I know that my life isn't that bad compared with some, but to me, it's been hell.

I have this vision of how my life was supposed to be, and it's nothing like I planned. The things that happened to me were not supposed to happen to me. I'm too smart for all that, right?

The one thing about my marriage I know holds true is that we love each other. We have our problems, but we still *love* each other. We've talked about getting a separation for a while, but neither of us has moved on it. We both want the marriage to work, but it's hard for us. He can't shake my infidelity; I can't shake his. The trust factor in our marriage is very thin. We've both had issues dealing with trust.

Writing this book has really opened my eyes to things I didn't see, especially when it comes to my husband and me. We are talking about my past, which I didn't totally reveal to him. He is understandably upset. I didn't tell him because I was afraid that he would leave me. I know that was selfish of me, but I don't know if I could have handled another man leaving me.

We are seeking help for our relationship. We agree that we need counseling, but we are unsure where to start. He wants the pastor; I want the therapist.

I've realized that I have this fantasy life in my head, and I lose my mind when my fantasy is not my reality, which has been virtually all my life. I'm a Pisces, a dreamer. All day long, I dream up different scenarios about how my life should be and how things should go. I'm thirty-three, with none of my fantasies fulfilled. I'm thirty-three, mother of two by two different men. I'm thirty-three, and in a lot of ways I'm still that little country gal from Arkansas who just wants to be loved. The true question is, what type of love can fill the empty space I have inside of me? What is it going to take for me to really be happy?

I'm married with two kids, I own my house, and I have a decent car. I'm doing quite well with my classes. On the outside, everything is kosher. On the inside, it's not enough. I want success, real success. Success being happiness, and career fulfillment. I want to be that one in my family who wasn't afraid to follow her dreams and go for something unconventional, not punching someone's else clock and living from paycheck to paycheck. I want my husband out of legal matters. I want my son to go to an Ivy League college, and I want my daughter to be Secretary of State one day. I want my marriage strong so that I can be a model for my kids when it gets to be their time to choose a mate.

Are my expectations too high? Will they ever be reached? Who knows. There is one thing I do know—the biggest life lesson ever is that the reality of life, true reality of life, is enough to make you insane, especially if you were not prepared for it. I am on the brink of insanity, and that could be the end of my story, but not really.

As a parent, it is my duty to show my kids, and talk to them about, the harsh reality of life. Whenever they have a question about something that my parents brushed off, I answer them, and I answer them frankly. I refuse to sugarcoat life, because I don't want any of them to end up like me, in their thirties still confused, unsure of whom to believe or whom to trust. My kids, all four, are my beacon light. I know that they have helped light my path. I want to show them that they can be whatever they want to be. I want to teach them to reach for what they want.

Sometimes, I may be hard and harsh, but that's the way life is. The real world isn't soft, and it can make you lose your mind. I want them to see my triumph. It took me until I was at least thirty years old to figure things out, and I'm still not so sure I've got them down. But what I do know is that, like any other parent, I don't want them doing what I did, as clichéd as that sounds. I want them to be their own person, to be independent, and to do what they feel is right in their lives. Just know that Momma is always here for them, whenever they need me, but I have to let their hands go and send them into the world to face it. My shoulders can't bear all of their troubles, but my ears are open to listen, and my heart is full of a mother's love.

My faith in God hasn't always been strong, but I found that in my darkest moments, when my faith was withering, He pulled me through. The Lord has opened my eyes to see things for what they really are, and I thank Him daily. Without God, there would be no me. I wouldn't have had the sense to do the things I've done to better myself. The old saying goes "He might not come when you call Him, but He's right on time." I find that to be true.

I've still got things to do, places I want to go. My life has been a setback of sorts, because of all the untold lessons I had to learn the hard way. I don't think I was prepared for this big revelation of life. I've always seen myself as a victim of circumstance, but I no longer want to be the victim. Making myself out to be one takes too much work, and it takes some of my dignity and peace. Being a victim also sets me up for failure.

I'm learning about myself more and more each day. I think I still care too much what people say about me, but that piece of me that wants to follow the crowd is dwindling. It all started with the decision to cut off my hair and grow locks. This may not have been a big deal for most, but for me it was a sign of my independence, a step away from the critical words of others. "Why did you do that, Reality?" "'Cause I wanted to."

I'm on a path of forgiveness, and that path is bumpy. I want to forgive my dad for not caring enough about me to stick around. I'm trying to come to grips with the fact that I'm not, nor will I ever be, Daddy's Little Girl. He will never dote on me. He will never be there when I call. He just won't, and it hurts, but the pain isn't as intense as it used to be. One day, it may not matter to me at all. I still talk to him, but the conversations are short, which is to be expected. I only talk to him if I call him. Still waiting for him to pick up the phone to say, "Hey."

Even though I want to forgive, I'm afraid that if I do, I lose my power not to let someone hurt me. I've heard that forgiveness is never about the other person; it's about letting go of the past and past hurts. It's about freeing yourself from the bondage of pain. It is a process, a slow process. It took years for people to hurt me, and it took years for that hurt to build the "woe is me" wall. It's gonna take some time for me to tear it down completely and be able truly to trust those around me.

My son most likely won't go to an Ivy League college and beat the odds. If he does go to college, he'll go to one right here in Indiana, and his successes and failures will be his own to bear, not mine. I have my own issues to handle, and while I am here to listen, I can't worry about everyone else's failures. My daughter is becoming a younger version of me, which I really don't like, but I know she can't help it. She wants to be a singer, a chef, and she wants to play basketball. She's a good student, as mindful as a nine-year-old could be, and lucky. Her dad loves her and breaks his neck for her at any time. She is Daddy's Little Girl, the one thing I could never be. That's why I encourage her to speak to him at least once a day, if nothing else just to say, "Hello." I told her that the relationship with her dad is important, and she should cherish it. I know she does.

I'm almost done with college, and soon my dreams will become my reality. My dreams are big, and I live in fear of "What if?" As in, what if I don't make it? I have to tell myself that no matter what, not making it is not an option. I don't *want* to make it; I *have* to make it. There is too much at stake, too much to lose. I know I said my story is at the end … I was wrong; it's only the beginning.

Hello, I'm Angenita LaShawn Williams Childs, Little Country Gal from Arkansas, Reality Checks In, and Growing Up Twice. I am a mother, daughter, sister, college student, wife, lover, and fighter. I thank you for reading my story. I hope it helps someone some day. Maybe it has helped you.

Reality's Epilogue

AS I FINISH WRITING MY PORTION OF THE BOOK, life still is in a sort of limbo. So, as you can see, I'm still learning. I'm still growing. I'm still locating who I really am. Although some things have been messed up, it could have been worse. I'm still feeling around on this thing, but I feel like I'm getting there.

My husband and I are working on our relationship. I'm still in college, and I still am working hard to pursue my dream of being an author. I guess finishing the book makes me an author, though, right?

To all those little girls who lack a father, understand that while you may feel alone and unloved because he is not there for you, someone does love you. Don't go from man to man in search of that love, because all you will find is heartache. Be cautious in your selections when dealing with men, and don't let a man deter you from the things you want or need. You cannot force a man, including your father, to love you. Your best bet is to love yourself.

To the little boys who have that void left by an absent Daddy, you can still grow and be your own man. His neglect of you should only make you a stronger person. If there is a man you look up to, follow his model. Promise yourself that you will be a better father than yours, and stick to it. You know how it is to be without one, so stay with your child, even if you and the mother don't agree.

To boys and girls, don't blame yourself for your parents' mistakes. Don't feel like things are your fault if they have nothing to do with you. Remember that if Mom and Dad can't get along, it's not your fault; it's theirs. Also, feeling alienated by Mom is hard to bear because she just might feel like you are the root of her problems. Just remember you did not ask to be born, and she can't put that burden on you. If Daddy wants you to keep a secret, especially one of infidelity, lies, or abuse, tell it. Don't stand by and watch and feel sorry for yourself. Be proactive about your life. We all want Daddy's love, but that doesn't mean that Daddy can do whatever he wants.

To the fathers out there, I just want to say it is so important that you are a part of your children's life. Be involved. If you are an abusive man, get help, because your children need you. You are the first man that your child looks up to, especially your daughter. She looks to you to gauge how a man should treat her. Seek counseling to help you, or, better yet, try God. Would you want your son to be that way? Would you want your daughter to be beaten? Ask yourself those questions before you raise your hand or say hurtful things. Anger is a normal, healthy emotion, but it's not an excuse for violence or belittling. Loving someone means you won't hurt them. If you hit, you hurt, and if you hurt, you don't love. Abuse stays etched in your children's minds, and they carry that into their own relationships. They may even think something is wrong if their partner doesn't hit or berate them because of the foundation laid at home. It's sick and twisted.

Tell the truth about how you feel. Don't bottle things inside and pretend like everything is okay when it's not. If you are hurting, let it out. Don't have it in your mind that no one will take you seriously or that the way that you feel is stupid. If you try to talk about it, and someone says it's bullshit, then go to someone else. Living with pain is not living. Using drugs to dull the pain doesn't help; it just buries it for a moment. If pain is there, no one can say that it's not. If you don't have a close person to talk to, pick up the phone to your nearest counseling center or pastor. The help is there for you. Don't let people say you are "crazy" for wanting to get your feelings out. Keeping them bottled up inside of you is what will make you crazy. Just like you go get a physical checkup, get a mental health checkup. It's just as important.

Love who you are before attempting to love someone else. Your heart may tell you that you love them, but really the feelings are trying to replace your emptiness. *Never* settle for less than what you are. Never let anyone tell you that you are stupid. No matter who you are, what you look like, or what your GPA is, there is something inside of you worthy of true love. An outside appearance is just that, outside. The inside really does count.

In closing, I just want to say that writing this book has made me deal with some of the issues that I still have inside. It hasn't been a cure-all, but it's a start. I will reach that true happiness, one day at a time. With persistence and perseverance, you can too.

Angenita

Dream

Superstar

I SPENT NEW YEAR'S EVE 1999 at church as usual, but this year I kept one eye closed and the other eye open during prayer. We were all anxiously waiting to see the lights turn off and the computers crash because of Y2K, but nothing happened.

I would visit Atlanta for the first time to secure my job relocation and find a place to live. I didn't really know anyone there. Angela's three brothers, Dennis, Keith, and Ned, and her mother Mable lived there, but I really didn't know them. I had only met them one or two times before.

I rode the Greyhound bus to Atlanta. It was a twelve-hour trip. I was excited, but a little nervous about what kind of people would be on the bus. I traveled at night and found a seat all to myself. I used my purse as my pillow and slept the whole trip. Ned picked me up from the bus station and took me to rent a car so I could get around.

The next morning, I went to my job interview and secured my position. The hiring manager said that not only could I have the job, but I was getting a three dollar per hour raise along with a four hundred dollar a month bonus for attendance and job performance. I would be making ten dollars an hour. I felt like I was rich. When I had first started working at sixteen, I made only four dollars seventy-five cents an hour. I was making seven dollars ten cents in my current position. "When will you be able to start?" I turned around and looked on the calendar. "How about the third week in March? That will give me time to wrap up everything at home and move down."

"Okay, great! March it is; see you then. Welcome aboard!"

The only thing that I was nervous about was being able to pay my rent on my own. I didn't want to have an apartment that took my whole paycheck, because it was just me and what if something happened? I had lived with Kim and Delta, but never totally by myself. I wanted to play it safe so that I wouldn't get in over my head and have to come crawling back to my mother's house. I searched some places online before I arrived in Atlanta and picked out a few that I thought I could afford. I went to four apartments and found one in a gated community. It didn't look as good as the others, but it was still okay from the outside, and you needed a swipe card to get in. That made me feel safe. Another selling point was that it was only ten minutes away from Jordan's family. If I ever needed anything, they wouldn't be too far away. I gave them my deposit to hold my apartment, and Mable and I drove around so that I could familiarize myself with my soon-to-be city. I had a great time and hurried home to wrap things up for the big move.

I had been hustling on my job as a customer service representative, getting paid commission from a lot of inside sales leads instead of giving them to the sales reps. I earned $110 for each lead on top of my base salary. My checks looked nice for five months because making extra money for my move was all that I focused on. I went into the work database and found everyone that didn't have a maintenance agreement. I mailed them a form to fill out to add it to their account with a prepaid envelope. For each one I received, I was paid ten dollars. My sister Kevia and I would rent movies, pop popcorn, and drink Pepsi as she helped me stuff all of the envelopes. Jordan was four, and he would stack them up in the box, ready to be mailed out.

I saved every dime that I earned, with the exception of paying for necessities. I called all of the moving companies and negotiated the cost for a moving truck and car hauler for a one-way trip to 'Hotlanta'. The price tag went down from $1,000 to $700. Everything was falling into place. Kim, O'Leta, and Ned were my moving crew. Ned took the Greyhound bus from Atlanta to drive the U-Haul back for me. I was going to rent a car for us and head out. Jordan would stay with my mother for the first week. The following week was spring break, and she would bring him down, along with Kevia and her friend.

I started paying my tithes at church six months prior to my move.

The last Sunday that I was in Indianapolis, the church took up a collection just for me and my moving fund. I was shocked as this was unexpected. I had some money saved to sit on. The pastor said, "Now, as most of you know, our babies Dream and Jordan are moving to Atlanta so she can pursue her dreams of singing. Let's all support her and send her off with something nice."

If I were the shy blushing type then I would've, but I just sat there in total amazement as they held the special collection. After church the treasurer counted the money and handed me a fat envelope with over $700 in it. I was really in shock then. The first thing that came to my mind was, *Wow I haven't even given this much through my tithing! It's true: God does multiply what you give.*

I was still on my spiritual high from my Kentucky revelation. Everything that happened was because of my deeper relationship with God. If the wind blew, it was because God wanted me to feel the wind at that moment. If the phone rang, it was because God wanted me to answer it, even if the call wasn't for me. Everything was because of God, and everything was for me.

Kim and O'Leta threw me a going-away birthday party at our favorite spot, a bar called Claude and Annie's. They would always talk about me because we had been hanging out at this bar for about two years and I never drank or smoked. They served Pepsi and had karaoke, and that's all I needed to have a good time. We had a great turnout for the party. My closest friends came out, along with some I hadn't seen in years. I wanted to enjoy the atmosphere and catch up with the old friends that I hadn't seen in years, but everyone was pressuring me to sing a song. I made my request, "Doo Wop, That Thing" by Lauryn Hill. I grabbed the microphone, and the music started to play. "It's been three weeks since you've been lookin' for your friend, the one you let hit and never called you again ..." When the hook came around I belted out, "Guys you know you betta watch out. Some girls, some girls are only about." I felt so powerful, like I had already became a superstar and like this was my song. Everyone chimed in, "That thing, that thing, that thing, that thing, that thing, that thing!" I performed the song, but my mind was elsewhere.

I am going to Atlanta. I am going to be a superstar. There is no one and nothing that can stop me. God told me to go, and I listened. I felt like I was on fire, and there was no doubt in my mind that things would work.

The morning of the move, I was running on pure adrenaline. We woke up early. I went to get the rental car and the Budget moving truck. As I signed my paperwork the clerk at the desk asked, "Do you want insurance on the truck?"

"No, thank you."

I headed to get the car hauler from U-Haul because they had given me a better deal. They hooked everything up, and I was ready to go. We drove to Angela's to pick up some things we still had there and to say goodbye. Her friend drove the truck as I went ahead of him. It was taking him a long time to get there. It was only about a ten-minute drive that took over an hour. When they finally got to the house they told me, "You will never believe what happened. The hitch fell off the truck, into this man's yard, and hit his truck. The guy called Budget and found out that you didn't have any insurance on the truck."

"Oh my God, are you serious? Was anybody hurt? I'm going back up there and get the insurance put on it. I'll be right back." The same guy helped me. "No, you can't add the insurance now. You already drove the truck off of the lot." He read me the legal mumbo jumbo that I really didn't want to hear. I was upset and really didn't know how to handle the situation. I left to finish loading the truck.

No one thought I was moving until I backed the truck into my mom's driveway. Mom started calling people, telling them, "You might want to come and say bye to Dream; she's about to leave for Atlanta." As me and 'my crew' put the boxes and furniture in the truck, people stopped by for a quick hug, words of encouragement, and whatnot. With all of our belongings loaded into the truck, we hit the road. We had a concert in the car listening to Mary J. Blige live, reminiscing to Jodeci's *Diary of a Mad Band* and Lauryn Hill. We got stuck in rush-hour traffic in Tennessee, and we got out of the car on the highway in the standstill traffic, turned the music up, and had a quick, miniature 'block party.' We were so happy and carefree. Our rocky morning turned out perfectly.

When we arrived in Atlanta, Ned was nowhere to be found. I had a toll-free pager, and he kept leaving messages, but I had to go to a pay phone to check the messages. He left me a voicemail on my pager. He was stranded in north Georgia. He had run out of the gas and money that I had given him. We turned around and headed back up the road. When we got to where he said he was, he was not there. He paged me again: "I sold your Discman for twenty dollars to put gas in your car. I took it off the hitch and I'm going back to the house." We again drove to Atlanta to pick him up and take him to the truck. What should've taken us eight hours took us twelve. None of us had cell phones. When the whole ordeal was over, we were drained, and the adrenaline was gone. We went to sleep at his house so we could start over the next day and move my things into my new apartment.

We arrived at the apartment complex in the morning. I went to the office, and the apartment that I was going to get was still not ready for a move in and wouldn't be ready soon enough for my taste. They put me in a cheaper apartment. I had no choice but to take it. I was in a rush. My moving crew had to go back to Indianapolis the next morning.

The complex was right off of Martin Luther King Jr. and Peyton Road. Everyone knows that all of the streets named after Martin Luther King Junior are in the 'hood. I, however, didn't know that I was in the 'hood until after I had my things moved in. The elevator smelled like pee; the people who lived there were a lot different from anyone I had grown up with. We cleaned the bathroom and the kitchen, wiped everything down as you do when you first move into a new place. We put everything in the right room and unpacked as best we could. We ate pizza and slept on the floor, which is our moving-day tradition.

The next morning, the crew headed back to Indianapolis. Kim was crying as they drove off. We reenacted the scene between Celie and Nettie in *The Color Purple*.

"Write!"

"What?"

"Write"

"Nothing but death can keep me from it!"

I smiled to myself, knowing that she was my sentimental friend, but I was happy. I was on my own, living in Atlanta, grown, and I would be a superstar soon—very soon.

My car had been reliable when I lived in Indianapolis, but it seemed like as soon as I got to Georgia, it would break down once a week. It always broke down on my way to work or on my way home. I would be stuck on the highway and a HERO (Highway Emergency Response Operator) would have to come and push my car onto the side of the road. AAA grew to know me very well and didn't need all of my information when I called. They'd send a tow truck to come and get me. I probably rode in the tow trucks more than I drove my own car.

In the summer, I learned why everyone called Atlanta 'Hotlanta.' It was scorching hot, and my car had no air conditioning. It was an hour's drive from work to home. Jordan and I would stop, get a cold drink, and try to pace ourselves drinking it. Jordan's never lasted. He would be sweating bullets and would need another drink. I made a promise to Jordan that we would have a car with air conditioning before the next summer.

I started to date a grease monkey mechanic from the 'hood named Chris. He kept my car running for free. I wasn't in love with him, but I met him within the first few months after I moved to Atlanta. It was a relationship of convenience. He needed a place to stay other than his sister's house, and I needed him to keep my car running, so I let him move in with us. He was a nice guy, just not for me.

Our relationship was short lived. I found out that he was cheating on me. I heard a message from his girlfriend on his voicemail. I was trying to be upset and pick a fight about it, but honestly I really didn't care. He had served his purpose, because just before I learned of his cheating I had bought a new car. A 2000 Mitsubishi Mirage. It was under warranty, so I really didn't need him anymore.

I had been in Atlanta for almost a year and started networking and making good progress. I moved into a much nicer apartment that was only a few minutes from my job.

Right after I moved, I met a management team who were looking to start a girl group. One of my co-workers knew them and told me about them. I got cute and went for my informal audition. I took Jordan with me. We were lined up at a long table. The management team: Damon, RayShawn, Linda, and Earl sat on one side of the table. Two other girls, along with Jordan and me, sat on the other side.

Across from me was RayShawn, a chocolate brother who looked good. He was in great shape. You could tell he was or had been a serious athlete at one time. *I love a man with muscles, not too many but just enough to hold me tight and protect me. Black and orange sure look good on him.* But then he smiled. *Uh-oh BLING BLING! Oh my God, this brother has two gold teeth right in the front of his mouth! Gold teeth are out of the question.* Even though he was fine, I got the thought out of my head. *I just got rid of the grease monkey, and I'm not looking for a relationship. I am here to sing and become famous. The only thing that will come before that is my son. I just need to stay focused and try to keep the ball rolling, but he is some nice eye candy.*

At the end of our meeting, we ordered desert. RayShawn bought Jordan ice cream with sprinkles and chocolate. That really made Jordan's day, and he was so happy. We went outside; I sang my audition song, and the other girls sang theirs too. It was pretty much a done deal; we had our three girl group. We exchanged numbers. "We will be in touch and get this group started." Jordan asked RayShawn, "Why is there an R and an M in your gold teeth?" If I were a white woman, I swear my face would've been as red as a tomato. He just laughed and said, "Those are my initials to my name. Initials are the first letters of your name. My name is RayShawn Moore."

"You can't remember your initials?" my know-it-all five-year-old replied.

Mmm mmm and you were being nice to him and bought him some ice cream, I thought to myself. "I am so sorry; kids say the first thing that comes into their head!"

"Oh, I ain't trippin' off of that; he's okay."

I had only been in my apartment for a week. I don't know why, but I decided to call RayShawn a few days after we met. "Hello."

"Hey, do you know who this is?"

"No, should I?"

"No, not really." I laughed. "I just really wanna know why you have your initials in your gold teeth." We both laughed. We talked for a while and learned that he didn't live far from me. "Do you mind if I come through for a little while?" he asked.

"Yeah, sure, that's fine."

We started out talking, then watched a movie. We joked how he was already sizing me up by buying Jordan ice cream. He claimed that he was just being nice and it meant nothing, but I knew better. One thing led to another, and we had sex. We had to keep it a secret because it wasn't the best impression for the management team to see. It just wouldn't look good if they found out that we had secretly hooked up. I knew our relationship wouldn't go anywhere. I wasn't looking for a boyfriend or a cut buddy either. I was focused. *I came to Atlanta to sing and entertain, and dag-on-it that is what I'm going to do.*

The group was set to record our first song, but we were unable to record as a group. Like always, one girl got pregnant. She confided in me, "Dream, can you believe Damon told me that if I want to stay in the group I have to have an abortion?"

"Are you serious?" No group was worth her doing something she was not comfortable with. She left the group, and so did the other girl. The team decided to manage me as a solo artist. The studio time was already paid for, and RayShawn insisted that I record the song by myself.

I recorded the song, and it was a success. The song was picked up to be on the ATL Bomb Squad compilation CD. After a few months, RayShawn and I decided that there was nothing more to hide about our relationship. We told everyone and started dating exclusively. My music career was progressing very well. They got me gigs, photo shoots, meetings with fashion designers. RayShawn and I got along very well, and Jordan looked up to him. He didn't break my focus, so it was cool.

I sent Jordan to Indianapolis to visit Allen's family and his godfather Ricky. RayShawn and I grew closer and became inseparable. We had such a good time. We'd spend the night at my place or at his, wake up, go to work, hook up right after work, and start all over again. We never argued or got on each other's nerves. We just naturally got along; it seemed like we had known each other forever.

We planned to drive to Indianapolis to pick up Jordan. I called my mother on the phone, "Mom, I'm bringing someone home for you to meet."

"Okay, dear, I'll be happy to meet him."

I have to prep her up. "But um, Mom, I gotta tell you he's got two gold teeth in the front of his mouth."

"Okay, sweetie, as long as he's a nice guy."

"Mom, he's got his initials, an R and an M, in his gold teeth!"

"Dream, it's okay!" she said calmly.

Well, she's been warned; she won't be in shock mode.

We got there, and my whole family immediately fell in love with RayShawn. Mom had him changing light bulbs and doing various other small projects. He helped my 100-year-old granny get around and played with my nieces and nephews. He genuinely was a nice guy. Tisha gave him the third degree, of course. "Are you a Christian? What are your intentions with my sister?" He stood his ground and answered every question with no hesitation. He didn't bat an eye or stutter. He was a soldier, and anyone who knows my sister knows that she can be one tough cookie when she's in the middle of one of her 'investigations.'

On our way back home, we were talking about all the fun we'd had. "Your family is so much fun to be around. They make me feel like I'm a part of the family too, like I've been around forever. But the first thing I noticed was there's hardly any men in your family. Only Tisha's husband and your aunt's husband, Lee. Where are all the men?"

"Hmm, you know, I never really thought about it before. Granddaddy is in Illinois, but I've only seen him twice. Aunt Caryn used to be married, but I'm not sure what happened to her husband. Wow! It's funny how you noticed that, because I never have. I guess that's because that's the way we've always been. We can pretty much hold our own. It's crazy, but so true. I really never noticed it though. Hey, what can I say, they are the only ones who stuck around."

After we returned to Atlanta, we went out to eat. He took my hand and looked me in my eyes. "You know, I'm falling in love with you. I didn't think that I would, especially this fast. I told myself that I wouldn't date anyone under twenty-five because they are immature, but you proved me wrong. I said I wouldn't date another woman with kids because of all the drama from my past, but you proved me wrong again. You are strong, and you have so many goals, and you don't let anything hold you back, and I love that too. I said all of that to say, Will you be my girlfriend?" I just smiled and giggled to myself. I hadn't been asked to be anyone's girlfriend in a long time, since high school even. I thought it was kind of cute, sweet, old school, and of course romantic. He was ten years older than I was. I was twenty-three; he was thirty-three. "I didn't know people still asked each other to be girlfriend and boyfriend, but of course I will, because I'm falling in love with you too!"

RayShawn would try to get Jordan to watch sports with him, but he was never interested. I wasn't either and would go into another room to watch something else. "Dream, you need to start exposing him to sports. Sports were so much fun for me growing up. It's what made me stay out of trouble, and I enjoyed it."

"Jordan is not a troubled kid. He doesn't like sports; he shows no interest, and I'm not going to force him. If he ends up wanting to play then I'll support him in that."

"How is he going to know if he likes it or not if he's never exposed to it?"

"I don't see the big deal, but I'll think on it."

I enrolled Jordan in soccer. RayShawn was proud, and we both stood on the sidelines cheering for him. Jordan stood in the middle of the field and barely ran toward the ball. After the game we asked, "Jordan, why didn't you run toward the ball?"

"I didn't need to because everyone else was running to it." We laughed, and RayShawn worked with him at home. Jordan looked to be bored out of his mind. "I need you to at least try to play soccer. We are going to put you in every sport so you can see what you like. You have to at least try to enjoy yourself, okay?"

"I'll try, but I'd rather read or draw."

"We can't force him to like soccer. Every few years or so, we'll put him in another sport until we find one he likes. You did the right thing, babe. Thanks," I told him.

On September 11, 2001, a co-worker received a call from someone in New York telling him that a plane had crashed into one of the Twin Towers. He made the announcement to everyone. We were in shock and started looking on the Internet for details. We thought that it was a freak accident and felt bad for the people on the plane and in the tower. Before we could digest the incident we got word that a second plane had hit the other tower. *It must be a mistake. They've reported it wrong. They have to be reporting about the same plane and the same tower.*

We turned on the TV in the break room and saw firsthand. We

were in total awe and disbelief; I couldn't believe what was happening. *This kind of surprise attack you only hear about in history books. We are Americans; no one attacks us; we attack everyone else.* For the first time, I was afraid for my life, and for the lives of Americans. I witnessed as people jumped out of windows on the top floors of the towers. The reporters on the scene explained what was happening as you heard the bodies plummet to the ground. It was horrifying. The world was coming to an end. "If you ain't right, then you better get right" was the message around the office. We couldn't do any more work, considering the events of the day. Our bosses let us go home early.

We picked up our children, held them tight, and held our loved ones close. I tried calling my family back home. The phone lines were overloaded. I got through to some, but not to all. I stopped trying because I figured someone else's call needed to get through more than mine. When RayShawn got off work, we talked about it and prayed.

Two days later he was laid off from his job where he had worked for ten years. He was devastated. He had just moved into a new apartment and signed a new lease. In the same breath, he couldn't be upset, because we were still dealing with the terrorist attacks. People were still missing and being rescued. His job didn't give him a severance package, and he didn't have too many options. I invited him to move in with me and Jordan. I asked Jordan how he felt about it before I invited RayShawn to stay with us. He was excited and thought that he would have a roommate to sleep on his bottom bunk. RayShawn and I laughed; I realized my son had never seen a real-life man and woman relationship. Everyone I had dated after his father passed was not around him, and if they did meet him they weren't touching or kissing on me.

We adjusted to living together pretty easily. That is, until one day I went to the bathroom and accidentally dropped my cell phone in the toilet. I yanked it out and pouted to RayShawn. "My cell phone is probably ruined. I'm gonna lose all of my numbers."

"Give it here; let me see." I handed him my phone and walked out the room. A few minutes later I smelled something weird and went into the kitchen to see what the strange smell was. When I walked in, RayShawn had a look on his face like a kid who did something wrong. "What's wrong? What's that smell?"

"I was trying to dry out your phone, and I made it worse."

"What do you mean you made it worse?" I looked closer and yelled, "Did you put my phone in the microwave?"

"Yeah, I took it apart, and I was trying to let it dry out before it was totally messed up."

"So, your solution is to put metal into a microwave? That is so stupid! I can't believe you did that!" I stormed off into the bedroom, pissed off. *This fool went and put my phone in the damn microwave. I don't have money to replace it! He doesn't have a job, so he doesn't need to spend the little he has on a cell phone. I'll be stuck paying for a monthly service that I can't use because I don't have money for a cell phone. What the hell was he thinking to make him put a phone in the microwave?*

I didn't speak to him the rest of the evening. The next morning, I went to work and wrote him a long letter. I told him how mad I was, how I was already stressed from carrying the financial load, and how stupid it was to put my phone in the microwave. I handed it to him and walked away. He read it and came into the bedroom with a smile on his face. "I knew you were mad at me, but I didn't think it was letter worthy. I understand where you are coming from one hundred percent. You have every right to be mad. I don't know what made me put it in the microwave. If I see that you need help with something, or something upsets you, I automatically try to fix it. I don't want you to ever be frustrated or unable to get something done. I didn't think it through. The next time you are mad at me, just talk to me, and don't write me a long letter. Talk to me and tell me what you are upset about."

"I always write. That's the only way I can make sure I get everything out that I want to say. When I started my period, I wrote my mother a letter. When I got pregnant, I wrote my mother a letter. If you don't want another letter, then don't do stupid shit like putting my phone in the microwave."

"I'm going to buy you a new phone."

"You don't have a job! I don't want you wasting your money on a phone."

"I'm going to buy you a new phone. End of story." I quietly rejoiced to myself because emotionally, that's what I wanted. Logically, it wasn't the best option.

Jordan adjusted to life in Atlanta very well, but he was home sick. He missed his family and friends from Indianapolis, but he had just started Kindergarten and was making new friends. The class used a stoplight system to symbolize each child's daily conduct. A green light meant that you had had a good day, yellow meant you could've done a little better, and red meant that you had had a bad day. At first Jordan brought home all green lights; all of a sudden every day he brought home a red light. RayShawn and I talked to him about his behavior. We even went as far as having Mable and Angela call him every morning before school to remind him to be good. But he still came home with red lights. "Jordan, if you come home with one more red light, I'm going to spank you!"

"Mamma, I'm trying. I don't know what's wrong with me, but I just can't be good!"

"Well, you better figure it out before I spank you! Do you hear me?"

"Yes, ma'am."

The next day RayShawn went to pick him up from school. It was a nice spring day, so I opened the balcony screen door to let some fresh air in. I sat on the couch to rest before I started dinner, but I fell asleep. I awoke to hear a child screaming, "Help me!"

I jumped up. *Is that Jordan?* I asked myself as I rushed to the door to look outside. I saw RayShawn pulling Jordan's legs from the back seat as Jordan frantically fought back. I opened the front door to run down and rescue him. *Wait, I need a knife.* I headed back to the kitchen, but I heard RayShawn chuckling. Jordan was flung over RayShawn's shoulder, still kicking and screaming. My heart was still pounding, but I suddenly realized that Jordan wasn't in any danger. "Why is he screaming like that?"

"He got another red light. He started cutting up as soon as I picked him up. You would've thought I was trying to kill him."

"Um, I kinda did, I heard him screaming and was about to run down and beat you up!" I laughed to myself because I realized how quickly I could've overreacted. He leaned over and kissed me. "I will never give you a reason to want to beat me up, okay. I'll prove it to you." Deep in my heart I knew he was telling the truth.

RayShawn was feeling a lot of financial burden. Not only had he lost his job, but he had been leasing out his house that he owned with his ex-girlfriend. It was a lease-to-buy contract, and he learned the tenant couldn't afford to buy it. The only option was to sell the house or let it go under foreclosure. In an attempt to help save his home from foreclosure, I decided to try to buy it. His best friend's wife, Theresa, was a real estate agent and told me the importance of home ownership instead of renting. She taught me things that I didn't know and had never thought of. I was so appreciative of my newfound knowledge. I let them run my credit, and I was approved for $110,000. His house was to be sold for $150,000. RayShawn got his CDL license and was driving trucks, but the financial damage was already done. We couldn't find another buyer, and the house went under foreclosure, but my eyes were open to a whole new world.

My lease was almost up in my apartment, so the timing was perfect. I was going to be a home owner. We began the hunt for a house. We found the perfect three bedroom, two bathroom home, with an attached garage, in Douglasville, an hour away from where we lived. We went through all the home-buying procedures. When it came time to put the money down on the house, I called the life insurance company regarding the policy that Allen had on Jordan. They sent me two checks totaling more than eleven thousand dollars. That was like one million dollars to me. I paid my car note for six months, I set some aside for a rainy day, and the rest I used toward my down-payment for my home.

The day we were set to move into our house, we packed both of our vehicles with miscellaneous things. RayShawn followed me down the highway, and I slowed down to get off of the exit ramp. I looked in my rearview mirror and saw RayShawn talking on his cell phone. *He is so into that conversation I bet he's not paying attention to where we are going.* No sooner had I finished my thought than he tapped the back of my car. *Oh shit!* I was stunned. "That fool wasn't paying attention." Jordan was sitting in the back seat and started screaming hysterically. "I don't want to die! I don't want to die!"

"Jordan, you are not going to die! It's okay! RayShawn just tapped the back of the car." He continued to scream, which sent me into a panic. I jumped out of the car to make sure there wasn't any damage. RayShawn jumped out, still talking on the phone and laughing. "Dang! I didn't realize I was that close! It's okay; it doesn't look like there's any damage though."

"It is not okay! Jordan is in there screaming his head off, and all you can do is laugh? I can't believe this, and you are still on the damn phone!" I snapped back.

"Ah man, let me call you back." He looked at me like I was a crazy mad woman. "Why are you overreacting? I didn't hit you that hard."

"Jordan thinks that because you hit him, he's gonna die! He's screaming his head off and you aren't acting on it at all!" He poked his head through the window and looked at Jordan. "Hey man, you are okay. I wasn't paying attention, and I didn't mean to scare you. Just because there is a car accident doesn't mean that you are going to die, okay?"

"Okay," he replied, through his tears. I hopped back in the driver's seat and drove off, still upset and in a frenzy.

Later that night we talked about it.

"Dream, I'm sorry that I upset you and Jordan earlier today. I didn't know that's how he reacted. I'm really sorry, but what I need for you to do is not overreact when he has a reaction. You only feed into it. If you know that nothing is wrong, then act like nothing's wrong and he'll follow you. You don't follow him; he's a child. Now that I see the bigger picture, I can see how he felt that way, but we are going to work on that."

"Okay, I'm sorry I snapped at you, but you know how I am about my baby!"

"Yes, I know how you are about that big ole boy that's not a baby. I already know I have to watch how I interact with him because you've always had to fight for him. I don't want you to feel you have to fight me for him. But we'll work on it."

This nigga must be crazy to think I'm not going to react when Jordan is going crazy about something like that. Man, please! He makes a good argument, but I'm Jordan's mamma, and I know what's best for my baby. He can go on with all the rest of that mess!

That summer we went to Indianapolis. I wanted to visit the people that I hadn't had a chance to see yet. "Babe, you ready to go visiting?" I asked.

"Naw, not really, I'm cool. I just want to sit down and relax, but you go ahead, have fun." I was a little thrown off because we always went everywhere together. I brushed it off because it wasn't a big deal, and it was certainly not worth fighting over. I went out visiting while he stayed at home with my mom.

The next day, we went to Grandmere's house for a BBQ. The whole family was there. Grandmere called everyone individually to show-case their talents. I enjoyed watching my cousins rap, sing, and dance. I, of course, sang, as well as my mom and my aunts. Grandmere and Aunt Caryn did storytelling. Mom called RayShawn up to showcase a talent. My heart jumped; I knew that he couldn't sing or dance. He had the gift to gab, he was good in sports, but I didn't know how he would showcase that. *Uh-oh, they love him now, but if he starts singing they are gonna have second thoughts!*

He stood up with a look on his face as if he was the proudest man in the world. "I've been around you guys for about a year; you all are so open, nice, and loving. I am so glad to have met you. I've never seen family members get together as often as you all do and not fight. You guys have done a great job raising Dream. She's everything that I've ever wanted and more. I feel like I'm at home around you guys." He turned to me, grabbed my hand, and stood me up. "You were there for me when I had nothing, when I lost my house and my job. I love you so much. You make me a better man. I want to always be here for you and Jordan." I watched as he bent down on one knee. "Will you make me the happiest man alive and marry me?" I was so shocked when he asked that, I didn't even answer. I just hit him and said, "I can't stand you!" and laughed. Everyone in my family said in unison, "So, is that a yes or a no?"

"Of course it's a yes!"

He placed a beautiful white gold diamond ring on my finger. I couldn't take everything in, because everyone ran to us hugging and screaming, wanting to see the ring. Then I found out that the day before, when he had stayed home with my mother, he'd got her permission to marry me. He said that he'd had to ask her because my father was not around. He had explained to her that he'd never intended for us to be 'shacking up,' but I hadn't left him when he'd lost his job and hadn't left him homeless either. He'd told her he absolutely loved Jordan and would be honored to raise him. Everyone but Jordan and I had known that he was going to propose.

This was nowhere near where I saw myself when I first left for Atlanta, or when I went to the audition and saw the gold teeth. I wasn't looking for love, a man, a husband, or a father for my son. God sent them all my way, and I gladly accepted.

He genuinely loved my son, and my son genuinely loved him back. He brought balance into our lives and into our home. He saw things and abilities I didn't see in Jordan, because to me he was still my help-less baby boy, even though he was five. I had heard of fairytale rela-tionships where the love is still as strong, if not stronger, years after meeting and marrying. When I moved to Georgia, I saw function-ing, happy, healthy couples who took care of their children and didn't harm them. I never believed it until I saw it over and over firsthand, because that was never my reality.

RayShawn also opened my eyes to the problems that I had constantly with Jordan's side of the family. Every holiday or break I would get tense because I knew they would call and it would be some type of drama. I would let Jordan visit Indianapolis for the summer. When I went to pick him up there was always a new issue. After I'd get there Delta would say things like, "Oh, I was going to let him stay another week." Or all of his clothes that I had sent would be missing and not have been replaced. They would send me nasty emails, voice mails, and aggravating calls that made me explode. One day, RayShawn asked me, "Why do you answer the phone if they are going to do you like this? You don't have to answer the phone, and he doesn't have to leave for the summer. He just doesn't have to. We can take care of him, get him in some type of summer program. He doesn't have to go away just because they want him to. If any of them have a problem with that, tell them I said he can't go."

It was like the light clicked on; I realized I didn't have to deal with them. I would answer the phone, and when they'd start going off, I'd just hang up. I stopped answering their calls, emails, and voicemails for a year. It was the most peaceful year of my life.

RayShawn wanted to adopt Jordan because he loved him like his own and so we could all have the same last name when we got mar-ried. We decided not to have him adopt Jordan, because he was his father's only child. We didn't want him to have to change his last name. RayShawn didn't want to rob him of the right to carry his father's name through life and marriage. We did agree that if any-thing ever happened to me, he would continue to raise him as his own so he wouldn't have to readjust his life again. He understood that I preferred Jordan not to live with his family because of their issues. The only other option would be his godfather Ricky.

RayShawn worked midnight to noon driving trucks. One night he left for work, I set the alarm, and I went to sleep. I was awakened to the alarm going off. I jumped up and started to run toward Jordan's room but was stopped in my tracks by a man standing and laughing in the doorway. As my eyes adjusted to the light and tried to make out the stranger in my house, I plotted my escape plan. *I'm gonna run into Jordan's room, grab him, jump out the window, run down the street to the neighbor's house, and call the police.* My plan was interrupted by the man laughing. I soon realized it wasn't a stranger breaking in to abduct me or steal all of our belongings. It was RayShawn. "What are you doing here?"

"I live here."

"But why aren't you at work?"

"Don't worry about it; just go back to bed."

"Don't tell me to go back to bed; you betta tell me why you are here!"

"I told you, I live here." My heart was racing, and I was visibly shaken.

"Look at you, you don't have a bat, knife, or gun, but you are looking like you are ready to kill somebody."

"You better be glad I don't, or it would be you I'd be killin'." He came over to hug me, and I pushed him off. I knew it was RayShawn, but I was still thrown off because he wasn't supposed to be home. He explained, "My load wasn't ready, so they sent me home to wait for it and I'll just go to work late."

"Next time, call before you come in. I was either gonna kill you or me and Jordan were going to be long gone down the street." I told him my escape plan with me and Jordan jumping out the window. He laughed, "Yeah, next time I'll call you before I get home. You would've been looking crazy running down the street in the middle of the night carrying that big ole boy." We laughed, and I eventually fell back asleep.

Through all of the wedding planning, we were heavy into my music. RayShawn would find gigs or people for me to work with. I was on TV, working with big producers, and going to the studio three or four times a week. I was on a compilation album, doing shows and photo shoots, and collaborating with other artists.

We hooked up with two producers through someone I knew on my job. Everything started out really well and positive. I was supplied with new tracks weekly, and I wrote and recorded dozens of songs. It was weird because I always knew that I could write well. Hearing my words fused with music and harmony was thrilling. The executive producer, Zeus, had worked with several well-known artists and was excited about my vocals, and especially my song-writing skills. The plan was to complete a full R&B CD and release it on our own.

I loved music, Jordan, RayShawn, and finally the way things were progressing in my life. I was in love with my life, and my life was in love with me. We would travel up the highway to Indianapolis to visit my family and down to Miami to visit RayShawn's family too.

We recorded for a year. We had over twenty songs complete. Toward the end of the year the vibe started to change. "Sing harder. Sing like Beyoncé. If Beyoncé was singing this she'd be screamin'."

"Yeah, but I'm not Beyonce. I love her and all, but we don't need two Beyoncés. I don't want to be compared to her. I just want to be me, Dream."

Soon after, we came to a mutual agreement to stop working together. Zeus wanted all of his tracks back and wouldn't give me my recordings. "I don't want you to leak my tracks."

"I wrote the songs, so my songs are just as much at risk as your tracks!"

"Yeah, but I know I won't leak them."

"I know I won't leak your tracks! Give me my vocals; only then I'll give you your tracks."

As great as things were going, I still had my issues I held inside. I knew that I couldn't carry these things into my soon-to-be marriage, because I wanted it to work. I started writing. I emailed a letter to Angela, Mable, and Delta to get everything off my chest. I wrote another letter to my father.

I hadn't talked to my father in years. He tried to hide from our family, but I always knew how to find him. When my mother's father passed, I planned on coming home and hand-delivering the letter to him. The letter was over twenty pages long. I had a lot to express, and in writing the letter I learned of more untapped feelings that I had to get out. I didn't want to forget anything, so I had to make sure that I didn't leave anything out. The letter was full of rage, love, confusion, and pain. I didn't want him to reply, but I had to let him know how what he did had plagued me and tried to hold me back from being truly happy. I had a great fiancé that I knew I could trust, but this wave of doubt was always in the back of my head, all because of the man who was my father. No one knew what I was doing except RayShawn, but it wasn't for anyone else; this was for me so that I could move on.

The day before the funeral I printed out the directions to my dad's house, and RayShawn and I headed out. We pulled into his subdivision. It was very nice, with two- and three-story homes. It was dark outside, so we squinted to read the street signs and addresses. We turned onto his street, and my heart started to pound. The lump in my throat that I used to get came back. My hands were shaking as I held the yellow envelope with the letter in it.

RayShawn slowed down to make sure he didn't pass the house, but it felt like he sped up. He stopped the car and I looked up at the numbers on the mailbox. *7446. It's the right house.* I gathered my nerves and got out of the car.

"I'm not going in; I'll be right back," I told RayShawn as he waited in the car. As I walked up the driveway various scenarios ran through my head of how the 'reunion' would go. As I got closer, I could see through the windows in the foyer, and there were toys on the floor that would be for a young child around the age of three or four. My game plan started to change. *I have to save this child.*

As I pushed the doorbell, magically all of my nerves went away. I was no longer his victim. I was grown, strong, and not afraid to talk back; not to mention my fiancé would whoop his ass if he tried anything. I waited and saw a lady coming to answer the door. The closer she came, the more familiar she looked. I soon realized who she was: my Aunt Mary. I'd heard through the grapevine they were married, but to see her in person was another story. I wanted to push the door open and shake her and say, "Aunt Mary, you've got to leave and never let a child near him again. He's a child molester, and he will never stop! Run! Run! Run!" I held my composure as she opened the door, "Hi, Mary. How are you? Is my dad here?" She looked a little confused, as if she couldn't remember who I was, but I looked familiar. It was no surprise. She hadn't seen me since I was five years old. "No, he's not; he's still at work."

"Oh, okay. Well, can you give this to him for me, please?"

"Sure."

"Thanks so much. Have a great night. Take care, okay?" I walked away, and even though he wasn't there and I didn't have an outburst, I felt fulfilled. *I hope she reads the letter before he gets home. I remember where he works. I should go up there and tell him to hurry home because I've exposed his dirty little secret. Who would marry a man who was a convicted child molester? Does she know why he and Mom broke up? Does she know that he went to jail? Does this make her my aunt stepmother? They are too old to be having kids; maybe those toys belong to her grandkids. Oh well, I did what I came to do. It's in God's hands now. Now I am free to get married and enjoy my life.*

"How'd it go?" RayShawn asked.

"Fine, he wasn't home …"

Started September 24, 2001; finished August 18, 2002

To the man who was my father,

First let me start off by telling you that every word in this letter are my undeniable, heartfelt feelings for you. I am sure beyond a reasonable doubt that I will never regret saying anything I've put in this letter, no matter how good or bad it may be. Everything in this letter is solely from my perspective, no one else's. I am finally old enough to speak my mind, finally mature enough to put all these feelings I've built up for so long together. Finally, I have found freedom and peace of mind within myself. I've been getting rid of all hurtful and unhealthy things that have been holding me back from being the remarkable human being that I am and was born to be. I threw out so much stuff, so much bad emotion, and so much pain that I could've had a garage sale. Better yet, a soul-cleansing sale. For the most part a lot of my issues stem from you. There are things that have not been uncovered, until now. Some feelings I threw out I never knew I had … (invisible luggage weighing me down). I didn't know I had it until I got older and things started affecting me in ways that they shouldn't have. You can't touch me, hurt me, or curse me any longer. The chains have been broken. Now at the age of 24, I can finally say today that I am free and happy without a single regret. If I were to die tomorrow, my soul would not be troubled by you or anything else for that matter. Soak in every word of this truth from my heart. Take every word to heart and let it run through your veins until you die. All these years of pretending like I was okay when I wasn't are gone. Always smiling on the outside, but really crying on the inside, gone. I am finally free.

About a week ago I got off of work, came home, washed my face, looked in the mirror, and smiled. It was there at that moment, that very second, that God gave me peace. I was finally 100% completely happy. I didn't have the 'invisible luggage' weighing me down. I had to smile because for the past twenty years or so it was never a 100% truthful smile. I was never truly *happy. Now twenty years is not a long time to live, but it is a long time to hurt and not really know why or how to ease the hurt. But twenty years of hurt is especially hard if that's all you know. I'm only 24 and that's all I knew. So through writing this it gave me peace, gave me the chance to sit down and sort everything out in my head. I was hiding my feelings so everyone else would be happy and believe that I was okay. Just trying to be a rock, but I'm not a rock; I'm a person, a human who can feel all emotions at any time and place. I realized it was okay to hurt and okay to move on. It's okay to remember and it's okay for me to feel however I feel. If I want to love I can; if I want to hate I can, because I have free will and the right to feel however I want. If my feelings all of a sudden change, it's okay. I don't have to hide anything.*

Now I can live my life. I can put all trust and faith into a man and marry him. If I want to have a million babies I can and be happy and not worry if they'll struggle or be abused. Because all this time of holding all my emotions in, nothing else could get in or out. No love, joy, or peace. Just a bunch of mixed-up emotions that I didn't know how to deal with. When I decided to write this letter I wanted to go off and curse your name; all that built up into pen, paper, and words. I started remembering things and forgiving things, accepting things and hating things. I don't expect or want you to be a part of my life. You've proven yourself unworthy.

Why this letter right now and why in so much detail? Because I needed some closure with you in my life, so I could go ahead and live my life the way I'm supposed to, and this is what this letter is about. It's long, but blunt and to the point, but hey that's just the way I am. But you wouldn't know that, would you? Because you don't really know me. I'm too big for you to like now, huh? You don't like us to talk back, do you? How many children have you abused? I've been sitting here trying to figure out if I actually hate you or not. Ain't that a bitch? Don't sound shocked at my language because you lost the privilege to father me and tell me what to do the first day you put your triflin', clammy, pedophile hands on my once so innocent body! I've been and still am struggling to see how I feel about you. I asked myself would I cry if the man I once called dad died? My honest to God answer is/ was no. If you were to drop dead this very second while reading this letter my emotions would not change. I would go on living my life as if it never happened, like you never existed. I would probably even be happy, because I wouldn't have to worry about you hurting other young kids and messing up their innocent lives. I wouldn't come to your funeral, nor would I shed a tear. So you can tell your family now not to notify me. Still, I am trying hard to feel hatred for you, but I can't seem to find it in me, and hating you is not worth my soul being in eternal damnation. I don't hate you, but I don't love you. So if that's hate in your book, then you have my permission to consider it so. But what I can say is, I did wish harm on you. I did deep down, probably still do. I wished you somehow a slow and painful death similar to the slow and painful hill I had to climb to get to where I am in my life now.

Mom called me the other day about an issue; she sounded like something was terribly wrong, and it was. She said, "Guess what happened." I automatically thought that she was going to tell me that you had died and I was pissed because I hadn't gotten this letter to you. Unfortunately, that was not what she told me. DAMN!

You haunt my everyday thoughts. I'm always coming up with obscene scenes in my head that are so unimaginably horrid. Scenes tacked on to my real-life memories. I'm always thinking of things that could possibly happen to my loved ones or even me. I am always making something out of nothing in little innocent gestures I see in everyone, even people in the grocery store. It's all your fault. I keep trying to move on with my life, but I have to settle the score with you for my soul and peace of mind to be right.

What is wrong with you? Do you have any excuse? Anything to say for yourself? I don't need to know now, it's too late. I don't need your bullshit half-assed rebuttal that's just full of more lies. I know now that I will survive regardless. I'll probably survive better if I don't ever hear from you again. My mother taught me how to stay strong through the storm.

Believe it or not, you, yes you, are my main life lesson. I've learned that all men are not created equal. Because you are not a man; you are less than a dog. You are pure evil; your name should've been Lucifer. To me you seem to have no remorse, no shame, no love; nothing's changed. Don't come begging and pleading to me for forgiveness or help. You don't love me, you never have, and you don't love yourself. You started a chain reaction of abuse to start happening to me. After all these things kept happening my mother had to assure me that she would ALWAYS believe me and ALWAYS fight for my protection. I knew that I was marked, because my daddy marked me ... his own flesh and blood. You tried to mark me like the mark of the beast that you are! Cursed. I was falling down hill first until I learned that I could fight back and it wouldn't be the end of the world. After I started fighting back it stopped.

The problem is that people always try to keep bad things in their family secret. Hide behind it and never talk about it. It seems that they are afraid to admit that there's a child molester in their family. That's all the more reason not to keep a secret. People need to learn to open up their fuckin' mouths, point you all out, so there will be fewer victims. Don't be embarrassed or ashamed if a family member got sent to jail or is always in jail! I mean, who really gives a fat lady's ass! The only people who are going to judge and criticize is someone who has done the same thing or someone who's too uppity or 'picture perfect' to admit it! WHO THE HELL CARES! You are a fuckin' freak, a damn pedophile, and I TOLD ON YOU! I told anyone and everyone who was in the sound of my voice and who would listen. So tell me, how many skeletons do you have in your closet? What are their names? What are their ages—17 or 5?

I remember that time you called me some years back. You told me you had a three-year-old you wanted me to watch. I thought that was a hint that I have another little brother, and wondered if you were expecting me to play a part in his life. But I've put it all together now and figure now that's my childhood friend Nyla's son. Are you doing the same thing to him? Are you sure her family will never find out? I'm not one to tell anyone who to be with, marry, or even what to do with their life, but I would think it would be smarter to marry someone that wasn't so close to the family. It would be easier for them to find out what you did. Don't you agree? Your dumb ass didn't think of that, did you? I think that you are far beyond the counseling/therapy stage. Only God can help you now. I went to different counselors, and that was cool for what it's worth. It did help in a way, because it let me know that I wasn't the only one this has happened to. It let me know that it was okay to talk about it, but it didn't give me closure. They tried to let us get closure with our offenders while writing them in jail. I wrote to you and got a bullshit reply. Even though I was a young child I knew that it was bullshit and that it didn't make any sense. How in the hell did you think that you were keeping the family together? What does that have to do with you molesting your children?

In therapy they even told us that we would either be very promiscuous and sexually active or not like sex at all. NO MEDIAN! They also said that some people who have been abused would probably abuse someone. I looked at those counselors like they had bumped their damn heads! Why in the hell would I ever put anyone through the hell I had to go through?

Dream,

I was glad to hear from you. And don't worry; your letters and questions did not make me mad. I am only mad at myself. I will be glad to answer your questions, but first I want to say that I am sorry for what happened and any harm that came because of it. Please forgive me. And thanks for being concerned about what happened and why.

Now to get to the part that you want (and answer your seven questions). Please understand that the answers may only be in part, and there may be more explanation, but I will try to give you the basics (what the answer is centered around).

Answers:

1. It happened because of my own thoughts and feelings. I really thought it was keeping the family closer.

2. No! I didn't start drinking

3. I didn't think that I was out of control, but apparently I was.

4. I didn't consider the consequences because I didn't think that any harm was being done.

5. I didn't know that it would break up the family. If I had known that (or given it more thought), I would have used other means to attempt to keep us (the family) together. I truly had it in my mind that nobody would get hurt.

6. Yes, I do feel guilty for what I did. I am guilty. I don't blame anyone but myself for my actions.

7. Yes, I am very sorry. I apologize, and I wish I could erase it out of His records.

I know that I haven't answered the questions completely, but I hope that it can give you a small understanding of what I am saying. I am not at all asking for sympathy from anyone.

I do hope and pray that you and the rest of the family can get the best out of life.

Thanks for still loving me through all of this. God bless you.

I love you, Dream.

Daddy

Did they rape you when you were in jail? Damn if they didn't. Great job if they did. Right up your fuckin' ass with no Vaseline is exactly what you deserve. Ripping all your insides apart, like you did mine. But you'd probably like that, wouldn't you?

Do you remember the first time? I do! Believe it or not. I mean, hell, how could I forget? You probably thought I didn't remember that much because I was so young, but how could I forget something like that? Would you? Wouldn't you remember if someone chopped your dick off?! But I'd better stop talking about it before you get a hard on and go find someone else to molest. Why did you shake when you did these things to me? Were you scared, nervous because you knew what you were doing was wrong? Did it make you feel good? Like a real man? Did you really get sexual pleasure from it? What kind of pleasure do you get from eating out a child? You are fucking disgusting! Were you really thinking that you would keep the family together when the same dick you stuck in my mother the night before you tried to stick in me? Or did you think it made me feel good? Dumb bastard! Children don't have those sexual longing feelings down there until they are older ... or was it just the thrill of the possibility of getting caught.

Would you believe that I made a vow not to have any children and never get married so that it wouldn't be possible for the things that you did to me to happen to my children, and I wouldn't have to struggle emotionally, financially, and physically like I saw my mother struggle? But God had to tap me on the shoulder and warn me that I would miss out on so much if I chose that route. He had to let me know that all men don't molest and abandon children and that He would send me one to prove it. But I still struggle with that; I still have my doubts.

I come up with a million excuses of why I wouldn't want to have more kids … "It hurts" … "I don't want to get fat" … "They could end up bad" … "too much responsibility …," but in all actuality you are the root of my issues with having kids. I hide it so good. I even hid it from myself! I don't want my child to abuse anyone, and I for damn sure didn't want them to come out looking like you. So there you have it. I'm fucked up, and would you believe I actually love children! (In a healthy way of course.)

It must be a pattern: you swoon the women, marry them, and molest the children. Does your wife know what you've done? I'm sure there's more to tell than the bits and pieces I've disclosed. Does she realize what she's gotten herself and family into? Do you all have kids together? Are you planning on having any? I remember Tisha telling me that one time she came to your house and there were teenage girls there. Who were they? What were they doing there? Why did you have them there?

It hurts me that I have your blood running through my veins and that I have to pass it on to my children. I'm worried about my whole bloodline because of your mentality. This is what goes through my head every day! Is this pedophile, sex offender thing hereditary, or is it just you? Is Uncle Steve the same way? Did you molest Tammy? I look at old pictures of you and want to throw up! How could you dare be upset at someone else messing with me and you did the same things. YOU HYPOCRITE!

Do you realize you haven't seen me in six years, and we haven't spoken in over three. All this time without you and you still haunt me! I had a nightmare about you just the other night . I dreamt that you were chasing me, stalking me everywhere I went, trying to fondle me as old as I am now. Everywhere I ran you were behind every corner. I saw you everywhere I turned, smiling the pedophile smile. You surrounded me. I couldn't go back to sleep. If I hadn't've told on you, would you have kept doing it until I moved out? Then how fucked up would I be? All the counseling I've had won't/can't and didn't erase the pain or memories or even the indecent fact that you got off on me when I was only five years old. If I ever find out that you are still abusing kids, I will mess up your whole life without ever talking to or touching you, and that's a promise. But then again I don't have to worry about that,

*because God has already said that He would make you pay. So have
you earnestly repented of your sins? That means that you've stopped
and won't do it again. That means that you don't have those lustful
feelings for minors any longer. Yeah right ... I'll never believe that.
I had my first Pap smear around the age of eight. A procedure usually not done until you are at least a teen who has started her period.
It hurt so bad because they had to literally open me up, poke and pry
with their hands and long Q-tips. I thought I would throw up, but I
didn't (just trying to stay strong). They were looking for damage. Can
you believe that? Damage like I had been brutally raped by a complete
stranger ... but it was my father instead. I was afraid to wash my privates because I thought it was something bad, because you made me
feel that dirty. The doctor who examined me had to tell me that I had
to wash my vagina or I would get an infection. HE had to tell me that
it was okay to touch it, that it wasn't bad, that it was mine. Another
man had to tell me that! Nobody knew that I had stopped touching it,
wiping it, all of that. After you touched my innocent womanhood, my
family, my whole world started falling apart. For the longest I blamed
myself for that. I figured it was my fault. I thought if I never would've
told, Mom wouldn't have had to struggle. I was afraid to ask for a few
dollars for after-school snacks, new shoes when mine were worn out.
I didn't want to ask my mom for book rental and money for school
pictures because I knew she didn't have it! I hated myself for being the
reason why Mom hurt so much. I thought I wanted to be the only one
in pain because I felt like I could handle it. That's what you did.*

*How were you happy to call yourself a man when these things you
were doing to us were so inhumane? How was I supposed to be happy
about being a woman if I didn't have time to learn what a woman
was? They sent me to the Guardian's Home; it was so horrible. I had
to share panties and clothes with runaways and other girls that had
been abused. That made me feel even dirtier down there. A vagina is
supposed to be, IS something sacred. Womanhood is a VERY sacred
thing, something you are supposed to save for your husband, and you
took that from me. I had to put my womanhood where others girls put
theirs. They weren't my sisters or cousins; they were complete strangers.
Sharing underwear with complete strangers who were probably afraid
to wash their womanhood as well. People would come to the Guard-*

ian's Home to look for a child to adopt. I would tell them that my mom was coming to get me. They would say, "Okay, dear." But I could tell by their eyes that they didn't believe me. So when I would see them coming I would hide in corners or the bathroom so they wouldn't look at me or talk to me. I didn't want them to get any ideas in their heads that I would be coming home with them. I did that until Grandmere came to get me. You caused all this hurt before I was even a teen. The years that are supposed to be the most innocent, the most precious and fun, were the worse years of my life because of you, and my teen years were two times worse than what they should've been. For a while I thought I was gay because I didn't like men, didn't trust them, didn't want them looking at me or near me. I was never attracted to a woman, but how was I supposed to know why I was feeling the way I was at such a young age?

You are so despicable I hate who you are, who I knew, and what you've become. TAKE THAT! Take a fucking picture and put it in your back pocket. Let it marinate on your brain because it's true. I used to hate the way I looked because I looked like you. I hated my hair because it is so nappy like yours. I hated being skinny with no shape for so long because that was like you. I hated my name because you gave it to me. I hated my widow's peak because that was like you. I used to think that I was so ugly, but I always smiled because I had my mother's pretty white teeth instead of your jacked-up ones! One day we were sitting around the table eating, and Keenan and I were fighting. He said, "That's why you look like your daddy!" I threw my glass of water in his face and walked away. I didn't want to be associated with you by any means, not looks, actions, characteristics, bloodline. NOTHING! I hated you SO bad!

I called the Marion County Police Department to see why you weren't on the sex offender registration list. I was going to have you hunted down by the Sheriff and have your papers served so your family, neighbors, and friends would know what you're capable of. Lucky for you (I guess) they have laws that protect you. If the offense happened before 1993 you are not required by law to be registered. So either you're a temporarily changed man or no one has told on you, or you just haven't got caught yet.

I started having sex at a young age, way too young. I felt like that's all boys/men wanted from me. I felt that was all I had to give. I would wear tight jeans. Sneak out of the house with things I had no business wearing. I wanted to feel loved the right way. I was too young to know what the right way was. Mom was gone busting her ass going to school and working long late shifts to keep a roof over our heads and food on the table. Trying to give us a little this and that to make each one of us individually feel special.

I have forgiven you the best way I know how, but that's between me and God. If I haven't forgiven you completely, then it's because I don't know how to. I can't say that I don't wish you harm, but I can't say I wish you happiness either. I've always heard that "there's a thin line between love and hate." And for the first time, I understand it. I guess I'm just stuck in the middle because I only feel emptiness toward you. I am walking on a tightrope and I don't know if I'll ever lean or fall off to the other side. Consider my feelings of emptiness for you. Consider our relationship way past dead.

If you ever happen to see me one day, just walk by. Don't acknowledge my presence, or pretend I'm not alive, I never existed. You owe me so much that you'll never be able to repay me. I'm not talking moneywise. I'm talking about emotionally, mentally, physically you owe me. But you can't repay your debts to me now. I've turned it over to my collection agency—God! So how you repay Him is between the two of you.

My pain goes deeper than the abuse. It's for everything you missed. Everything that I was afraid of because of the things you did to me. Every mistake I've made that you'll never know about. Every conversation that we should've had. Everything you were supposed to teach me. Everything you were supposed to protect and shield me from. EVERYTHING! All of my feelings of being this dirty little unloved girl. It's deeper than the abuse. The abuse is only the cover of it all.

I'm tired of struggling and fighting with these demons in my life. You have put so many demons on me without realizing it. I've been fighting them off one by one. Until now is the only time I've been able to breathe. You've caused so much unnecessary pain. So I'm throwing all your demons and curses back at you. Did you feel it? You get them off. Struggle like I did. It's not that easy, so I've been writing this letter for about a year now. To get everything I'll ever have to say to you off my chest. This is the last you'll ever hear from me. I command that evil spirit to leave my family alone. It all stops here, right now, today. I rebuke that evilness. It can no longer cause hurt, pain, and grief. You have to let it out because it started in you. Don't pass it on. It's like that movie Fallen *with Denzel Washington. The evil spirit flows through everything it touches. STOP! STOP! STOP! IT ALL STOPS! I'm finally a woman. Enjoying my womanhood in the right way. When I want, how I want, and with someone I want. You can't touch me. You can't hurt me ever again.*

Remember this letter on your deathbed. This is not a hate note by any means. This is a letter from my heart. May God bless and protect any underage child that comes in your eyesight or reach. I feel so much better now, 100% better. Eleven months and 26 days getting all this that has been built up for the past twenty years off my back. So there you have it, just in case you ever wondered how I felt, which you probably haven't. But now you know anyway, but this letter wasn't for you, it was for me, for my healing. Funny how all the counseling didn't change things for me, but the only thing that did was confronting you. The girl you once called Dream is gone. Well, that's it. This is it; this is all I'll ever have to say to you.

The wedding plans progressed. We decided who would be in the wedding party, along with who would play what role. RayShawn's first realization about my family was more visible then ever: I had no male to walk me down the aisle. "I'll walk myself down the aisle. I don't need anyone to walk me down." RayShawn kept telling me, "No, I want you to have the full experience. We will find you someone special to walk you down the aisle."

"Well who? You already said it. There are no men in my family. Uncle Lee is waiting for his first grandson to be born; Markus isn't going to be able to make it. You know him and Tisha have all of those kids! Who else is left? Reverend James will be officiating with Reverend Day. There's no guys left except Jordan."

"He's a kid; he can't give you away."

"Yes he can; it will be sweet. It's always been just me and him, so he can give me away."

"Okay, let's ask him."

"Jordan, come here."

"Yes, ma'am."

"I wanna know if you will do Mommy a favor. When we get married, will you give me away?"

He started to cry, "If I give you away, who's going to be my mommy?"

"No, baby, I'll always be your mommy, no matter what. I'm just asking you to give me away in the ceremony. I'm not going anywhere. We are going to be a family." He sniffed and wiped his tears.

"Okay, as long as you are still going to be my mom."

"I will, stinky boy. I'm not going anywhere, promise." I looked at RayShawn and smiled.

"I guess that's settled; Jordan will give you away."

"Yep, case closed."

It had been a few months since I had sent out my letters. I felt fresh, new, and confident. It was July 26, 2003; our wedding day was finally here. RayShawn had family that came from out of town, and the majority of my friends and family had come down as well, most of them for the first time. They were so happy to see that I was doing well and loved our house and environment. RayShawn's two brothers were supposed to be in the wedding, but neither one of them could make it. His younger brother, Lamont, had had a stroke a few months prior. His older brother, Maurice, had just been in a motorcycle accident the week before the wedding and was still scarred and bruised. We had to have our two ushers be part of the wedding party, but that just meant that we didn't have any ushers. I wanted everything to be perfect and was worried about the lack of ushers. "Don't worry about it; I'll handle it," RayShawn told me.

Kevia and I got our hair done that morning and then went home to gather our belongings and go to the church. We were the first ones there. We got dressed and waited. Everyone else in the wedding party was running late, even RayShawn and Jordan. The people who were invited arrived before the actual wedding party. They showed up one by one as Kevia and I sat and waited. "Don't worry; everything is going to be okay!"

"I'm fine. I'm just waitin' on ya'll!"

An hour later, everyone was finally ready. I watched the procession on the TV monitor in the back before it was time for me to walk out. I saw two white men ushering Mom and our aunts down the aisle. I didn't know who they were and could only see the back of their heads. "Who are those white men walking with my mamma and aunts?" I asked my wedding coordinator.

"Girl, you know RayShawn worked it out. That's your friend's boyfriend and the limo driver!" We chuckled to ourselves.

That's why I'm marrying him; he always makes sure everything is handled, so I don't have to worry about it. There's no doubt that I'm marrying the right man for me. My friend's daughter sang her song. Then my cue came to enter. They opened the church doors as "Amazing Love," a song I wrote and recorded, started to play. I walked down the aisle with Jordan holding my hand to give me away. I've heard brides say that they were nervous the day they got married and had second thoughts. I didn't have that problem. I was happy and excited. There was not a nervous bone in my body. I was ready to become Mrs. Moore and rushed down the aisle. It was a wonderful day, perfect to say the least. My pastor from Indianapolis and our local pastor both took a part in performing the wedding. My friend Ni'chelle, who was in my group MSST, sang the Lord's Prayer and had the whole church in an uproar. Raya, another girl from the group who was a bridesmaid, made eye contact and knew we were thinking the same thing. I'ma take off my shoe and hit her in the head if she don't stop singing like that! After the song was over, RayShawn and I gazed into each other's eyes and exchanged vows and rings. We were pronounced man a wife. We took pictures and headed out for the reception.

The reception was so much fun. Our first dance was to "Made to Love You" by Gerald Levert. Reverend James started everyone dancing. We danced nonstop from seven p.m. until midnight. Mom and Kevia got on the dance floor. We all did the electric slide and had a great time laughing, talking, and taking pictures.

After the reception was over, our friend drove us to the Georgia Terrace Hotel for our wedding night. We consummated the marriage without holding back anything. It was beautiful and magical. I was his, and he was mine; we belonged to each other.

The next day, we spent time with our family and went to Stone Mountain. We went out for breakfast before they headed back home. We packed our bags and left for Savannah.

Savannah was fun and very relaxing. You could do as much or as little as you wanted, and we ate the best crabs that I have ever tasted. We did do some sightseeing, but mostly we stayed in the hotel room.

A month after we were married, RayShawn left for work around five a.m. He called five minutes after he left the house. "I don't want you to worry; you don't have to come, but I just wrecked my car."

"What! What do you mean don't worry, don't come, you just wrecked your car? Are you crazy? Where are you?"

"I'm right around the corner. I left the house five minutes ago. The police are here already. I'm not hurt, but I think my car is totaled." I jumped up. "I'm on my way." I went into Jordan's room, picked him up, and put him in the car. "Jordan, we have to go see about RayShawn, okay? He's okay, but he wrecked his car. I don't want you to worry."

"Okay." He was still half asleep. When we turned the corner you could see all of the flashing lights and a policeman redirecting traffic. Jordan started screaming, "I don't want RayShawn to be dead! I don't want him to die!"

"Jordan, he's okay; he's not dead. Please calm down. I'm going to go get him." Unable to stop his emotional tirade, I jumped out of the car and ran through the grass. RayShawn looked up and saw the look on my face. "Are you okay?"

"Yeah, I'm fine, but Jordan is going ballistic back there. Can you just come and show him that you are not dead. I don't think he will believe me until he sees you." He asked the police officer, "Could you excuse him for a moment? I have to check on my son."

Wow, his son? I know we are married and all, but, hmm, he's never said that before. He rushed over to the car and opened the door.

"Jordan, come here. Give me a hug." He picked him up and squeezed him tightly. "Look, I'm okay, nothing happened to me. I'm not going anywhere I promise okay." Jordan looked over him as good as any six-year-old could.

"You're not going to die?"

"No, man, I'm not going to die. Look, I don't have any scratches or scars on me, but I'm going to have to buy a new car though." He chuckled. I smiled in disbelief. *Just a year ago I had to bite his head off for not reacting the way I wanted him too. I sure do love me some of him.* He finished his police report. We gathered his items, put them into my trunk, and drove off.

Later that night, I had no choice but to thank him for the way he had handled the situation with Jordan. He thanked me for not over-reacting and letting him handle the situation.

"I'm so glad I married you," I told him.

"Me too, sweetie. I'm glad I married you too."

One evening, we were relaxing on the couch and the phone rang. I looked at the caller ID and saw that it was Angela. This was the first time I'd heard from them in a year. I figured they had learned their lesson, especially after the letter that I had written. I picked up the phone. "Hello"

"Um, hi! Oh my God, how are you?" Angela gasped.

"I'm good. How are you?"

"I'm fine. Um, I'm so glad you answered the phone."

"Mmm hmm."

"How is Jordan doing?"

"He's fine, doing good in school. He's on the honor roll."

"That's good! Well I was really calling to ask you if it would be okay if me and Mable came down for his birthday with Delta's kids."

"Well, let me check with RayShawn first, and I'll let you know."

"Okay, that's fine."

I figured that Jordan would enjoy it, and they came down. Little did I know they would bring Delta with them. She didn't tell me that she was coming until they were already in Georgia and she called me from her cell phone. I was pissed. *How dare this heifer not acknowledge my letter, and then just assume that it's okay to come to my house.* I knew I would have to confront her—really all of them—face to face. I gathered my thoughts. After they settled in, I sat them down. "I am Jordan's mother; RayShawn is Jordan's father. We take care of him. If there are things that you don't like about the way that we are raising him, keep it to yourself. I am not the same little girl who gave birth to him. You guys got away with treating me anyway you wanted because I was so young and didn't know any better. No more! Please know and believe that if we ever fight about Jordan again, I guarantee you will never see him again. You won't know what's going on with him, and he won't know who you are. The drama that you guys keep up is just not worth it. I want him to have a relationship with you guys, but I have no problem with cutting you completely off; I mean it. Don't ask if he can come to visit for the spring and summer because I'm just not comfortable with that yet. Every time he did it was a big argument or a fight. When I feel that he and I are both ready, I'll let you know, and he can come up. So I hope you guys have a great time here for his birthday, but this is my position on this, and I'm serious." Angela tried to laugh it off in her usual manner by saying, "Girl, ain't nobody trying to disrespect you, ha, ha, ha. Give me a hug." I backed up and told her, "I'm serious, Angela. Please don't force me to prove myself!"

Mable chimed in and said, "You should respect her; she's doing a very good job with Jordan; he's growing into a nice young man." Delta cried and apologized, "I'm so sorry, Dream, for everything, and I mean everything. Being married has been so good for me. My husband already told me that I can't keep doing things to you like I have been. His father's family did the same thing to his mother, and now he doesn't know his father's family."

She apologized and admitted her wrongdoing and crazy ways. She didn't try to make excuses for it; it was what it was, a bad situation. We were on our way to healing our relationship. "I can't speak for everyone else, but just know that with me, we will never fight about Jordan again. You are doing an amazing job with him, and I'm so proud at how far the both of you have come."

Delta and I had made a pact to have a good relationship. The next summer, Delta asked if Jordan could spend a few weeks with them. I still had my reservations, but I wanted him to know his family and have fun with them. On the other hand, I wanted to protect him from all of my issues with them. I asked RayShawn: "Delta wants Jordan to spend a few weeks there for the summer. I don't know if I should let him go though. What do you think?"

"What's your reasoning to not let him? Are you worried for his safety, or do you just not want him to go?"

"I don't think they'll physically harm him or nothing, but you know they are crazy. What if they have a birthday party for Allen? What if they try to take him to the cemetery? I ain't havin' it. They are gonna be sittin' around holding séances, no sir, not with my baby. I don't want to put any bad thoughts in his head, because I want him to feel comfortable around them, but I want him to realize when things aren't right."

"Well, if you don't think he's in any physical harm, then let him go. Don't tell him what to watch for, because those are your issues. They know how you feel from that long ass letter you sent. But if it makes you feel better, tell Delta and Angela your dos and don'ts. If they do things you are not comfortable with, then he doesn't go back."

"You are the best hubby and dad in the world. You are right. I guess he's going to Indianapolis." I sighed. I was happy, nervous, and anxious at the same time. *Stay strong. It's gonna be alright.*

Life was great; we were happy. We had our share of ups and downs. Most of them were us against the world, never with each other. We were still very compatible. I could read him, and he could read me. My family loved him; his family loved me and my son. We survived the death of his youngest brother and my 102-year-old Granny. We were so in love that we decided to have another baby. I never thought that I would plan to have a baby; I honestly didn't think black people did.

We got pregnant, and this time being pregnant was fun. We knew that we were pregnant for a month before we told anyone. We didn't want to tell anyone locally that we were pregnant before our family knew. We decided to go to Indianapolis and tell my mother and family first. We bought an announcement card and gave it to my mother. We watched anxiously as she read it and realized that I was pregnant. "Are you serious?"

"Yep! But don't tell anybody. You are the first to know. We'll tell everybody tomorrow over Nanny Re's for Christmas dinner."

"Awwww, I'm so happy for you. Remember you swore up and down that you weren't having any more children."

"I know, Mom. Don't talk about it. It's RayShawn's fault!" I laughed.

The next day the whole family came together for Christmas dinner. Mom said, "Okay, everybody, I have a special announcement." Everyone stopped and waited to hear the news. "I'm going to have another grandbaby soon." Everyone's eyes turned to Tisha, who had six children. "It's not me!" she said; they turned and looked at Kevia.

"Noooo!" she said laughing.

"Um, yeah, I guess that leaves me, huh?" We chuckled and were greeted with hugs. We were soon interrupted because Jordan started crying and ran out of the room.

"Noooo! I don't want you to have a baby!" RayShawn and I ran after him. "Jordan, what's wrong? Why are you crying?" He wrapped his arms around me. "I always wanted to be the only child."

"Well, it's a little too late for that now, but it's okay. You are going to be such a good big brother," I replied.

"Just because there will be another kid in the house doesn't mean we are going to love you any less. We loved you first remember?" RayShawn said in a reassuring tone.

He started to calm down. "Well, can you make it be a boy?"

"Well, we don't have any control over that. Sorry, but you will love the baby even if it is a girl."

"No I won't." We giggled and hugged him and went back into family room. "All's well guys. Jordan is happy again … so long as the baby is a boy!" We all laughed and joked. I was happier than I had ever been before. *Thank You, God, for giving me this joy.*

I only got sick four times. RayShawn made me feel beautiful the whole time I was pregnant. I loved to buy maternity clothes and having him rub my stomach and kiss the baby until I fell asleep. Mable came to stay with us and was going to watch the baby for the first year so we wouldn't have to take the baby to daycare.

We started looking for a bigger home to accommodate our growing family. About a month before we had our baby, we moved into a beautiful five bedroom, three bathroom home. It had a fenced-in backyard, with enough room for our dog, Cookie, a pool, and a swing set if we wanted one.

On August 10, 2005, I woke RayShawn at six forty-five in the morning. "You're not going to work today."

"Are you in labor? Are you ready to go to the hospital?"

"No, I'm not having any pain yet. I just know the baby is coming today. Go ahead and call in."

"How do you know if the baby is coming today if you aren't having any pain?"

"I don't know; I just know." He reached over and grabbed the phone off of the night stand to call into work. My hospital bag had been packed for months, but nothing in the bag was what I wanted to wear to the hospital. I rummaged through the closet and drawers and changed clothes three times.

"What are you doing? It doesn't matter what you are wearing.

You won't be dressed long. They aren't looking at what you wear," RayShawn fussed.

"I know. I just want to be comfortable," I replied. I was walking through the room and felt a pain that I couldn't walk through. I held my stomach and closed my eyes.

"Get in the car." I looked up at the clock; it was seven eighteen.

"Right now?"

"Yep, get in the car; let's go." As soon as the pain stopped I rushed to the car. *I have to hurry up and get to the hospital. I don't want to feel any labor pains.* I was about to get in when I felt another sharp pain. "I wanna get in the back. I don't want to sit down 'cause the baby's gonna fall out."

"Dammit, Dream, you didn't tell me you were having pain! We should've been gone." He fussed as he helped me get into the back seat.

"I wasn't having pain; the pains just started. Just drive." RayShawn headed out, speeding through the subdivision and in the middle of the main road. "Okay, so I don't want to die on my way to the hospital! Slow down and drive like you have a CDL license! I promise you I'm not having the baby in the car."

"You say that, but all of a sudden you are feeling pain. Don't worry. I got this." He kept speeding, and every time he turned the corner I felt another pain.

"Ease up on the turns, man!" *Epidural, epidural, epidural.* The pains weren't unbearable by any means, but I didn't want them to get to that point. I'd witnessed Tisha in labor with all six of her children. I remembered the pain Mom was in when she had Kevia.

At seven forty-five, we pulled up to the Labor and Delivery ward, and nurses ran out with a wheelchair to admit me. *How long before I can get an epidural? I hope I'm not too late. Epidural, epidural, epidural.* They admitted me and rushed me in to be checked by the nurse. RayShawn wheeled me into the pre-labor room and helped me lie on the bed. As soon as I sat down, my water broke.

"See, I told you if I sat down, my water would break." I giggled. No turning back now. I wonder if the baby will look like me or him. *Epidural, epidural, epidural.*

Another pain came. "Nurse, can you find out if I can get an epidural, please? This baby is going to be here real soon."

"How many is this for you?"

"This is my second."

"Oh well, that baby may not be here for hours. Most times they like to take hours before they are ready to come out." I gave her the fakest, most understanding smile I could. "I don't believe in long labor. Get in, get out, get on with your life is my kind of labor."

She hooked me up to two monitors. One showed my contractions; the other showed the baby's heart rate. Then she pulled back the white cover over my legs and checked to see how far dilated I was. "Oh, you were right. This baby will be here soon. You are just about ready." I was already dilated eight centimeters.

"So, how long before I get my epidural?"

"I'll call the anesthesiologist right now. If we wait much longer, you won't be able to get it."

"Okay, well then, let's get to it." I smiled.

RayShawn leaned over and said, "You are silly. You are in labor and still joking around with this lady. I'ma call you the epidural lady from now on."

"I'm not pushin' without my epidural! The doctor better come on!" I chuckled.

"I love you, sweetie."

"I love you too, babe. I can't believe we are actually about to have a real live baby!"

Around eight a.m. the anesthesiologist administered the epidural. He was a cocky guy, and RayShawn watched him closely as I leaned over to give him access to my spine. Instantly the pain was gone. "Mmm, you're good!" I smiled. "Okay, let me know when I can start pushing. I'm ready when you are. I'm tired of being pregnant."

"Give us a few minutes and we will be ready."

"Okay." We waited, talked, and sent out text messages to our family and friends. Soon after, the doctors were ready. "It's baby time. Scoot your bottom all the way to the end of the table. When I tell you to push, I want you to bear down real hard and push for ten seconds. When you are done, take a few deep breaths and wait for me to tell you when to push again."

"Okay." Wow, I feel so much better, relaxed, much happier than when I was pregnant with Jordan. I wonder if it's going to be a boy or a girl. I hope it's a boy. I know it's a boy. Wow, this is what it feels like when married people plan to have babies. Who would've thunk.

After only a few pushes, we learned that we were proud parents of a precious eight pounds eight ounces baby boy. We decided to name him RayShawn Lamont. RayShawn after his father; Lamont after his younger brother, who had just passed. We called him Ray for short. We were very happy.

We enjoyed our new addition. Jordan adored him and always kept a watchful eye on him. He enjoyed playing with him and keeping his little brother company. "See, Jordan, I told you you'd love the baby."

"Yeah, he can drive me crazy sometimes, but I'm glad he's here."

"Well you are a good big brother, and I know he will always look up to you and want to be just like you."

Ray was a whole different breed of child than Jordan. Even before he could walk or crawl, he could climb. He was very active and had to be seen. He was a natural born athlete. The first time he held a football in his hand, he could throw it far and in a straight spiral. RayShawn would get excited: "Whew! That boy is good. I can't wait until he's four or five so I can put him in sports." Jordan would make little hints of liking sports, but we already knew that he didn't. "Jordan, it's cool, man. I'm not gonna bug you about playing sports. I still love you, and your talent is not sports. You can draw your butt off and have a great imagination. That is your gift, and that's what I'm going to help you do. We are going to do a comic book and sell it to all the kids your age."

"Really!" Jordan exclaimed with his big brown eyes.

"Yeah man, I wanted you to like sports at first, because that's what I loved to do, and I wanted you to love it like me. But hey, I can get down with the comics too, okay? You are gonna have to take care of me and your mamma when we get old, and I think I'll like all that cartoon money you're gonna get." They laughed, and I silently watched and enjoyed the moment. *I got it right. It's all coming together.*

A little over a year after Ray was born, I felt off. After a few months of feeling that way I went to my OBGYN to see if it was something she could detect. It's kind of hard to explain, because I wasn't in any pain or uncomfortable. My body just felt off. She ran tests; I wasn't pregnant and had no STDs.

"Dream, there's nothing physically wrong with you. You probably just need to drink more water, exercise, and not be stressed."

"I don't exercise much, but chasing after Ray is exercise enough. I'm not stressed at all; I'm the happiest that I've ever been in my life. I can drink more water, but I know that something is wrong, and none of the stuff you are telling me is going to help."

"Are you still taking your birth control pill?"

"Yes, it's the only medicine I take."

"Maybe it's your hormones; I'll write you a prescription for another pill. Maybe that will help."

"It's not going to make me gain weight or nothing, is it? I like my pill I'm on. I've been on it for four years with no problems."

"No, it's another low-dosage pill."

"Okay, I'll try it."

For the next two months, I took the new pill religiously, but I still felt off. I scheduled an appointment with our family doctor to see if she could detect something. I explained to her all of my symptoms and issues. "Well, it's very rare, but maybe you are going through early menopause."

"Wow! Really?"

"Mmm hmm, but let me run a variety of tests so we can get to the bottom of it all."

"Alright." She left the room, and I patiently waited for her to return.

I wonder what kind of tests she's going to run. I hope it's nothing major wrong. Probably not; I eat healthy. I don't feel sick, just off. Something's going on, though; that's for sure. Shortly after, she re-entered the room with a Cheshire-cat smile on her face. "We can't run any tests today, but I think I know what's wrong." I glared at her with a questioning eyebrow.

"What do you mean?"

"Congratulations!" she beamed.

"Congratulations for what?" I quickly replied.

"You're pregnant!"

"I'm what? No, my last name is Moore. That must be the lady down the hall in the other room. Did you check the name on the cup?"

"Not the answer you were looking for?"

"Definitely not. I'm on the pill and just saw my OBGYN two months ago, and she switched my pill. I wasn't pregnant then, but I was already feeling off."

"Well, after you have the baby, if you still feel off, come back and we will run tests on you then. But I can't run them while you are pregnant. Are you happy?"

"I don't think happy is the word. I'm not unhappy; I'm just shocked. This is not why I came to the doctor today." I put my clothes back on and went home. RayShawn greeted me at the door.

"So, what did they say?"

"Congratulations."

"Congratulations for what? You're healthy?"

"Healthy enough to get pregnant." His facial expression changed.

"Wow! Are you serious?"

"Yeah, you said exactly what I said to her."

He pulled me in and hugged me. "It's okay, baby. It wasn't planned, but Ray was a rare thing. I still don't think people plan to get pregnant. We are happily married; I ain't goin' nowhere. How do you feel?"

"I'm fine. I'm just in shock. That's not what I went to the doctor for. I think I'ma have to get a second opinion."

A few days later, I was back at my OBGYN's office and it was confirmed that I was pregnant. Since I was still having regular periods they did an ultrasound to see how far along I was. I was eight weeks pregnant. *Wow, that's exactly how long I've been taking these new pills. I oughta get that doctor for these bootleg pills!* When the ultrasound technician looked on the screen she said, "Have you been feeling a little off lately?"

"Yes, that was my whole point of going to the doctor to begin with and for me switching my pills."

"Well, I can see the problem right here." I looked at the screen to see if I could see what she saw. "Your ovaries are enlarged. You have polycystic ovarian syndrome; that's just a fancy term for enlarged ovaries. Basically, you are predisposed to have diabetes and things like that. But you can also control it by what you eat. You can't have too much starch or sugars, but you need a lot of protein."

"Why didn't the doctor tell me that before? She just switched my pill!"

"Well, it's something that flares up and then can go down. It really depends on what you eat. You probably got pregnant because they were so flared up and your hormones were fighting the pill and they eventually won. But the baby looks to be very healthy and okay, so everything will be fine."

"Well, I'm not taking the pill anymore after this baby comes! You can tie my tubes right now!" We joked, and she gave me the information I had been looking for from the doctors. "I should've come to see you first instead of the doctors! How much do I owe you?"

Even though the pregnancy was not planned, I didn't feel the same way as I had when I was pregnant with Jordan. RayShawn was right. We were happily married, and I wasn't by myself. *Wow, what a difference it makes when you do things the right way. If I had've known then what I know now, Lord have mercy. And I really thought I was grown and knew what was best for me.*

We found out we were having a daughter. We decided to name her Sa'dia Uriella. Sa'dia means sweetly singing. Uriella means light of God. It was a beautiful name with meaning. Although I was happy and more content than I had been during my first pregnancy, I was still scared that my past would somehow resurface. *God, why are You doing this to me? Why does it have to be a girl? I trust RayShawn and all, but a girl? Really? Can You just go ahead and change it to a boy? No? Come on, God, You can do anything. I know a child molester is a child molester and they don't care if it's a boy or a girl. But with a girl I have to worry about everybody all the time. Are you serious, God? Well, I will pray for strength. I guess it was meant to be, just like Jordan. I was on the pill this time and still got pregnant. This little lady is coming no matter what, huh?*

God whispered back to me and said, "Dream, stop worrying. Your life is not your children's life. Have faith in me. I will protect you and your children. RayShawn is the man for you. If you had any doubts, you wouldn't have married him, because you already had Jordan." He was right. I had been doing so good and following what He told me to do. I had been so blessed and happier than I had ever been in life. I didn't want to block any blessings that He would bring to me, so I stopped fighting my worries.

On November 15, 2007, I gave birth to a precious baby girl who weighed in at eight pounds fourteen ounces. Once again, I hardly had any labor pains. I made them rush to give me an epidural because I didn't want to start feeling pain. I didn't want it be too late to have my drug of choice.

Sa'dia was the biggest baby I had ever seen. Her face wasn't wrinkled, and she didn't have a lot of extra skin all over her like most babies. When the doctors handed her to me, RayShawn and I both sighed. "Oh my God, she is beautiful."

All of my children were beautiful, but Sa'dia was a different kind of beautiful. She was the beautiful I had always wished I was when I was growing up. She had long, thick, curly, jet black hair. From her ears you could see that she would be a nice light-brown color. She opened her eyes and smiled at us, and she had the biggest, brightest, happiest eyes anyone had ever seen. "Uh-oh, RayShawn, I think we have a readymade diva on our hands."

"You know it. That's okay. Daddy will spoil her. She can be a diva if she wants." As happy as he was, I could still see sadness in his eyes. A sadness that I knew I couldn't fix. He missed his firstborn, his oldest daughter. *Man, seems like we'd have the perfect life if we could have a relationship with her.*

From day one, Sa'dia proved to us that she was a prissy little diva. Even her cry was different from the boys'. If you turned away from her, she would scream as if you had pinched her. The boys adored her and watched over her. She would boss them around before she could talk. Everyone was drawn to her, and she would stare at you with her big eyes and make your heart melt. RayShawn would say, "I'm gonna have to get a gun or something. Whew, when those boys come around, ain't gon' be no joke!"

One day she was crying and nothing would get her quiet. I started singing the first song that popped into my head. "Oh who mistreat it? Oh who mistreat it? Oh who mistreat that little girl? Oh who mistreat it? Oh who mistreat it? Oh who mistreat that little girl? Was it your Nanny Re, or your sister, or your brother? Was it maybe even your father? Who mistreat it? Oh who mistreat it? Oh who mistreat that little girl?" The song worked, but RayShawn looked at me very strange. "Are you paying attention to what you just said?"

"What do you mean? Mom made up that song for me when I was little. She made all of us a song of our own."

"Wow. You said who mistreat it, was it your father. Your father was the one who mistreated you."

"Yeah, I used to think about that when they split up, but it's okay.

She can have my song. Her life is not my life, and, hey, she stopped crying." I realized that my family was like the other families in Georgia that I had seen. My children's lives were not mine. After so many years of fighting, that part of my life was over.

PDA Journal Entry

March 17, 2009, one a.m.—my birthday

I usually get my best ideas, songs etc. in the shower, car (when the radio's not on), being close to a constant humming noise of a fan, or times like now when I should be asleep but a forceful urge won't let me sleep & I'm forced to jump up & jot down my ideas. Right now the house is quiet, the children and hubby are sleep. It's one a.m. & the only things up & running are me, my thoughts, God, & oh yeah my PDA! Ha!

This whole book writing experience has been like a dream to me. I'm not shocked that I did the book (because I've known since I was a young girl that I would do it). I'm just shocked at how it came to pass. I always KNEW—yes KNEW—that I would have to be at a certain stage in my life so that when it came out it would be a success. Since I've always strived to be a superstar I thought that is what I would have to be in order for it to be a success. These past few weeks I started to think different. I started MY STORY when I was a teen. I had already been through and lived through a lot, not to mention more than my fair share of hard knocks. I started an updated REVISED version if you will some time before I moved to Georgia. One of my co-authors, whom I have known since I was a teen, whom I was always cool with but usually talked to on again off again, sent me an email in July 2008 about writing a book with three other women just about struggles in our lives ... One dropped out ... we picked up two more & for various reasons they fell off too, but the original three remain. It is now my 31st birthday, even though I still claim 25 & we are in the editing stages of our book. All three of us are married with children who all have their agendas & needs, but we pushed through all of these things to come up with this beautiful finished project that I am more than proud to be a part of. No matter what obstacle we came across ... AND WE DID COME ACROSS THEM ... we never gave up. But then I think to myself, MAYBE, just maybe I don't have to be a superstar for this book to be a success. Maybe this book is the gateway to superstardom. But I do know that I am in a different place than I was 9 yrs ago before I moved to Georgia, I'm in a different place than I was when I was a teen writing my story. Maybe THIS is the time and I am in the place where I need to be in life for this book to be successful. Not just physically, but emotionally & spiritually with a WONDERFUL support system. My outlook on life is so different. Maybe this is what God was telling me but once again I was only seeing things MY way.

You see, things didn't come to pass the way I EVER planned or thought they would, but God had it all worked out before I was born. Our paths crossing & this final project were in God's plans long before I breathed my first breath 31 years ago. EVERY trial, tribulation, heartache, moment of confusion, chaos, success, & 'failure' all led up to this! I say all that to say NEVER GIVE UP! The moment you give up is when your breakthrough is coming. The more you fight, the stronger you will be! God may not come how you thought or when you wanted Him to, but TODAY HE'S RIGHT ON TIME! There are SO many more blessings that HE has done for me than I can put in this book. And I have no choice but to give thanks to Him for all of the dark moments in my life because if I didn't have them I certainly would not be the woman I am today & I wouldn't be able to feel the way I do & be compassionate & help all who I come in contact with, whether it's through this book or with a simple smile as we cross paths. I am so grateful & so ready to receive everything else that God has in store for me. This is my season; I claim & accept it. IF YOU LEARN NOTH-ING ELSE FROM ME, please take away never give up … no matter the situation or circumstance … You can't see the light at the end of the tunnel, but it's there! It's just not for you to see yet! You've got to go through some stuff first. He knows how much you can handle, but you have a choice to quit & fail or push on & succeed. When my middle-class family was broken up and I was in the Guardian's Home and then we were on welfare I THOUGHT THAT I WOULD ALWAYS BE POOR. When men KEPT 'messing' with me, I thought that was my purpose in life. When I got pregnant at 15 I ABSOLUTELY KNEW my life was over. (My son ended up being my biggest motivator, my reason to see beyond my current situation, because I didn't want him to have to deal with my situation. He deserved better.) The smallest being in my life became my biggest gift! When my son's father died I ABSOLUTELY KNEW that I would never love another man, and that my son and I would forever be in the 'grieving mode.' When I would date men that I KNEW weren't right for me, but I just didn't want to be alone, I DIDN'T BELIEVE that I would find a loving husband who would be more than honored to do right by me and my son. Through all of this I had to keep striving and keep pushing ... and thru all of the pushing and striving I started to change my mindset. After I changed my mindset and realized ... POOR IS A STATE OF MIND. VICTIM IS A STATE OF MIND. SETTLING IS A STATE OF MIND. I AM WORTH SO MUCH MORE AND I AM NOT MY PAST SITUA-TIONS! I DESERVE EVERY GOOD THING THAT COMES MY WAY! *When I realized that MY God is not a god of lack and that I could have ABSOLUTELY WHATEVER I WANTED, I started WORKING more toward my goal. (A family, children, mental health, stability, my entertainment career, and yeah money is nice too, but the others are more important.) I refuse to become a statistic because of what I've been through. If I never would've listened to God by stepping out on faith and moved to Atlanta, I wouldn't have a chapter three to my story. Jordan would not have a father in his life and be so well rounded. My two youngest kids would not be here. I wouldn't have the fullness of the support system that I have now. We have to learn to keep fighting and trust God. Just last night my hubby asked us (the authors) who was our target audience ... the obvious answer for my story is children who have been molested and are emotionally unstable. For the teen who is looking for love because she feels the lack from her fa-ther. For the teen who has a child at a young age and doesn't know how to cope with the responsibility. Any woman who's struggled in her mar-riage. For the mother who can't understand or feel what her teenage daughter is going through. BUT in an even bigger picture ... my target is you. If you picked up this book and read all or some, that is what was meant. If you FELT what I felt when I was going through, it's for you. If you haven't been through what I have but know someone who did and now you can understand better, it's for you. No matter who you are, or what your reasoning is to pick up this book, I hope it helped you in whatever way you needed to be helped. That is my target and*

*goal: to help whoever reads this book, and I thank you from the bottom
of my heart for taking the time out to read it. Today is my birthday…
this book is the best gift that I could have this year. Thank you, God, for
my gift!* ☺

I am Poor Little Rich Girl, Sixteen and Grown, Superstar. I am a
dreamer; I am Dream. I am Delina Rochelle Hill-Brooker. My story
has never been a secret. Being able to be straightforward and talk
about it was one of the benefits of counseling. The more I talk about
it, the more I heal, even to this day. Don't be afraid to think and dream
big. Dare God to surpass your wildest wants, dreams, and ambitions.
You have to be willing to work for it too.

Dream's Epilogue

AT TIMES, I OFTEN FELT like God was treating me like a mouse He was trying to catch. He would put a piece of cheese in my path. Once I had consumed and digested it, He would put another piece in my path, until I followed His plan step by step and piece by piece. There is no one in this world that can make me believe anything less than the omnipotence of my God. He is almighty and powerful. You can't tell me that my God ain't good.

Let me also add that although the stories about my son's father are true and he was irresponsible on many occasions, I do not fault him. Not because he is deceased and unable to defend himself, but because he was still a boy. He was not mature enough to be a father. I truly believe that he was incapable of being the father that Jordan needed at the time. I do know that he loved him dearly. Love and responsibility are two separate things. I told this story like I did to illustrate to younger readers what could and often times does happen in these types of situations. Not all teenage fathers are deadbeats and immature. There were things that I did that were immature. The only difference is I had no choice but to take care of my son, go to work, stay up at night, and find babysitters when needed. If I didn't do it, then who would? No one. To this day, I still believe that no matter how things go down in most instances it always falls on the mother. Of course, there are always exceptions to the rules, but I can only tell the story of how my life was. I also believe that if his family had not made it so easy for him to still live his life without responsibility, the story would've been somewhat different.

I have dealt with all of my issues as best as I can. I have made amends and started fresh with the relationships that I felt were most worth it. My mother is my best friend. Jordan's family are my in-laws and my friends. I was never legally joined into the family, but they accept my children, and I accept theirs. As far as my father is concerned, I'm not sure if there is a word to describe how I feel about him. I don't hate him anymore or wish him dead. I know I did love him; whether or not I still do, honestly I'm not sure. I don't think that you ever stop loving someone once you love them, so I guess there is some part of me that does. I just think that the dynamics of my love for him have changed, and I'll leave it at that. It is what it is.

As a side note, in the black community especially we often shun the thought of therapy and counseling. For whatever reason, we think that people will look down on us or think that we are crazy, or that it's only for white people. I believe that we all need counseling at one point or another in our life. So many tragedies could be avoided if we would just seek and ask for help. Let the people look down on you if that's what they choose to do, but just know you will overcome and rise above by learning how to cope with certain issues. Believe it or not, they probably want counseling too, but are too ashamed or prideful to admit it.

As I finish this book, my baby girl Sa'dia is almost two, Ray just turned four, and Jordan is fourteen. I just started singing and writing again. I'm going all-in like I always do. I am finally comfortable in my own skin, comfortable enough to speak my mind not only when I am asked, confident in my ability to be a great mother. As I looked back in my diary and journals to add things to my story, I was so grateful and thankful for God's grace in my life. I'm thankful that I had sense enough to listen to God when He told me to move. It gave me the strength to know that I can do anything that I set my mind to.

My stories are only a few of my testimonies. I am only one of mere hundreds of millions of living witnesses. My life is nowhere near perfect, and I still have obstacles. I just have that bold faith to believe that my wildest dreams will come true. I thank God every night for my husband, who takes such good care of me and my children. He supports my dreams and pushes me to keep going. I never thought that I could love a man unconditionally, but I do, and he unconditionally loves me. He showed me all men are not the same, and I let him. One thing I can say about my life is that I have lived and I'm ready to live some more.

I hope this book as a whole makes you think, laugh, cry, and rejoice, gives you hope, provides answers, and gives you an insight into how life can be, with the good and bad things. Most of all, I hope this book helps you and inspires you. Thank you for reading our stories. Writing is such a great therapy and a great outlet. The more I write, the more I learn about myself and the more insight I have into my situation.

Delina